MORALITY AS LEGISLATION

"What would happen if everyone acted that way?" This question is often used in everyday moral assessments, but it has a paradoxical quality: it draws not only on Kantian ideas of a universal moral law but also on consequentialist claims that what is right depends on the outcome. In this book, Alex Tuckness examines how the question came to be seen as paradoxical, tracing its history from the theistic approaches of the seventeenth century to the secular accounts of the present. Tuckness shows that the earlier interpretations were hybrid theories that included both consequentialist and non-consequentialist elements, and argues that contemporary uses of this approach will likewise need to combine consequentialist and non-consequentialist commitments.

ALEX TUCKNESS is Professor of Political Science at Iowa State University. He is the author of *Locke and the Legislative Point of View* (2002), *The Decline of Mercy in Public Life* (with John Michael Parrish, Cambridge University Press, 2014) and *This is Political Philosophy* (with Clark Wolf, 2016).

T0384777

MORALITY AS LEGISLATION

Rules and Consequences

ALEX TUCKNESS

Iowa State University

CAMBRIDGE
UNIVERSITY PRESS

CAMBRIDGE
UNIVERSITY PRESS

Shaftesbury Road, Cambridge CB2 8EA, United Kingdom

One Liberty Plaza, 20th Floor, New York, NY 10006, USA

477 Williamstown Road, Port Melbourne, VIC 3207, Australia

314–321, 3rd Floor, Plot 3, Splendor Forum, Jasola District Centre, New Delhi – 110025, India

103 Penang Road, #05–06/07, Visioncrest Commercial, Singapore 238467

Cambridge University Press is part of Cambridge University Press & Assessment,
a department of the University of Cambridge.

We share the University's mission to contribute to society through the pursuit of
education, learning and research at the highest international levels of excellence.

www.cambridge.org
Information on this title: www.cambridge.org/9781009055611

DOI: 10.1017/9781009052542

© Alex Tuckness 2021

First published 2021
First paperback edition 2023

A catalogue record for this publication is available from the British Library

ISBN   978-1-316-51140-4   Hardback
ISBN   978-1-009-05561-1   Paperback

For Anastasia

Contents

Acknowledgments

This project began in 2015 when a student at Iowa State asked to do an independent study on the Scottish Enlightenment that led to me reading Francis Hutcheson's *System of Moral Philosophy* for the first time. There were interesting parallels to Locke, and I originally thought I might write a book on Hutcheson's political philosophy. My colleague Cullen Padgett-Walsh shared his insights on Hutcheson with me; both of us were interested in him in part because he didn't fit neatly into traditional categories such as "consequentialist."

When, several months later, I realized I could do a larger project that traced rule-based and act-based consequentialist thinking over the last four centuries, I reached out to John Michael Parrish, my coauthor on *The Decline of Mercy in Public Life*. His comments, insights, and patient listening have been invaluable from the beginning of the project to the end.

As I worked on the project I had the benefit of three excellent students who worked as research assistants: Elaina Conrad, Brody Tritle, and Rachel Lentz. Brody deserves special thanks for turning a room in his apartment into a small library annex so that citation checking could continue during a global pandemic. Their work checking citations, formatting, indexing, and editing has made this a better book. The funds to employ them, and also to present papers at conferences, were provided by the Koch Foundation, which sponsored a small grant for work on the philosophical foundations of well-being, and by three sources at Iowa State: the Department of Political Science, the College of Liberal Arts and Science, and the Whitaker-Lindgren Faculty Fellowship. I am grateful to my chair, Mack Shelley, and my dean, Beate Schmittmann, for their support and assistance.

I am grateful to the audiences that provided feedback on various chapters of this book at the American Political Science Association, the Association for Political Theory, the Northeast Political Science Association, the Iowa Association for Political Science, and the Midwest

Political Science Association. I also got very helpful feedback from a presentation to the Department of Philosophy and Religious Studies and a separate presentation to the Department of History, both at Iowa State. Several members of the Philosophy Department deserve special thanks. Clark Wolf has provided extremely important feedback at multiple stages, especially on the late twentieth-century utilitarians. Joe Kupfer suggested that the term "hybrid," which now figures very prominently in the book, might better capture my meaning than the term I was originally using. Stephen Biggs helped me tighten the language and logic of Chapter 7. Margaret Holmgren helped me think through the framing of Chapter 7. Greg Robson read more of the manuscript than anyone else and had countless helpful suggestions.

My greatest debt is to my wife Anastasia. Her antipathy toward logical contradictions helps keep my mind sharp, and her friendship, advice, encouragement, and patience have helped me more than I can put into words.

Abbreviations with Method of Citation

Parenthetical references in the text are by author, year, and (where applicable) page number, except in the cases listed below. Author names are omitted in the text when the name is present in the sentence introducing the quotation or when the full citation has been previously used in the same paragraph.

Abbreviation	Reference and Citation Method
Austin	Austin, John. (1832) 1995. *The Province of Jurisprudence Determined.* Edited by Wilfred Rumble. Cambridge: Cambridge University Press. Cited by page number.
Bentham Analysis	Bentham, Jeremy. 1822. *Analysis of the Influence of Natural Religion on the Temporal Happiness of Mankind.* London: Carlile. Cited by page number.
Bentham Deontology	Bentham, Jeremy. (1834) 1983. *Deontology together with a Table of the Springs of Action and Article on Utilitarianism.* Edited by Amnon Goldworth. Oxford: Clarendon Press. Cited by page number.
Bentham PML	Bentham, Jeremy. (1789) 2007. *An Introduction to the Principles of Morals and Legislation.* Mineola, NY: Dover. Cited by page number.
Berkeley	Berkeley, George. (1712) 1901. "Passive Obedience, or the Christian Doctrine of Not resisting the Supreme Power, proved and vindicated upon the principles of the law of nature." In *Works of George Berkeley.* Oxford: Clarendon Press, Vol. 4. Cited by paragraph number.
Butler	Butler, Joseph. (1867) 2006. *The Works of Joseph Butler: Containing the Analogy of Religion and Sixteen Celebrated Sermons.* London: William Tegg [reprinted by Elibron Classics]. Cited by volume and page number.
Cumberland	Cumberland, Richard. (1672) 2005. *A Treatise of the Laws of Nature.* Translated by John Maxell and edited by John Parkin. Indianapolis, IN: Liberty Fund Books. Cited by chapter and section, and then page number.

Abbreviation	Reference and Citation Method
Grotius	Grotius, Hugo. (1625) 1925. *The Law of War and Peace*. Translated by Francis W. Kelsey. Indianapolis, IN: Bobbs-Merril. Cited by book, chapter, section, and (where applicable) subsection.
Hume E	Hume, David. (1751) 1998. *An Enquiry Concerning the Principles of Morals*. Edited by Tom L. Beauchamp. Oxford: Oxford University Press. Cited by section (or appendix) and part, and then page number.
Hume PW	Hume, David. (1777) 1994. *Political Writings*. Edited by Stuart D. Warner and Donald W. Livingston. Indianapolis, IN: Hackett. Cited by page number.
Hume T	Hume, David. (1737) 1978. *A Treatise of Human Nature*. Edited by Lewis A. Selby-Bigge and Peter H. Nidditch. Oxford: Clarendon Press. Cited by book, part, section, and then page number.
Hutcheson Illustrations	Hutcheson, Francis. (1728) 2002. *An Essay on the Nature and Conduct of the Passions and Affections, with Illustrations on the Moral Sense*. Edited by Aaron Garrett. Indianapolis, IN: Liberty Fund. Cited by page number.
Hutcheson Inquiry	Hutcheson, Francis. (1725) 2008. *An Inquiry into the Original of Our Ideas of Beauty and Virtue*, Revised Edition. Edited by Wolfgang Leidhold. Indianapolis, IN: Liberty Fund. Cited by treatise, chapter, and page number.
Hutcheson PMIC	Hutcheson, Francis. (1745) 2007. *Philosophiae Moralis Institutio Compendiaria, with a Short Introduction to Moral Philosophy*. Edited by Luigi Turco. Indianapolis, IN: Liberty Fund. Cited by page number.
Hutcheson System	Hutcheson, Francis. 1755. *A System of Moral Philosophy, in Three Books*. Glasgow: R. and A. Foulis. Cited by book, chapter, section, and then page number.
Kant G	Kant, Immanuel. (1785) 1997. *Groundwork of the Metaphysics of Morals*. Edited by Mary Gregor. Cambridge: Cambridge University Press. Cited by page number.
Kant M	Kant, Immanuel. (1797) 1996. *The Metaphysics of Morals*. Edited by Mary Gregor. Cambridge: Cambridge University Press. Cited by page number.
Locke ECHU	Locke, John. (1690) 1975. *An Essay Concerning Human Understanding*. Edited by Peter Nidditch. Oxford: Clarendon Press. Cited by book, chapter, and section number.
Locke Letter	Locke, John. (1689a) 1983. *A Letter Concerning Toleration*. Edited by James Tully. Indianapolis, IN: Hackett Publishing Company. Cited by page number.
Locke PE	Locke, John. (1703) 1997. *Political Essays*. Edited by Mark Goldie. Cambridge: Cambridge University Press. Cited by page number.

(cont.)

Abbreviation	Reference and Citation Method
Locke TT	Locke, John. (1689b) 1988. *Two Treatises of Government*. Edited by Peter Laslett. Cambridge: Cambridge University Press. Cited by treatise and section number.
Locke Works	Locke, John. (1823) 1963. *Works of John Locke*, 10 vols. London: Thomas Tegg [reprinted by Scienta Verlag Aalen]. Cited by volume and page number.
Mandeville	Mandeville, Bernard. (1732) 1988. *The Fable of the Bees or Private Vices, Public Benefits*, 2 vols. Edited by Frederick Benjamin Kaye. Indianapolis, IN: Liberty Fund. Cited by volume and page number.
Mill CW	Mill, John Stuart. (1969) 1985. *Collected Works*. Edited by John M. Robson. London: Routledge & Kegan Paul and Toronto: University of Toronto Press. Cited by volume and page number.
Mill OL	*On Liberty* found in Mill, John Stuart. (1969) 1985. *Essays on Politics and Society*. In *Collected Works*, Vol. 18. Edited by J. M. Robson. London: Routledge & Kegan Paul and Toronto: University of Toronto Press. Cited by volume and page number.
Mill RBP	*Remarks on Bentham's Philosophy* found in Mill, John Stuart. (1969) 1985. *Essays on Ethics, Religion, and Society*. In *Collected Works*, Vol. 10. Edited by J. M. Robson. London: Routledge & Kegan Paul and Toronto: University of Toronto Press. Cited by volume and page number.
Mill S	*A System of Logic Ratiocinative and Inductive* found in Mill, John Stuart. (1969) 1985. *Essays on Ethics, Religion, and Society*. In *Collected Works*, Vol. 10. Edited by J. M. Robson. London: Routledge & Kegan Paul and Toronto: University of Toronto Press. Cited by volume, book, and chapter.
Mill U	*Utilitarianism* found in Mill, John Stuart. (1969) 1985. *Essays on Ethics, Religion, and Society*. In *Collected Works*, Vol. 8. Edited by J. M. Robson. London: Routledge & Kegan Paul and Toronto: University of Toronto Press. Cited by volume and page number.
Mill W	*Whewell on Moral Philosophy* found in Mill, John Stuart. (1969) 1985. *Essays on Ethics, Religion, and Society*. In *Collected Works*, Vol. 10. Edited by J. M. Robson. London: Routledge & Kegan Paul and Toronto: University of Toronto Press. Cited by volume and page number.
Moore	Moore, George Edward. (1903) 1954. *Principia Ethica*. Cambridge: Cambridge University Press. Cited by chapter, section, and then page number.
Paley	Paley, William. (1785) 2002. *The Principles of Moral and Political Philosophy*. Indianapolis, IN: Liberty Fund. Cited by page number.
Parfit	Parfit, Derek. 2011–2017. *On What Matters*. Oxford: Oxford University Press. Cited by volume and page number.

(cont.)

Abbreviation	Reference and Citation Method
Shaftesbury	Shaftesbury, Third Earle of (Anthony Ashley Cooper) (1711) 1999. *Characteristics of Men, Manners, Opinions, Times*. Edited by Lawrence E. Klein. Cambridge: Cambridge University Press. Cited by page number.
Sidgwick Methods	Sidgwick, Henry. (1907) 1981. *The Methods of Ethics*, Seventh Edition. Foreword by John Rawls. Indianapolis, IN: Hackett. Cited by book, chapter, section, and then page number.
Sidgwick OHE	Sidgwick, Henry. (1902) 1988. *Outlines of the History of Ethics*. Indianapolis, IN: Hackett. Cited by page number.
Wittgenstein	Wittgenstein, Ludwig. (1953) 1958. *Philosophical Investigations*, Third Edition. Translated by Gertrude Elizabeth Margaret Anscombe. Englewood Cliffs, NJ: Prentice Hall. Cited by section number.

Introduction

But is it not monstrous to suppose that if we *have* worked out the consequences and if we have perfect faith in the impartiality of our calculations, and if we *know* that in this instance to break [rule] *R* will have better results than to keep it, we should nevertheless obey the rule? Is it not to erect *R* into a sort of idol if we keep it when breaking it will prevent, say, some avoidable misery? Is not this a form of superstitious rule-worship (easily explicable psychologically) and not the rational thought of a philosopher?

J. J. C. Smart (1956)[1]

outsmart, v. To embrace the conclusion of one's opponent's *reductio ad absurdum* argument. "They thought they had me, but I outsmarted them. I agreed that it *was* sometimes just to hang an innocent man." [Satirical reference to utilitarian philosopher J. J. C. Smart.]

The Philosophical Lexicon by Dennett and Steglich-Petersen (2008)

The Metaphor of Legislation in Ethics and Politics

In ethics, one of the most common exercises is to ask, "What would happen if everyone acted that way?" and to then consider what consequences would follow if everyone actually did. There is a potential tension between the two steps. "If" emphasizes the hypothetical, and indeed counterfactual, nature of the thought experiment. My action will not magically cause everyone in the world to act similarly in similar situations. "What would happen," on the other hand, derives much of its significance because we care about the actual

---

[1] This book covers a four-century timespan, and norms regarding spelling, grammar, formatting, punctuation, and capitalization have changed quite a bit over the years. I have chosen to reproduce the original texts in quotations as they appear in my sources except that I have silently removed some extra spaces. All italics are from the original source unless otherwise noted. Where these differ from modern usage, they are a reminder that we are in conversation with voices from a different era but with whom we can still converse.

consequences that will affect the lives of actual people, not hypothetical or counterfactual consequences. If we think that our answer to this question helps determine what is right for ourselves and for others, our question can be reframed in legislative terms: "If you were legislating a code of conduct for all to follow, what code would be best?" In this book I will explore the historical reasons why this common and intuitive way of thinking about ethics came to be regarded as morally problematic and I will suggest a less paradoxical way it could be incorporated into contemporary moral deliberation in ethics and in politics.

We can say roughly that the legislative perspective is one where deliberation is aimed at rule selection: "What general rule would be best for situations like this one?" In stating it this way, I am consciously excluding some other sorts of activities and considerations that are relevant to real legislators. In a democracy, a legislator might weigh the impact on their reelection chances of voting yes or no on a piece of legislation in terms of reactions of voters, campaign contributors, and the media. They might need to consider trading their vote on the proposed legislation to gain votes for a different bill that they think is more important. I am excluding these sorts of considerations insofar as they are simply prudential questions about what is best for the legislator but I include them insofar as they relate to the public good. A legislator who believes law A would be best, but who also believes that there is little chance of A being adopted, might choose to propose law B instead, which would still be a substantial improvement over the status quo, though not the best, especially if proposing A would decrease the chances of adopting B. This sort of thinking also counts as use of the legislative perspective since it is still oriented toward an action-guiding rule. It aims at the best attainable rule.

My particular interest is in the use of this deliberative frame outside of the obvious context of actual legislators deliberating on the merits of actual laws. It can be used in quasi-legislative activities, or as a heuristic for helping resolve ethical dilemmas of individuals, or as a source of moral guidance and constraint for those who have more traditional legislative power. The following contemporary example will illustrate what I mean by the legislative point of view and the moral questions that arise when we consider using it in some contexts as opposed to others.

Ethics and the Legislator: Stepping Out of the Chamber

Imagine a thoughtful legislator sitting in the legislative chambers thinking about whether to support a proposed piece of legislation. The legislation, if passed, would give more latitude to immigration officials to grant asylum requests. In deciding whether to support the bill, they will think about the probable consequences of its adoption. If more asylum seekers are accommodated, how much better (and longer) will their lives be compared with returning them to their home countries? If the law increases the number of asylum seekers without increasing the funding for investigating and processing their cases, will the result be longer waiting times for applicants? What implications will there be for the economy of the legislator's own country, including the welfare of its workers? If discretion increases for immigration officials, what if they use that discretion to the benefit of applicants from some countries rather than others? What if the use of discretion is affected by racial bias? What if the latitude leads to more mistakes and, as a result, dangerous criminals are accidentally let into the country? The legislator is particularly moved by the plight of asylum seekers from a specific country in the midst of a religiously motivated civil war and wishes the law made it easier for immigration officials to grant asylum in such cases, but they also know that the law would apply to applicants from all countries, not just that one.

All of these questions raise ethical issues and there are a variety of ethical frameworks the legislator might use to decide what they ought to do with regard to their vote on the proposed legislation. One approach is consequentialism, the view that consequences alone determine what is right and wrong. The legislator has a sense that some outcomes are better than others and that in at least some cases they can weigh these against each other so that they can determine whether the new legislation or the status quo is more likely to lead to better consequences. They might look at the actual frequency of crimes committed by those granted asylum compared with the rest of the population and compare that with the likely harms experienced by those denied asylum, and decide that the consequences of the proposed bill would be, on balance, an improvement. What is of particular interest is that the sort of decision the legislator is faced with (to support proposed legislation or not) gives them a particular perspective from which they think about those consequences. They must think of the consequences of a new law being adopted, not just of a particular set of worthy applicants being admitted. The new law will give discretion to people other than the legislator and they have to think about how these others will likely use the discretion rather than about how they would use the discretion if they were making the decisions about specific applicants. Those who will interpret and apply the law will be fallible and make mistakes. The new law, once known, may influence the behavior of those potentially affected by it.

Now suppose that our legislator steps out of the chamber after voting in favor of the bill. They receive a call from an important campaign contributor who wants the legislator to use their influence to help them secure a lucrative government contract. Suppose the legislator thinks consequentialism informs them regarding which action is right in this case as well. They might reason that a general practice of legislators helping donors in this way would have overall negative consequences. The government could end up with inferior value for the contract and public trust in the fairness of the system would be undermined. There would be obvious beneficial consequences for the legislator in keeping the contributor happy. Let us suppose the contributor would likely provide reasonable value to the government in return for the contract. These situation-specific benefits are vastly outweighed by the negative consequences of a political system where legislators systematically use their influence to get governmental contracts for campaign contributors or their friends and family. The legislator might, therefore, have good consequentialist reasons to say no.

Or they might not. They might instead, as a consequentialist, assess the chances that use of their influence will become publicly known and conclude that the chances are very small. They might, therefore, assume that the chances that their action will contribute to the formation of a new norm that then influences other legislators or public perceptions is also quite small. Looking only at the consequences of this one particular decision, they might think about the benefits to their reelection chances that would come with keeping the contributor happy and the important legislative causes (like helping refugees) that they think they will be able to advance if they continue to serve. If there is little reason to believe that there will be a significant causal link between their actions and those of other legislators or public perception, they might question why counterfactual consequences matter. What matters instead are the probable consequences of this specific action.

In the two scenarios above we see a legislator confronting ethical dilemmas and trying to use consequentialism to resolve them. In the first scenario, the context in which the legislator must make their decision (voting on potential legislation) structures their consequentialist thinking in a particular way that focuses on the consequences of the adoption of a publicly known rule that will be interpreted and enforced by fallible, biased people. From their view in the chamber, questions about the probable consequences of a publicly known rule are not counterfactual since the result of passing the legislation is the adoption of a new public rule.

In the second scenario the legislator leaves the chamber. Although they could take a situated perspective and look only at the morally relevant features of the specific acts they might perform, many people find it ethically appealing to use something like the legislative perspective outside the chamber. Many people's moral intuitions resonate with something like the golden rule with its demand that our actions be consistent with reciprocity. We should not do what we would not want others to do, and imagining a general public rule that would approve of our actions is a way to think about our actions as reciprocal. Moreover, even if many people think that consequences are not the whole of ethics, few people think them irrelevant to ethical decision-making. John Rawls remarked that "All ethical doctrines worth our attention take consequences into account in judging rightness. One which did not would simply be irrational, crazy" (Rawls 1971, 30). It is possible to account for many widely held moral and ethical beliefs by noting that a given rule regulating our actions would produce better consequences than alternative rules or no rule at all. If a rule would be beneficial if adopted and followed by others, that gives me a moral reason to act on it.

This line of thought, though intuitively attractive, has been found deficient, at least insofar as it is thoroughly grounded in the most well-known form of consequentialism, utilitarianism. Although the definition of utilitarianism is disputed, we can for now define it as an approach to ethics that judges the rightness of actions by the likely or actual impact of those actions on happiness (or pleasure, welfare, or satisfied preferences). Consequentialism is a broader term referring to approaches that define actions as right or wrong based on whether those actions produce good outcomes but that may have a broader or more complex account of what counts as a good outcome. A lot of ink was spilled in the twentieth century debating the merits of "act-" and "rule-" utilitarianism, and this debate tracks along with the two scenarios above. Rule-utilitarians argued that one should not apply the principle of utility ("maximize happiness") directly to specific, situated actions. Instead, one should use the principle of utility to select rules for behavior and decide specific actions with respect to those rules. This indirect form of utilitarianism can more easily explain why the legislator should not use their influence to help a donor get a government contract. There was a small cottage industry generating hypothetical examples where act-utilitarianism seems to lead to troubling ethical conclusions, especially if one believes one's actions can be kept secret (framing an innocent person to prevent a riot, harvesting organs from a healthy patient without their consent to save the lives of five other patients, etc.). If one looks only at the specific action, one can construct a scenario where utilitarianism seems to compel unethical action. We can add to this cases where the harms or benefits of a single act are negligible but where a general practice of many people performing that act could lead to real harms (not voting, walking on the grass of a pristine lawn, etc).[2]

This rule-utilitarian line of thought was found wanting because it seemed inconsistent with its utilitarian foundations. If I care about maximizing happiness it seems I should care about the probable consequences of *this* action and not worry about counterfactual consequences that would occur if I were legislating a rule for everybody, given that I am not actually legislating a rule for everyone (Lyons 1965). Put another way, a utilitarian has no trouble explaining why an actual legislator should utilize a legislative perspective when actually legislating. If you really are enacting a public rule, think about the impact on happiness of adopting that rule. What is puzzling is why a theory committed to producing the best actual consequences would tell you to think like a legislator when you are not legislating.

The Historical Emergence of Counterfactual Use of the Legislative Perspective

This puzzle was at the center of the twentieth-century debate between "act-" and "rule-" utilitarians, a debate nurtured in part by some interpreting Mill as a rule-utilitarian (Urmson 1953). The quote from Smart (1956) in the epigraph summarizes in three devastating questions the basic problem: to obey the rule in cases where you could produce better consequences by breaking it seems to treat the rule idolatrously, even worshipfully, rather than rationally and philosophically, since the rule has no inherent authority of its own, it is only a pointer to what normally produces good consequences. The second epigraph shows the problem for act-utilitarians like Smart: he really is forced to say that the rule "don't use your discretion to bring about the execution of a person you know to be innocent" should be broken in exceptional cases when doing so produces more utility than following the rule. It is such counterintuitive conclusions that have often motivated the

---

[2] On framing the innocent see Rawls 1955. Early discussions of doctors killing patients to harvest their organs are found in Harris 1975 and Harman 1977. Though not originally conceived of as a contribution to the debate about act- and rule-utilitarianism, nonconsensual organ harvesting became a typical instance of something that is not utility maximizing as a general practice though it might be in particular instances. Harris's survival lottery proposal arguably could be affirmed by rule-utilitarians, not just act-utilitarians. Harman's version (page 3) is the one that became canonical.

desire to treat rules with more reverence. In this book, I will argue that Smart's linking of rule-utilitarianism to religion is telling, probably more telling than he knew. The instability of rule-utilitarianism can be better understood if situated within a different historical frame that shows how the secular, realistic, consequentialist, and counterfactual rule-utilitarians of the twentieth century are the heirs of a theistic, realistic, weakly consequentialist stream of thought that was not thought, by its practitioners, to be counterfactual at all.

What I have called the legislative perspective descends from a particular way of thinking about what is right and about justice that was popularized by thinkers whose starting point was a divine legislator motivated by benevolence. In its original formulation, people might think about what rules would be rational from God's perspective in order to discover the laws they were to follow, but they would not have thought of themselves as the legislators of the moral law. While they used a legislative lens to reason to their conclusions, the heuristic was a way of understanding what was independently true for others as well, rather than a decision-making strategy for themselves alone. For them, the move from the situated perspective to the legislative perspective was not hypothetical or counterfactual as they assumed the existence of an actual God promulgating actual moral laws. They also assumed a moral obligation to obey God's law. Their focus on morality in terms of obligation to obey law is characteristic of much of modern moral philosophy (Anscombe 1958).

Since I am ultimately interested in hybrid approaches, I will use the phrase "weak consequentialism" to designate approaches that adjust the content of rules and principles to produce better consequences but that can also include nonconsequentialist commitments. The term "consequentialist" was not in use when these authors were writing so they were not participating in a defined movement of that sort. The theological character of many of their works would keep them from being classified as thoroughgoing consequentialists today by many people. They might be better classified as hybrid theorists in that their moral thinking relied upon nonconsequentialist theological commitments to frame their consequentialist reasoning. I will use the term "hybrid" in this book as a broad category for theories that include both consequentialist and nonconsequentialist elements. Many of these thinkers, for example, held to a belief that God's moral law should be obeyed, which was not explicable in purely consequentialist terms while using consequentialist reasoning to fill out the content of the moral law. Part II of this book will argue for the viability of a modern hybrid approach that is available to people who reject the theological assumptions of the earlier approaches.

In the seventeenth and eighteenth centuries this theological tradition of morality as the will of a divine lawgiver was increasingly separated from its original biblical context and joined to the idea of a benevolent divine lawgiver. Important figures in this line of thought include Hugo Grotius, Richard Cumberland, John Locke, Francis Hutcheson, William Paley, and John Austin. Their more religiously-minded critics at the time complained that God's holiness or justice had been lost due to an overemphasis on God's benevolence. The excitement over scientific theories that could explain natural phenomena by means of "laws of nature" may have encouraged these authors to try to find a similar approach in ethics. If we start with the assumption that there is a moral code willed by God that defines what is right and add the assumption that the overriding goal of that God is bringing about good outcomes, one has a theological version of the rule-consequentialist position. The moral rules need not be discovered from the Bible. Instead, one can determine the correct moral action by asking what moral code a benevolent God would promulgate to human beings. One can even stipulate that God, as a benevolent legislator, must attend to the same kinds of considerations as a human legislator. The divine moral code's content must account for the selfishness, fallibility, and other limitations of the mere mortals on whom it is imposed. In other words, the figure of the divine legislator allowed theorists to develop a weak version of rule-consequentialism that, unlike its secular counterpart, was not, from their perspective, counterfactual. In the religious version it is assumed that there is in fact a benevolent legislator who has enacted a welfare-maximizing moral code.

In the nineteenth century, John Stuart Mill and Henry Sidgwick, building on the earlier thought of David Hume and Jeremy Bentham, worked to figure out what the standing of rules could be in a thoroughly secular and utilitarian philosophical system. Their solutions came with costs that many subsequent philosophers were unwilling to pay. In the twentieth century, there was a resurgence of explicitly secular, rule-utilitarian thought that tried to use legislative reasoning to avoid some of the counterintuitive conclusions of act-utilitarianism. These philosophers were often criticized, along the lines of Smart's quote in the epigraph, for being inconsistent utilitarians. In fact, a number of the prominent twentieth-century philosophers who are often thought of as rule-utilitarians are better characterized as adopting hybrid approaches that are, in a way, descendants of the hybrid theological approaches of earlier centuries. Hybrid approaches represent the best opportunity for continued use of the legislative perspective in cases where the agent is not literally legislating.

Different Forms of the Legislative Perspective

So far, I have been talking about the legislative perspective as if it is just one way of looking at things when, in fact, it is a family of ways. (I use the phrases "legislative perspective" and "legislative point of view" interchangeably.) In this section, I describe how conceptions of the legislative perspective can vary across four dimensions. In the next section I will describe four contexts in which the legislative perspective could be employed. The historical study will reveal differences, not just similarities. My interest in Part II is in asking how a particular version of the legislative perspective is justified. It is thus important both for framing the historical inquiry and for thinking about the contemporary relevance of the legislative point of view to specify the different forms the legislative perspective can take. Our present concern is with the sort of deliberation one engages in when thinking legislatively, that is, the sorts of considerations that are morally relevant. This is separate from the question of the contexts in which it is appropriate for a person to employ the legislative point of view, however construed. That will be addressed in the following section. What all of the variations of the legislative perspective discussed here have in common is that they are about the selection of action-guiding rules that apply to a whole set of cases. By contrast, a situated perspective (the main alternative to the legislative perspective) is interested not in identifying the rule that would be best to direct a set of cases but in identifying the action that would be best in this particular situation.

The first dimension along which the legislative perspective can vary is how realistic or idealized legislative deliberation is. By "realistic" I mean how closely does it track with the considerations a legislator would typically use in deciding whether to vote in favor of proposed legislation. Immanuel Kant wrote, *"Act only in accordance with that maxim through which you can at the same time will that it become a universal law"* (Kant G, 31). In another formulation he wrote, "act in accordance with the maxims of a member giving universal laws for a merely possible kingdom of ends" (Kant G, 46). While Kant was open to thinking of the moral law as, in a sense, the will of a supreme being, duty to God "is not objective, an obligation to perform certain services for another, but only subjective, for the sake of strengthening the moral incentive in our own lawgiving reason" (Kant M, 230).[3] Kant's formulation, as commonly interpreted, is explicitly

---

[3] Kant also wrote, "A law that binds us *a priori* and unconditionally by our own reason can also be expressed as proceeding from the will of a supreme lawgiver, that is, one who has only rights and no duties (hence from the divine will); but this signifies only the idea of a moral being whose will is a law for everyone, without his being thought of as the author of the law" (Kant M, 19).

legislative and highly idealized. I need not worry about whether my opinion is the one that will prevail in the legislative chamber since I can act as if my maxim once adopted is a universal law. I legislate for an idealized kingdom of ends where people act in accord with their duty even though I know such a kingdom is "merely possible" and not actual.

By contrast, consequentialist approaches that tend toward a more realistic conception of the legislative point of view would consider it relevant that the best option on the merits might be one that few people would adopt and that this might be a relevant reason for rejecting it. It is similar to the way that a legislator might decide that it is better to support a law that has a higher probability of becoming law even though it is not the best law that could conceivably be adopted. A realistic approach would consider how fallible and sometimes self-interested people would interpret and apply the law and might reject a proposed law because of foreseen errors. Legislators, using the realistic approach, are not the ones who interpret and apply the law and must anticipate how other people with different values and judgment will interact with the law. They must also consider the likelihood that people can be brought to comply with a law and the costs involved in attempting to bring about compliance, including voluntary compliance. My interest in this book is primarily in the more realistic theories that more closely mirror the deliberation of human legislators. Part II will explore ways in which Kantian approaches can be combined with this sort of realism.

A second dimension along which use of the legislative perspective can differ is with respect to consequentialism. How does a legislator judge which law would be best? A pure consequentialist would take the expected outcomes of the various options to be the only relevant consideration. Kant insisted that legislators should not worry about the likely consequences of their laws when legislating (Kant M, 109). John Stuart Mill claimed that even Kant was a consequentialist in the end, since Kant rejects maxims by considering the consequences of the universal law (Mill CW, 1:207). Most have thought Mill was wrong about Kant, but Mill was certainly right about real legislators. One can hardly imagine them being indifferent to the likely consequences of a proposed law, especially since "consequences" is here used very broadly and could include things like the outcome of more people's rights being protected. In this book, my primary interest is in theories that take the likely consequences of different frameworks of rules to be morally relevant to deciding whether those rules rightly influence our decision-making and our understanding of what is right and wrong. Theories need not be wholly consequentialist, but they must be at least weakly consequentialist. In Part II we will see that nonconsequentialist approaches can supply premises that realistic and consequentialist uses of the legislative perspective need.

A third dimension along which theories that use the legislative perspective vary is the degree of weight that they give to the legislative perspective. Both the textbook Kantian approach and the textbook rule-utilitarian approach are similarly strict in that the position chosen from the legislative point of view just is constitutive of what is right. Once I rationally determine the content of the universal law, I must, as a Kantian, obey it. Otherwise, I act wrongly. Once I determine the appropriate rule on utilitarian grounds, that rule is the standard of right and wrong, and I must, as a rule-utilitarian, obey it. Otherwise, I act wrongly. It is also possible to have a weaker position where deliberation from the legislative perspective has significant weight but where the situated perspective also has some moral weight. In other words, not only is there a continuum for how consequentialist we are in deciding the content of the rules (second dimension), there is also a continuum about how decisive the rules so derived are in determining what is in fact right or wrong, ranging from always to never (the third dimension). Those who opt for never have rejected the legislative point of view, but both "some" and "always" assume that the dictates of the legislative point of view meaningfully influence what is right or wrong.

Debates among proponents at different points along this continuum track with debates about how rule-like morality is. Some virtue ethicists might object to placing significant emphasis on rules. While they might agree that in identical situations the same right act should be performed, they might deny that situations are ever identical and question the ability of a rule-based approach to ethics to capture all of the morally relevant particulars of our decisions (Dancy 2004). That ethics is primarily about rules of conduct is controversial, and many virtue ethicists have made a point of criticizing that assumption. "What if everyone did it?" might still be a helpful question to ask in order to think more clearly about the implications of an act, but it need not lead to framing our deliberation as if we were legislators. A different way of arguing for the "none" answer comes from act-consequentialism. Some act-consequentialists would hold that while rules are useful tools for improving the speed and accuracy of our decisions, we ultimately make moral decisions as situated individuals in particular situations and what matters is which decision, in that particular situation, will produce the best consequences. Thus we have extreme versions of virtue ethics and act-consequentialism on one end of this spectrum and extreme versions of Kantianism and rule-consequentialism on the other. In specifying this as a continuum rather than a dichotomy, we note the possibility that compliance with legislative rules might be a right-making feature of an action but not the only right-making feature.

The fourth dimension, and the one of particular interest, is the admissibility of counterfactual reasoning. Counterfactual reasoning, in general, is simply reasoning on the basis of suppositions that we think will not actually be true in the real world. Consequentialist counterfactual reasoning gives weight to consequences beyond their expected likelihoods. Rather than estimating the expected change in outcomes that is likely to happen when I perform an action, I might reason as if my decision has more influence over the decisions others will make than it actually has. To take the simplest case, a consequentialist legislator contemplating whether to vote for a law does not need to engage in any counterfactual reasoning. The legislator would simply try to estimate the expected consequences of the law in comparison with the status quo or other laws that could likely be enacted. By contrast, a person who is about to act secretly in a way that will never be known to others could still ask what the consequences would be if the principle on which the person was about to act were adopted as a general rule. In this second case, counterfactual consequences are considered as morally relevant reasons. One might think that this dimension is simply about whether one is a legislator or not, but that is not quite right. Whether I am in a context where my actions are causally connected to the adoption of a rule that will influence the decisions of others is about the context in which I deliberate (see the next section) rather than what sorts of considerations are relevant when I deliberate. In the counterfactual case, one generalizes to a larger group for which one does not actually have the power to legislate and asks what rule or principle would be best for that larger group. Suppose a legislator is contemplating what law to adopt for authorizing military interventions. If the legislator simply asks what law, here and now, is best to adopt, it would be a factual expression of the legislative point of view. If, instead, the legislator asks what rule would be good not just for their own country but for some larger group of countries including their own to adopt, knowing that the rule adopted in their own country will not significantly impact the rules adopted elsewhere, their deliberation is counterfactual but their context is legislative. The proposed law is directed toward the adoption of an action-guiding rule (legislative) and is counterfactual because consequences that would happen if other countries adopted the rule are considered, even though there is no causal link between the new law and changes to other countries' laws. The factual deliberation cases are not particularly interesting because there is nothing difficult to justify. Our interest here is in the counterfactual deliberation cases, which are always open to the objection of why one should let hypothetical and counterfactual consequences influence what is right in a particular case.

Legislative and Political Contexts

We also need to specify the contexts of the legislative point of view both to identify those that are of special interest and to note contexts in which the legislative point of view may be easier and harder to justify. Here we can note two contextual dimensions: legislative versus nonlegislative and political versus apolitical. Combining these two dimensions yields four different contexts, each representing an ideal type. The first dimension specifies whether the agent is in a position to meaningfully shape a new rule (a legislative context) or not (a nonlegislative context). For all of these contextual contrasts, it is helpful to think of them as continuums rather than dichotomies. In the case of the legislative context, agents vary both in the degree to which the activity they are engaging in would be characterized as trying to change or maintain a rule and in how much influence the agent has over changing the rule. Legislative action aims at the establishment of a rule or principle while nonlegislative action aims at some other exercise of discretionary power. There are many instances in which public officials are in a position to make decisions where it is better described as the exercise of discretion in a particular case than as enacting a general rule or principle. Persons in a legislative context can also vary in the degree of control they have over the rule that will emerge. A legislator representing a very small and isolated party, for instance, may have little realistic chance of changing the content of legislation. This legislator is still in a legislative context. There are also people who are in quasi-legislative contexts. If widely accepted moral norms are general principles that are often used as the basis for allocating the reward of praise and the sanction of blame, then attempts to change, defend, or reinforce those norms are quasi-legislative activities.[4] Similarly, private persons (parents and private employers, for example) are often in situations where they are in a position to enact rules

---

[4] From the legislative perspective, the person who publicly states, "X would be wrong to do Y in situation Z" is trying to persuade others to affirm the same norm and thus create a new rule that will "punish" transgressors, perhaps with public shame. If, following Mill (OL, 18:241), we agree that public opinion can be an even more powerful force restricting liberty than public laws, public moral expression by private persons becomes analogous to legislation. We find ourselves

that will direct the actions of others (children and employees). They formulate rules that will cover a set of cases. Whether voting in a legislative chamber, writing a book to encourage the adoption of a new moral norm, or setting limits on how much time children in a family may use a given technology, a person is aiming at the adoption of a new rule or principle and attempting to exert causal pressure toward that end. All of these are examples of legislative contexts.

The second dimension specifies whether the rule, principle, or decision in question is political or apolitical. Introducing this dimension raises questions about what is or is not political, a perennial and perhaps "essentially contested" concept. To try to provide a definition with precise necessary and sufficient conditions is, fortunately, unnecessary for our purposes. Functionally, I will argue in Chapter 7 that the more political a decision is, the greater the weight accorded to the legislative point of view, all else being equal. What is needed is a focal case for what counts as political rather than a clear dividing line between the political and apolitical. I assume being political is on a continuum where things are more or less political rather than simply political or apolitical. Several factors push a context closer to the focal case: that it concerns the use of the state's coercive power, that it concerns the laws or norms that regulate the public lives and basic rights of persons, and that it is performed by a person who holds public office.

Practically speaking, coercive rules that are adopted by governments are more political, all else being equal, than rules adopted by private citizens in nongovernmental contexts. A law regulating immigration is political; a rule specifying how much time the children in a family can spend playing video games is apolitical. The point of this distinction is to note that we might have two individuals, a legislator and a parent, who are both in a position to meaningfully adopt a rule that will have consequences for others but that we do not think of these as equally political. Attempts to influence the state's ability to intervene in areas that have been thought of as private would be political.

Below is a two-by-two table (Table 0.1) illustrating the interaction between these two contextual distinctions. Not all legislative contexts are political and not all political contexts are legislative. Of particular interest is the fact that a person in an apolitical context can also be in a legislative context, and a person in a political context can also be in a nonlegislative

---

simultaneously subject to the public opinion around us and members of an enormous legislative body (the public) that has the power to change those opinions.

Table 0.1

	Legislative context	Nonlegislative context
Political context	Voting on actual legislation.	Using discretionary political power that will not set a precedent or deciding whether to comply with publicly adopted rules.
Apolitical context	Setting rules for one's family or club.	Using discretionary power in one's family or club.

context. The examples are focal cases and are not exhaustive of the categories.

It is worth noting how these contexts interact with the factual/counterfactual dimension discussed in the previous section. The factual/counterfactual dimension is a moral choice the agent makes to think about a moral question in a particular way rather than a fact about the particular context in which one makes the decision. Two legislators faced with the same legislative question could respond differently, one using a factual legislative point of view and the other a counterfactual one, asking what rule or principle other states or provinces should adopt as a way to decide what is right to adopt in this case. Remember that, in our sense, persons in apolitical contexts can also face this same legislative dilemma. Parents deciding about the use of technology and social media by their children might do so by setting rules the children are expected to follow. In doing so they are engaging in a legislative enterprise but one that, if it is political, is only weakly so (perhaps it will affect the opportunities of their children to interact about politics with their peers). The parents, who are engaged in rule setting, are using the legislative point of view in a noncounterfactual way by simply trying to select the best rule for their particular family, and there is little that is theoretically interesting about the case for our purposes. On the other hand, parents in such a situation might think about what principles they would want parents in general to use and consider the difficulties of enforcing the rules and the accompanying penalties given children who may desire to break the rules or parents who may have different interpretations of what counts as "social media" or "screen time." Here there is a counterfactual context since they are not actually in a position to set rules for other families and they might adopt different rules for their own family given the less-than-ideal rules of the other families with whom they interact.

In the two legislative contexts (political and apolitical), interesting philosophical questions arise in the counterfactual cases but not the factual ones. Legislating based on what principle you would want some larger group to follow makes sense if you are in a position to legislate for that group. By contrast, in the two nonlegislative contexts, any use of the legislative point of view is necessarily counterfactual and stands in need of justification. One of the contentions of the concluding chapter will be that the arguments for using a counterfactual version of the legislative point of view are stronger in political contexts than nonpolitical contexts.

My interest in this book is thus particularly in versions of the legislative perspective that are counterfactual, realistic, and weakly consequentialist in the senses noted above. They are counterfactual in the sense that the person using the legislative frame is considering the consequences of people acting on the rule that go beyond the actual causal impact of the agent's own actions, either because one imagines a rule adopted more widely than one's actual scope of legislative influence or because one's actual legislative influence is negligible. Though counterfactual, these theories are also realistic in that proposed rules are evaluated using the best estimates of what would happen if such a rule were promulgated to fallible and imperfect agents who can disagree in their interpretation of the rule, question its legitimacy, and fail to act rightly even when they know the right thing to do. These theories are consequentialist at least in part; it makes a moral difference whether a proposed rule would lead to more or less of the legislator's preferred outcomes coming into existence. The judgments that flow from such a legislative perspective need not be so stringent that they exhaust the field of morality, but they must have some moral weight that goes beyond what purely situated reasoning generates.

Goal and Objectives of the Book

The goal of this book is to explore approaches to ethics that assess actions as right or wrong, at least in part, based on their conformity with rules where the content of the rules is chosen from the legislative perspective. The emphasis will be on ethical approaches that make these moral rules closely analogous to human legislation with all the typical concerns about interpretation, enforcement, demandingness, bias, and fallibility that are the stock and trade of deliberation from the legislative perspective that seeks to improve the well-being of citizens. Part I will trace the development of this approach from the seventeenth century through the twentieth century to better understand the reasons why this approach is thought to be paradoxical. Part II will sketch reasons why we might still find this approach helpful today and suggest ways it might be defended. In doing so, the book will attempt to accomplish several objectives.

First, it will provide an alternative historical frame for understanding the contemporary debates about the relationship between rules and consequences in our ethical thinking. In a common telling, the classical version of utilitarianism is Jeremy Bentham's act-based account. Rule-consequentialism appeared later (perhaps with Mill, perhaps in the twentieth century) to try to save utilitarianism from the disturbing moral conclusions to which it leads. The rule-based approach was then rejected by the majority of moral philosophers as inconsistent with utilitarianism. Instead, this book offers a different version of the story. It is the rule version of consequentialism that came first. What is of particular interest about authors like Hume and Bentham is their determination to keep much of the earlier consequentialist logic while decreasing the importance of God in the explanation of those beliefs. Twentieth-century rule-utilitarianism was actually a return to an earlier formulation, without the theological underpinnings.

Second, an important part of this story is the significance of the secularization of conceptions of justice. It is in the sphere of justice that act-consequentialism has often been criticized for being insufficiently emphatic about the importance of rules and practices. Secularization affected both the reasons to act justly and the structure through which we think about the content of justice. Normally, all the attention is on the former. When the story of utilitarianism has been told in a way that gives a significant part to the theological versions of the approach, the emphasis has normally been on the issues of moral motivation and moral obligation. Many, but not all, of the utilitarians operated within a framework where human behavior is motivated by the desire for pleasure and aversion to pain. Since a utility-maximizing rule may conflict with my own private utility, God provided a convenient solution to the motivational problem. One could stipulate that God will punish vice and reward virtue in the next life such that moral behavior and self-interest are necessarily aligned. An issue is whether actions that are right are therefore obligatory absent a God who commands us to do what is right. The big question that Bentham, Mill, and Sidgwick faced was how to explain moral motivation and obligation without recourse to divine sanctions or divinely imposed obligations. This was emphasized by the most influential historians writing at the turn of the previous century. Sidgwick himself emphasized this problem in his *Outlines for the History of Ethics* (OHE) and highlighted the

problem of explaining moral motivation without God as the big outstand-
ing question at the end of his most famous work, *The Methods of Ethics*
(Methods). Leslie Stephen (1900) thought the absence of divine sanctions
was the only real difference between Bentham and the more theologically
inclined William Paley. Albee's valuable history of utilitarianism (1901)
similarly focuses on the problem of why we will act morally in the absence
of God.

Modern interpreters who affirm the importance of the "theological
utilitarians" have also tended to focus on the issues of moral obligation
and moral motivation rather than the shift to a legislative perspective and
the changes to the content of our moral beliefs that come with it. James
Crimmins (1990), who has been very helpful in highlighting the secular
turn of Bentham and his followers from the earlier theological versions of
utilitarianism, focuses on the problem of sanctions rather than the shift to
a legislative perspective. The theological utilitarians were defined by
T. P. Schofield in terms of their "adoption of a religious sanction for the
enforcement of moral obligation: virtue would find its reward in the
pleasures of heaven, and vice its punishment in the torments of hell"
(1987, 4). Bart Schultz says the main difference between Paley and the
secular utilitarians was "his reliance on God's command, with the prospect
of heaven or hell, rather than on the visible or invisible hands of social
institutions." He continues, "It was Paley's fame that spurred both Jeremy
Bentham and William Godwin to publicly defend a secular version of
utilitarianism, taking the doctrine off its conventional religious foundations" (Schultz 2017, 11). The closest view to mine is found in a few pages of
Schneewind's book on Sidgwick in which he discusses William Paley. He
notes Paley's theological utilitarianism as important and also that Paley was
"the forerunner of the utilitarians who were later to develop rather sophisticated versions of rule-utilitarianism" (1977, 126). He does not, however,
note the connection between the two, namely that the theology helps
justify the rule-based approach.[5]

While the absence of divine sanctions is certainly part of the story, the
present book will highlight a different aspect of the secularization of justice
that has remained in the background. A secularized justice faces not only
a motivational problem but also a perspectival problem. The content of
justice changes depending on whether we assess actions from the situated
perspective of an individual decision maker or the general perspective of

---

[5] Schneewind does argue that Paley quixotically thought his rule-based approach could solve the
problem of whether God's will determines what is right or is determined by what is right (1977, 127).

the legislator of a code of justice. This is true even for theories that are otherwise the same in their commitment to consequentialism. In the theological versions, the legislative perspective was understood to be factual since they believed there was, in fact, a divine legislator issuing binding decrees. In the secular versions, individuals must make a counterfactual perspectival shift, shifting to the perspective of a legislator even though they are not legislators.

This shapes the link between ethics and rationality. In the late twentieth century, formal theory, or game theory, popularized the notion that under certain circumstances individual rationality leads to collectively suboptimal outcomes. The "prisoner's dilemma" is the most famous example of this phenomenon. In such a scenario the cost/benefit is such that no matter which option the other person picks, one always gets a better outcome for oneself by implicating one's confederate. The result of both confederates choosing this course is much worse for them than if they had both remained silent. "Tragedy of the commons" scenarios have a similar structure where it may be rational from an individual perspective to overfish a lake but where the collective outcome of many people doing so is quite bad for all concerned.

Interestingly, two of the more common solutions to these problems, repeated iterations and legislative intervention, were already being explored in the early modern texts. The divine legislator was a way to solve collective action problems when human legislation was unavailable or ineffective. Secularized accounts of justice often appealed to repeated interactions to solve the problem, but with a richer and more complex psychological account than the twentieth-century versions. What is of special interest is to see that the problem is not ultimately one rooted in the "selfishness" sometimes postulated in game theory. Even strong consequentialists who seek the good of all concerned may find that their actions are suboptimal if they and others think from the perspective of a situated individual rather than taking on a legislative perspective. Derek Parfit's book *Reasons and Persons* was enormously influential in analyzing the ways consequentialism might be self-defeating or self-effacing. In one example he notes: "Consequentialists should claim (C9) Suppose that each of us has made the outcome as good as he can, given what the others did. Each has then acted rightly. But we together may have acted wrongly. This will be so if we together could have made the outcome better" (Parfit 1984, 73). Thinking in a consequentialist manner from a situated perspective can lead to suboptimal outcomes for very unselfish people. Larry Temkin argues that this may be the case with attempts to help the poor around the world (Temkin 2019).

Some consequentialists argued that if thinking from a legislative perspective leads to better outcomes than thinking from a situated perspective there is no real paradox because consequentialism would then instruct us to use the legislative perspective or adopt some other decision-making procedure rather than directly employ consequentialism. Parfit calls these forms of consequentialism "self-effacing" since they direct us to believe some theory other than consequentialism in order to bring about the best consequence. The parallel to prisoner's dilemma scenarios suggests that more argument is needed here since some forms of rationality (perhaps including consequentialism) can create situations where we can see the suboptimal outcome looming but are unable to avoid it within the constraints of the form of rationality in use. Knowing that if we all think a certain way we get suboptimal outcomes is not always sufficient reason for me not to think that way, absent a strong moral reason to shift perspectives.

Third, the book will draw upon this story to consider the proper role of this legislative approach to morality today. I will argue that it does have a number of attractive features but that in order to adopt it one needs commitments that go beyond utilitarianism and, more broadly, consequentialism.[6] I will advocate for a hybrid approach in which the legislative point of view rests on a combination of consequentialist and nonconsequentialist commitments. If one is going to justify the perspectival shift, one needs either to revert to a theological formulation or find alternative nonconsequentialist grounds for justifying the perspectival shift. Since I assume that most of my readers will find the former option problematic (Mackie 1982), I focus instead on working out how one might make a nonconsequentialist case for the needed perspectival shift. In doing so I will return to the elements contained in the perspective of an actual legislator and show how different elements of that perspective contain attractive normative elements. One way of thinking about nonconsequentialist theories of justice, such as that of Rawls, is that they use deontological constraints such as publicity requirements that are designed to approximate a legislative point of view, albeit not one concerned with maximizing utility overall. Nonetheless, these approaches force us to imagine ourselves articulating principles that will then guide future decision-making in a legislative way.

[6] Some of these themes were explored in a different context, specific to Locke, in Tuckness 2002.

In making this argument I do not claim (or believe) that the legislative perspective captures the whole of moral thinking, nor do I think that conclusions reached from that point of view must be decisive in every situation. In the same way that citizens are sometimes morally justified in breaking the law, so too there may be some instances where persons are justified in acting contrary to the rules that would be selected from the legislative perspective. What I will argue instead, and explain in more detail in the final chapter, is that rules generated from a legislative perspective should be given more weight than can be explained from a situated perspective alone. Someone reasoning from a situated perspective has reason to think about the value of a norm or practice and about how failure to adhere to that norm might undermine it, causing harm. Someone reasoning from a situated perspective might recognize the efficiency gains and validity gains that a rule-based decision-making procedure has over a case-by-case decision procedure. I will argue for a commitment to the legislative perspective that gives the moral rules discovered from that perspective a weight that cannot be explained if one begins reasoning from a situated perspective alone. In other words, the goal is to justify a shift to a different starting point for moral reflection.

The argument I will make is constructed so as to be ecumenical on metaphysical questions such as the disputes between, for example, moral realists and constructivists. One might adopt the legislative point of view because one thinks doing so gets one closer to truths that are antecedently there, that it is an attractive framework for constructing moral principles, or that it makes good sense of one's moral sentiments. The sorts of reasons I will give do not depend on a particular metaphysical view.

The argument will also be ecumenical regarding the content of the beliefs adopted from the legislative point of view. People who are persuaded that the legislative point of view at least partly informs what is right may have strong disagreements about what principles would be selected from the legislative point of view. My argument is, in a sense, an argument for why we should imagine ourselves to be entering a legislative chamber, not an argument for which specific proposals will be adopted there. A legislative chamber is a place where people disagree about which rule is best. Nonetheless, it is important that we think the debate that takes place within a metaphorical legislative chamber is a debate worth having. The questions we pose have a substantive impact on the conclusions that we reach. Asking the question "which act?" leads to different answers than asking "which rule?" Similarly, asking the question "which rule is best for us?" yields different answers than the question "which rule is best for us as

well as others?" Each of these shifts of question often involves counterfactual thinking and I explore the reasons why these counterfactual questions
are important ones to ask.

Framing the Argument: Scope and Method

There are several definitional and methodological issues that need attention before beginning our historical account. The first has to do with
consequentialism and utilitarianism. I will focus on theories that have
a significant consequentialist aspect, even if they are not thoroughly
consequentialist, since the thinking of actual legislators almost always
includes at least some consequentialist aspect. My interest is in consequentialism more generally rather than in utilitarianism specifically, but much
of the literature I will explore focuses on this issue within the framework of
the meaning of utilitarianism and the debates between act- and rule-
utilitarianism. The basic dilemma I study applies to most forms of consequentialism since the basic dilemma of maximizing consequences from
a situated perspective versus a legislative perspective can still arise. In
general, I will follow the language of the authors I study. Parfit and
Hooker prefer to talk about consequentialism and so when discussing
them I will use that language. Utilitarians from Bentham to Sidgwick
consciously embraced the label "utilitarian" and so I will use it when
discussing them. In Part II where I discuss the contemporary implications
of the historical analysis, I will follow the now accepted distinction where
utilitarianism is a subset of consequentialism that has a more restricted
scope of what consequences count as good. As noted, the main interest
there will be in consequentialist theories more broadly and in ways nonconsequentialist considerations might help motivate a shift to the legislative perspective.

A related issue is the problem of defining utilitarianism itself. Traditions
evolve over time and it is misleading to impose a single definition on
utilitarianism and then criticize thinkers for not adhering to a definition
that is ours, not theirs (Rosen 2003, discussed below). Moreover, as will
become apparent in what follows, even among those who today study the
history of utilitarianism one finds widely varying definitions. Often this is
because a given writer is interested in a particular historical tradition and
different writers are drawn to different facets of a multifaceted movement.
William Paley provides an interesting test case. As we will see, Mill denied
that he was a member of the utilitarian movement largely because he was
not a sufficiently zealous advocate for progressive reform. Undeniably, the

reformist mission of utilitarianism from Bentham to Sidgwick is crucial to understanding their project but it is not obvious that "conservative utilitarianism" is a logical contradiction. Others think utilitarianism is, by definition, secular. Here again Paley would not count as a utilitarian since, as we will see, God plays a crucial role in his theory. That the move toward secularism was momentous in the history of utilitarianism is both true and one of the main points of this book. That said, building secularism into the definition risks obscuring the very thing this book wants to illuminate, namely the way in which the secular progressive movement of Jeremy Bentham had roots in and was reacting against a theological perspective that shared many of the same assumptions.

This book will therefore try to acknowledge these other issues while using a definition that tracks the issue most relevant to our inquiry, one that understands utilitarianism primarily as a standard of right and wrong. When Sidgwick wrote about utilitarian ethics, what he primarily meant was that utility provided a rational standard for discerning what makes actions right and wrong. With that emphasis in mind, I will use a broad definition where utilitarianism is a theory that defines right and wrong with reference to actual, intended or likely impact on happiness (or a related notion of well-being). Utilitarian theories may assess actions directly with respect to their likely impact on happiness or indirectly, for example with respect to a rule justified by its contribution to happiness. This definition is loose with respect to the details of what is being maximized because, as noted above, the real interest is in consequentialist theories more generally and so there is little to be gained by arguing about whether satisfied preferences, or retrospectively satisfied preferences, or desirable states of consciousness, or some other goal is what "real" utilitarians seek to maximize.

A related issue is chronological scope. Wherever one starts a historical study, one enters midstream. For this project I find it most helpful to begin with three seventeenth-century thinkers: Hugo Grotius, Richard Cumberland, and John Locke. I choose Grotius because he arguably starts a new and distinctively modern way of thinking about ethics and politics. He was forced to think about the principles that should govern war, peace, and much else without assuming a mutually recognized moral authority. He consciously engaged in ethical inquiry by thinking through the likely consequences that different sorts of rules would generate when acted upon by biased, fallible people. The natural law tradition of which Grotius was a part, by the time of Locke and Cumberland, was such that one could employ a thought experiment where one asks, "would a benevolent God enact this moral code?" to answer questions about what is right and what is wrong. Whether they were the very first to do so is less important than capturing a particular view of ethical decision-making and rationality. The conjunction of three beliefs set in motion the basics of the legislative approach to morality: that right and wrong are defined by a system of rules, that those rules are chosen by God in order to increase human happiness, and that these rules can be known through the use of reason and not only through special revelation. I am less interested in discovering the date when "utilitarianism" began than in describing a particular way of thinking about ethics that was crystalizing in late seventeenth-century England in the work of Cumberland and Locke, both of whom drew upon Grotius.

A similar logic governs the choice of the other thinkers studied. My goal is not to comprehensively discuss every thinker of the last three hundred years who employed the morality-as-legislation approach but rather to focus on key moments in a tradition that runs from the seventeenth century to contemporary debates in Anglo-American philosophy and political theory about rules and consequences. For that reason, I focus on authors from that tradition, most of whom are British. A project that looked more broadly at similar phenomena in continental thought or in nonwestern cultures would be welcome but is beyond the scope of this book.

As a final methodological point, let me address the problem of anachronism. Rosen (2003) notes a tendency in discussions of utilitarianism that is both unhelpful and that can be replicated in discussions of other topics. The error is to decide that a particular thinker, say Bentham, is the paradigm of a particular school of thought and then to criticize related thinkers who were either before or after (Hume or Mill, for example) as being "inconsistent utilitarians" because they depart from Bentham in some way or other. In doing so we are anachronistically imposing on them an understanding of utilitarianism that was not theirs. In the case at hand, if one takes the act/rule-utilitarianism distinction and applies it retrospectively to thinkers who never used the distinction one risks distorting their thought in the process. At a minimum, one may emphasize things that were not the emphasis of the original thinkers. Acknowledging this, it is nonetheless true that one of the reasons to look at these questions historically is to notice the questions people were not asking or the assumptions that were so widely shared that they didn't need to be stated. Noting this can help us make better sense of the debates that arise later when these issues are disputed. The question "what happens to your theory of morality if God is removed?" is not anachronistic in the least. It is a question that the thinkers of this era thought about often. Their different answers (and their varying levels of enthusiasm for finding out) drive much of the story that follows. Yet it is noteworthy that from Locke to Sidgwick they focused on how the removal of God undercut an important incentive for moral behavior, the threat of future rewards and punishments. Bentham was perhaps the most optimistic that such incentives could be done away with and little of importance would be lost. My goal is to foreground something that is clearer in retrospect than it was to the original participants in the debate. While the phrase "reflective equilibrium" originated in the twentieth century, the basic idea that one could discredit a moral theory by showing that it leads to conclusions that "everyone knows are wrong" has a long history indeed. To this day, asking how a moral theory matches with our moral intuitions is a common part of ethical discourse.

I hope to show that the thinkers we will study frequently utilized a legislative perspective on morality and were thereby able to arrive at what they thought were more satisfactory moral conclusions as a result. Some of this was undoubtedly unconscious. If one begins with the assumption that there is a divine law that prohibits bearing false witness, it will make intuitive sense to think that what one does in thinking about ethics is to find a route, by reason alone, to that same law. That one arrives at the acceptable conclusion solidifies one's confidence in the theory. Many of these thinkers were, in part, trying to come up with a rational basis for thinking about ethics that would account for enough of their existing beliefs to give them confidence in its validity while having enough critical purchase to provide meaningful guidance on the contested issues of their day. Their religious beliefs often led them to assume that morality has a law-like character without feeling the need to argue for that claim explicitly. One could imagine a God who judges people based on whether they produce the best consequences from their situated perspective, but that was not the God that they typically imagined.

Overview of the Book

Chapter 1 begins with Grotius, Cumberland, and Locke and argues that in them we see the basic elements of the theological version of morality as legislation. Grotius used a framework of evaluating the consequences of different possible rules for fallible, biased people as a way of determining what ought to be done. Cumberland provided a theory of right in which all the content of all divine laws could be traced back to one divine attribute, benevolence. Locke, while less systematically consequentialist than

Cumberland, had a hedonistic theory of the good, an account of God that also emphasized benevolence, and (most interestingly) a willingness to press very hard on the legislative metaphor in order to establish the correct content of natural law when it was in dispute. Locke imagines God as a legislator using precisely the structure of rationality that a human legislator would use in contemplating which law to pass, including problems of biased and fallible execution of the law. Locke's use is clearly counterfactual. It is probably not a coincidence that both Locke and Cumberland were strong supporters of new scientific theories that sought to understand nature by means of natural laws.

Chapter 2 examines the first important stage in the secularization of this theory culminating in the work of David Hume. During this time, two metaphors were in competition with the legislative metaphor, the architect, and the spectator. Shaftesbury emphasized what I will call the architect metaphor where one assumes that God, the divine architect, has so designed human beings that we know what is right without needing to use the legislative paradigm. Human beings are endowed with a moral sense by the divine architect. Francis Hutcheson tried to synthesize the legislator and architect metaphors while adding that of the spectator. The perspective of the unbiased spectator, or a sufficiently numerous group of spectators, helps us determine what is right. Hume is helpfully contrasted with his more theologically inclined predecessors as he rejected the legislative and architectural metaphors and secularized the spectator metaphor. Hume's skepticism about the existence of divinely implanted moral sense led him to seek other ways of explaining our sense of justice. Hume was very aware of the basic dilemma that adhering to the rules of justice in particular cases did not always produce the most good but that it was nonetheless important that people obey the rules of justice even in those cases. We will explore what Hume thought motivated people to act on rules that would be approved from the legislative perspective without recourse to divine intervention.

Chapter 3 examines the decisive break between religious and secular utilitarianism in the thought of William Paley and Jeremy Bentham. Paley, the better known and more widely respected thinker of the two at the time, is in many ways the paradigm case of the theological version of morality as legislation. Paley, like Locke, used human legislative deliberation as a paradigm of rationality for thinking about the content of the divine law. Bentham's project must be understood in part as motivated by a desire to reject the theological assumptions of theories like Paley's that stood in the way of radical reform. It also encouraged a reframing of moral expression as a kind of legislative act. Bentham saw reputational sanctions as one substitute for religious motives for moral action, but this also required a perspectival shift, when making moral statements, to a more legislative perspective.

Chapter 4 explores the development of Bentham's approach by his successors J. S. Mill and Henry Sidgwick. Both of them were grappling, explicitly now, with the perspectival problem that Bentham's full rejection of the theological justification for the legislative point of view entailed. Mill's intriguing suggestion that "wrong" refers to that which should be punished by law, public opinion, or private conscience, combined with his assumption that all three are open to revision on utilitarian principles, leads to the interesting conclusion that our moral statements about right and wrong are tacit legislative proposals and that in deciding whether to voice our moral opinions we must think like legislators. This was in tension with the idea that our public expressions of moral judgment should be spontaneous reactions to the poor choices of others. It is hard to see how we can do both at once. Sidgwick grasped the implications of this issue more clearly and more self-consciously than Mill did, since it meant that there was a potentially deep disjunction between what is right according to utilitarianism and what utilitarianism tells us to publicly state as right. Must we condemn an action we think is right if we don't want to encourage people to act in similar ways in the future? Sidgwick's defense of an esoteric morality is the final outcome of the attempt to secularize morality as legislation.

Chapter 5 looks at the twentieth-century debates about rule-consequentialism with an emphasis on the rule-utilitarian theories that dominated the debate. In the twentieth century, secular philosophers explicitly defended rule-utilitarian theories as alternatives to act-utilitarian theories that, they thought, led to implausible moral conclusions. This approach was powerfully criticized by people like David Lyons and J. J. C. Smart who thought rule-consequentialism was paradoxical because it awarded rules a weight that could not be justified on consequentialist grounds. In the mid- to late twentieth century there were philosophers who attempted to challenge the boundaries of utilitarian orthodoxy by expressly using nonconsequentialist moral premises to justify the shift to a legislative rather than a situated perspective. The focus on the failure of rule-utilitarianism in terms of strict utilitarian orthodoxy has obscured the importance of hybrid theories that draw on both consequentialist and nonconsequentialist premises. A number of thinkers who are classified as rule-utilitarians (and sometimes criticized for betraying utilitarian orthodoxy) in fact expressly acknowledged nonutilitarian aspects of their theories (including R. M. Hare and John Harsanyi). They are the heirs of the earlier hybrid approaches and provide a bridge to the contemporary use of hybrid approaches that is the focus of Part II. The chapter ends with a summary of the main historical claims of Part I. Rule-utilitarianism was not a revision of traditional utilitarianism but rather an attempt to return to the rule-based consequentialism of earlier theories without the theological foundations. Because God, in these earlier theories, did more than threaten people for disobedience, the secular versions struggled to explain why right action should be defined on the basis of rules that counterfactually would be chosen if one were legislating. The most successful ones consciously adopted a hybrid approach.

Part II of the book looks at the prospects for justifying the shift to the legislative perspective today. Chapter 6 looks at three prominent consequentialist strategies that have been employed more recently to justify different forms of the legislative perspective, as well as a fourth option that is Kantian. The first option, exemplified by Robert Goodin, Conrad Johnson, and Frederick Schauer, is to restrict legislative consequentialism's scope to the design of rules, policies, and institutions. The second option, pursued by Katarzyna de Lazari-Radek and Peter Singer, is to follow Sidgwick and accept a disjunction between moral rules and moral right (or between decision rules and the standard of right). The third option, used by Brad Hooker, seeks to justify a consequentialist legislative perspective based on its fit with our moral judgments using something like a reflective equilibrium approach rather than having consequentialism itself be the foundation. The chapter then considers a very different fourth option where the shift to a legislative point of view depends on Kantian claims as seen in the work of Thomas Hill, Jr. and Derek Parfit. Each of these approaches, however, includes serious drawbacks. Option one cannot help us in cases where we are not legislating, the counterfactual cases that are the emphasis of this book. It also risks being ad hoc. Option two will be unappealing to many because of its esoteric morality and rejection of a publicity principle. Option three raises questions about why, if nonconsequentialist moral considerations are used in selecting rule-consequentialism as a theory, we might not incorporate those nonconsequentialist considerations into the set of reasons used in determining the content of the moral code. Option four can justify the perspectival shift to the legislative perspective, but its rejection of consequentialist reasoning (at least in its more strictly

Kantian versions) makes the perspective unlike that of actual legislators and yields its own set of hard-to-accept moral conclusions.

Chapter 7 argues that the best option for defending the use of the legislative perspective is a hybrid approach that includes both consequentialist and nonconsequentialist commitments. Given that the theory in its original theistic form combined nonconsequentialist religious commitments with weak consequentialist reasoning, a successful adaptation of the legislative perspective to appeal to contemporary secular audiences will need to address both types of moral commitments. The chapter begins by reiterating the type of legislative perspective that is required: one that is moderate in its strength, realistic, at least weakly consequentialist, and applies to counterfactual cases where one is not literally legislating. I then sketch the reasons why a counterfactual use of the legislative perspective might be attractive. Next, I identify six moral commitments that one must endorse in order to use the legislative perspective in the specified sense. I argue that all six are plausible, but also note that they require a hybrid approach that is neither solely consequentialist nor solely nonconsequentialist. I describe the benefits of this hybrid approach and conclude by arguing that the nonconsequentialist reasons that justify the shift to the legislative perspective are stronger in cases where people are making decisions in political contexts, even if those contexts are not legislative contexts.

PART I

The Emergence of the Rule-Consequentialist Paradox

CHAPTER I

God and Consequences
The Path to Locke

I choose to begin the historical survey in the seventeenth century. While one can perhaps find earlier versions of the legislative perspective, the goal of the historical survey is not to provide a complete genealogy of the idea but rather to map a transition from one way of thinking to another. This chapter describes the use of the legislative perspective in a school of thought interested in natural law and natural rights with an empiricist aspect. They argued for the existence of transcultural, transhistorical moral principles but also believed that in order to identify those principles one needed to know something about the likely consequences of people trying to act on a rule. It is with John Locke that I think this way of thinking is most clearly specified and in this chapter we will examine how Locke did that, building on the prior work of Hugo Grotius and Richard Cumberland. There are others who could be mentioned here, such as Suarez, Hobbes, and Pufendorf, but since the goal is not to give a comprehensive account, the briefer treatment here should be adequate for our purposes. My goal in treating Grotius, Cumberland, and Locke will be to explain the role of consequentialist thinking in their thought and the extent to which that thinking takes a legislative form. In Locke we see the most developed form of the argument, but all three of them contribute to the development of the concept.

Grotius promoted a general framework of thinking that assumed the existence of international laws where the underlying justification for those laws is related to the likely positive consequences of the law existing. Grotius attempted to show that various legal conventions were justified on such a basis. He also thought that widely held opinions about what is right could themselves constitute a form of law. His most important work, *The Law of War and Peace*, will be our focus.[1] The form of argument

---

[1] Some translations take the title to be *The Rights of War and Peace*. While the difference is very important in a number of contexts, it is not important for this inquiry. Rights of the sort Grotius had in mind would still constitute general principles about what is right and wrong and could still be thought of as legislative in the same sense that a law is.

Grotius used for explaining the law of nations would be used later by Locke in specifying the law of nature.

Cumberland and Locke were both born in 1632; both were interested in medicine and both became famous for their writings on natural law. Ernest Albee (1901, 19) saw Cumberland as the founder of English utilitarianism. Cumberland argued that we have duties of benevolence to all rational beings and that the right action is the one that produces the most good. He also thought that the moral law was obligatory because it was promulgated by God. We would thus seem to have the basic ingredients in place for a theistic, rule-based consequentialism. Nonetheless, Cumberland did not grasp the implications of the perspectival shift in a way that would lead to different conclusions when one shifts to the rule-based perspective. Instead, in Cumberland's version, the two perspectives – that of the moral agent and that of the moral legislator – seem interchangeable. Moreover, there are questions about whether Cumberland understands consequences in the right sort of way to generate what I call the legislative point of view.

Locke's work on religious toleration, by contrast, forced him to face the ethical implications of the perspectival shift. One reaches different conclusions if a king asks "which, of all the actions I could perform, will most promote the true religion," rather than "which rule would God command all kings to act on in order to most promote true religion, recognizing the epistemic limitations of those kings." In Locke we see the basic logic of rule-consequentialism being used to determine the content of the moral law as it applies to politics. Before discussing these three, I will begin by clarifying the issues that will be our focus since there are competing narratives about the jural or legislative turn in early modern political thought that are different from the question I pursue.

Different Senses of "Legislative" or "Jural" Thinking

Others have discussed the question of whether a distinctively legislative or jural way of thinking about morality emerged during this period. Sidgwick, for example, makes this argument in his history of ethics (OHE). More recently, Terrance Irwin (2008) has discussed this question in detail. The question I will be pursuing is different from their primary questions, though it has some affinities. It will, therefore, be helpful to situate my question against these other questions at the outset.

What Sidgwick has in mind with his distinction is the idea that, for the ancient Greeks and Romans, the big ethical questions were about what the human good is and how to attain it. With the introduction of Christianity, the idea of moral law became more prominent in western philosophy and this moral law came to be thought of in ways similar to an actual legal code (Sidgwick OHE, III). By the time of Hugo Grotius, natural law had emerged as a primary focus of ethical thinking, at least in terms of interpersonal behavior. Irwin thinks that Sidgwick overstates the importance of Grotius. Irwin focuses on the longstanding debate between naturalists who take natural law to be merely indicative (indicating things that are already right or wrong by their very nature) and voluntarists who take things to be right or wrong just because God has decreed them to be so. Since God's decrees were normally thought of as general rules, voluntarism can be thought of as a legislative or jural approach to ethics. Irwin notes that we can distinguish between the content of natural law and whether it is obligatory. Irwin thinks Grotius follows Suarez (with less precision) in taking things to be right or wrong on naturalist grounds, in that there is something morally important prior to God's legislation that explains why the action is right or wrong. Nonetheless, what is right becomes binding on us because of God's legislative command. We should therefore differentiate between being a voluntarist with regard to the content of morality and being a voluntarist with regard to the obligation of morality.[2]

The debates about voluntarism were extensive, as is the secondary literature pertaining to them, and my goal is not to add to those debates. For present purposes, it is important that the version of the legislative point of view that is our focus depends on a theory in which the content of natural law is not subject to arbitrary specification by God. Strong forms of content-voluntarism are incompatible with the legislative point of view because the basic structure involves reasoning to what moral laws God has legislated based on both empirical facts and an understanding of God's moral character and purposes. We need, in some sense, to be able to think God's thoughts along with God. We need to be able to use the legislative metaphor for discerning what God has decreed through reason rather than through direct revelation. A God who might specify that benevolence is a virtue and then change to specify that it is a vice is not the sort of God whose will could be determined in this way. To discern God's will by reason we must be able to gain knowledge of God's moral goals and empirical facts about human beings and their contexts.

---

[2] See chapters 30–33 in Irwin 2008. On the distinction between the content and ground of natural law as it relates to voluntarism, see also Tuckness 1999.

If we turn from content-voluntarism to obligation-voluntarism, the situation changes. There is some commonality between obligation-voluntarism and the concept of a divine legislator because of a shared assumption that morality requires the existence of a lawgiver in order for morality to be binding, and this certainly is one way of thinking about morality as analogous to legislation. While it is true that the thinkers we will examine in this chapter believed that obligation depended on divine decree, the question I am pursuing in this book is a different one. Sidgwick and Irwin are interested in questions of moral motivation or moral obligation. (Is it in my interests to act morally? Am I obliged to act morally?) I focus instead on a different way in which God as legislator might impact ethics, namely by justifying a particular framework for working out the content of morality where the relevant question is whether or not the rule on which one acts is one that God would command, given a God who incorporates consequentialist thinking when specifying that content. That the commands of God give us reason to act morally was of course central to the way of thinking I am describing, but my goal in this book is not to provide yet another assessment of the cogency of divine theories of moral obligation or moral motivation but to highlight a third and much less understood shift.

Hugo Grotius

Grotius is famous both for his contributions to the field of international law and for his contribution to the idea of natural rights (Tuck 1979, 1999; Schneewind 1998, 66–81; Bull, Kingsbury, and Roberts 1990). The idea of reciprocity is inherent in the structure of his natural law theory. The law of nature was, for Grotius, "a dictate of right reason, which points out that an act, according as it is or is not in conformity with rational nature, has in it a quality of moral baseness or moral necessity; and that, in consequence, such an act is either forbidden or enjoined by the author of nature, God" (Grotius, I.I.I0.I). The first crucial question is therefore how we know God's will. Grotius began by reflecting on the sort of nature that God chose to create for human beings. God's creation is an expression of his will. The two most important aspects of human nature for Grotius were that human beings are strongly inclined to preserve themselves but also sociable creatures who want to live in community. Since God created us with these desires, acting in accordance with these desires is part of natural law. Grotius thought these drives are generally harmonious since if we act against the principles that preserve community, we are undermining one of our own key interests.

Given this framework, there are two different ways of establishing that a principle is part of natural law. The first is by showing "the necessary agreement or disagreement of anything with a rational and social nature" (Grotius, I.I.12.I). The other is by showing that the principle is universally, or almost universally, endorsed by all nations, or at least by the civilized ones. Grotius needed these qualifications ("almost" and "civilized") in order to get traction given the difficulty of finding literal unanimity among the nations on matters of moral right. Widespread agreement is indirect proof that the precept flows from the human nature that God chose to bestow. In other words, it is not that common consent directly creates obligation, but rather that it is evidence that a given precept is not merely one adopted in a particular place, but one that flows from our human nature.

Grotius thought that these principles promoted our living together and are rational expressions of our sociable nature.

> This maintenance of the social order, which we have roughly sketched, and which is consonant with human intelligence, is the source of law properly so called. To this sphere of law belong the abstaining from that which is another's, the restoration to another of anything of his which we may have, together with any gain which we may have received from it; the obligation to fulfil promises, the making good of a loss incurred through our fault, and the inflicting of penalties upon men according to their deserts. (Prolegomena.8)

Grotius thought that these principles described the sort of code that we would understand, based on reason, and that are necessary for creatures who want to live sociably with each other. He thought that although there will be differences of detail, we should expect to see these principles embodied in the laws of civilized nations.

The role of God in Grotius' theory is controversial. A few paragraphs later, he wrote: "What we have been saying would have a degree of validity even if we should concede that which cannot be conceded without the utmost wickedness, that there is no God, or that the affairs of men are of no concern to Him" (Prolegomena.11). Given the nature that we have, we do in fact desire to preserve ourselves within human community and thus we already have an internal motivation to affirm these principles even if we have no belief in a divine legislator who commands us to obey and will punish us if we do not. This does not mean that Grotius was denying the existence of God or denying that God's commands give an important reason to obey natural law, but it does highlight an idea that will become important later, which is that given certain assumptions about human beings, people might have self-interested reasons to promote norms that have beneficial consequences. Grotius also believed that God has the freedom, through special revelation, to impose additional obligations on people. The Old Testament law placed additional obligations on the Jewish people, and the New Testament places additional obligations on Christians (1.1.15–16, 2.1.10–13). God can, therefore, legislate in a more direct way for particular groups of people, revealing his commands to them directly or allowing us to discover more general rules that apply to all people.

Grotius was not using the legislative point of view in the form that Locke later will. Grotius did not suggest that we do a thought experiment where we consider different possible rules, think about the likely consequences of each, and then discern which one God has in fact legislated. Rather, God communicates his will to us by giving us desires for preservation and community. We need not think in an explicitly legislative way, we need only to act on our natural desires in a reasonable way. Given this framework, the existence of God is less important than it will be in Locke's version of the argument. Irwin is right in saying that in the passage quoted above concerning the necessity of God that

> Grotius refers to God as creator, not as legislator; he does not endorse voluntarism about natural law or morality. Like Suarez, he acknowledges God's creative will as the source of human beings with their nature, and hence as the source of naturally right and wrong actions; but this does not imply that natural right and wrong are the result of divine legislation. Though it is up to God whether there are any human beings, and hence whether any human beings act rightly or wrongly, it is not up to God to decide what is good or bad, or right or wrong, for creatures with the nature that is essential to human beings. (Irwin 2008, 92)

Grotius here used what will, in the next chapter, be called the architectural metaphor, which is an alternative to the legislative metaphor. Since we are designed by God, so the argument goes, reflection on our natural desires is a clue to God's will.

The consequentialism of Grotius' theory can be seen in the rationale he gives for reducing the moral requirements of natural law. Natural law did not require human virtue so much as bar acts that were clearly destructive of social relationships between human beings. Higher moral requirements were acknowledged by Grotius but generally treated as imperfect duties rather than as obligations one may be compelled to honor. Grotius also allowed self-preservation to take priority over duties to others when they were in conflict, at least as far as natural law was concerned (Forde 1998). Consider Grotius' initial discussion of whether war is permissible or not. He began by appealing to our created nature, in common with other animals. "The end and aim of war being the preservation of life and limb, and the keeping or acquiring of things useful to life, war is in perfect accord with those first principles of nature" (1.2.1.4). He then argued that

> Right reason, moreover, and the nature of society, which must be studied in the second place and are of even greater importance, do not prohibit all use of force, but only that use of force which is in conflict with society, that is which attempts to take away the rights of another. For society has in view this object, that through community of resource and effort each individual be safeguarded in the possession of what belongs to him. (1.2.1.5)

The second step hints at the legislative point of view. It is only unjust use of force that is contrary to society; things like punishment, or using force to restore what has been stolen, or to defend oneself from attack, are consistent with living in peaceful community. There is a sense in which a principle like "one may kill in self-defense" is affirmed because the general principle, when affirmed, promotes the goal of peaceful society. Yet we should not overstate the link between Grotius and the legislative point of view, since the main thrust of Grotius is to find these initial principles already widely affirmed and then give further confirmation by noting their compatibility with society. This is still different from considering multiple rules and selecting one based on consequences. Grotius' last step looked for confirmation of this position in history and the writings of various authorities and legal texts (1.2.2–3). This fits with his earlier claim that if something is part of the law of nature, we should expect to see it widely adopted.

Another precursor to the legislative point of view is Grotius' explanation of how natural law interacts with human laws. Grotius did not believe that everything that is wrong according to natural law must be prohibited by human law or vice versa. Human laws, whether civil law or the law of nations, make things directly enforceable and not everything that is wrong should be punished. Grotius noted two senses of "permissible." Morally permissible can mean that an action is not morally wrong (though perhaps not morally best) or it can simply mean that an action should not be punished (3.4.2). Grotius made this distinction because, in selecting rules and assessing their compatibility with the overall goal of sociability, the power to enforce a valid right is sometimes counterproductive.

The best example of how this works is seen with respect to conduct in war. According to the standard of right conduct, the side that is the unjust aggressor in a war should lay down its arms immediately and make reparations to the state it has harmed. We have already seen that such actions are commanded by the law of nature. Given that understanding, only the state with justice on its side is allowed to use force in self-defense. The state that launched an unjust war has no right to use violence. Nonetheless, the law of nations rightly treats conflicts differently. The problem is that states rarely consider themselves unjust aggressors and are in any case unlikely to comply with such a requirement. Any attempt to enforce the principle must confront these facts. Grotius confronted them by declaring that, in many cases in which third parties are contemplating punishing one side of a dispute for going beyond what natural law permits, the question of which side is actually in the right must be set aside. Grotius wrote:

> The reason why such effects met with the approval of nations was this. To undertake to decide regarding the justice of a war between two peoples had been dangerous for other peoples, who were on this account involved in a foreign war ... Furthermore, even in a lawful war, from external indications it can hardly be adequately known what is the just limit of self-defence, of recovering what is one's own, or of inflicting punishments; in consequence it has seemed altogether preferable to leave decisions in regard to such matters to the scruples of the belligerents rather than to have recourse to the judgments of others. (3.4.4)

It is not that there are no moral questions about how far a state can go in defending itself, but rather that if we allowed third parties to punish a state for going beyond what morality, strictly interpreted, permits, this would only drag more nations into the war and increase the bloodshed. Because judgments about what constitutes going "too far" are so contested, it is safer to deny that third parties have the right to enforce this moral principle.

Grotius here allowed nations to declare certain parts of natural law unenforceable through the law of nations. There are two possible views of this power. One is that there is a general power that states have to suspend the enforcement of natural law through the law of nations.[3] This is possible, but it is also possible that the power is more restricted. Grotius

---

[3] Forde (1998, 645–6) questions whether the permission to kill women and children in war can properly be thought of as minimizing suffering. He takes Grotius to claim that international law

looked favorably on this enforcement restriction because it plausibly contributes to the main purpose of natural law, which is maintaining peaceable society and includes decreasing bloodshed. Parallel to this would be his view that it is right to set aside strict application of a rule if strict application would undermine the rule's original purpose (2.16.26–8).

This concession has important implications for the practical application of his theory. Grotius went on to list a series of actions often taken in war (killing civilians and prisoners of war, for example) and declared that they may be performed with impunity even though they are wrong (3.4.6–14). Grotius worried about the following scenario: since most wars will involve the use of such means, wars will never end. Both sides will be guilty, thus entitling both sides to inflict punishments on the other, and likely commit further violations while trying to do so.

Grotius' approach to the law of nations thus involved a kind of consequentialism. If allowing states to punish other states for violations of the laws of war will only increase the bloodshed, the actions must sadly be regarded as having (earthly) impunity. Grotius claimed that declaring some offenses non-punishable is the least bad alternative.

While Grotius did not use this same procedure to justify particular laws of nature, he clearly thought the law of nations is compatible with the law of nature despite seeming to contradict it. The contradiction is only seeming because Grotius could explain that the law of nature makes separate judgments about what is right and about what should be punished, and that there can be an action X which is not in agreement with peaceful community while it is also the case that a general permission to punish X would undermine the prospects for peaceful community even more. This is an early version of what we will later call the disjunction strategy. The law of nations, backed by the law of nature, thus provides a way of looking at these questions from a more legislative and less situated point of view. From a situated perspective one would only look at a particular instance where intervention might be attempted and ask whether the intervention is justified based on the particulars of the case. One might decide that a given state is the unjust aggressor and that, therefore, every act of war by it is effectively a war crime. Grotius rejected

---

can limit the application of natural law without showing a consequentialist benefit. While I share Forde's intuition about whether such a permission is truly justifiable on consequentialist grounds, it is quite possible that Grotius had in mind that such violations were so likely to happen in practice that making them punishable would make things even worse by starting an escalating cycle of retaliation.

this. The law of nations must be framed as a general rule that many nations will try to follow, and actions must be assessed with respect to that rule.

The law of nations emerges, not from the will of a particular person, but from widely held norms adopted by a large number of people. Those who find themselves in a position to help shape these international norms are in a factual, rather than counterfactual, legislative position. Their position is analogous to Locke's "law of opinion," discussed below, and to a position we will discuss in later chapters called "moral expression as legislation" where moral norms that have law-like characteristics emerge by an informal process. What Grotius did not do, however, was make an explicit argument for the counterfactual use of the legislative perspective. Rather, his argument is that the men who formed the current law of nations thought in legislative terms and thus had good reasons for their choices, such as the choice to declare some wrongs unpunishable as a matter of international law. Laws of this sort are rational because they are in accord with the overarching goal of peaceable society. Locke, we will see shortly, used similar ideas and applied them directly to the law of nature itself. First, however, we turn to Cumberland who more thoroughly emphasized benevolence and the common good for thinking through the content of the law of nature.

Richard Cumberland

Given this chapter's focus on consequentialist approaches to natural law, Richard Cumberland is an important figure. He is thought by some to be the true founder of utilitarianism, and the figure of the divine legislator features prominently in his thought. Cumberland is important, for our purposes, because of his emphasis on benevolence as the essential characteristic of God and the primary virtue for human beings within a moral theory that emphasizes divine law. Nonetheless, there are important differences between his thought and Locke's version of the legislative point of view.

In broad overview, Cumberland argued that we have a duty to promote the good of all "rationals," that is all rational beings (including God). While there are disputes about the sense in which Cumberland was or was not a hedonist and the nature of his views regarding our motivations for acting benevolently, Cumberland was adamant that all our duties can be traced back to this fundamental idea. He claimed that

> all those Propositions, which deserve to be rank'd amongst the general Laws of Nature, I have observ'd *they may be reduc'd to one* universal one . . . "The

> Endeavor, to the utmost of our power, of promoting the common Good of the whole System of rational Agents, conduces, as far as in us lies, to the good of every part, in which our own Happiness, as that of a Part, is contain'd." (Cumberland, Introduction.9, 256)

As Schneewind notes, it is significant that Cumberland began the book by quoting two key passages from the Bible, one by Jesus and one by the Apostle Paul, indicating that our various moral duties are summed up in the command to love others as we love ourselves (1998, 102). Love, understood as benevolently seeking the good of all, is the fundamental principle from which all our moral principles can be drawn. In chapter 8, for example, Cumberland showed how the standard moral virtues such as generosity, frugality, hospitality, courteousness, truthfulness, moderation, and chastity can all be derived from his main principle.

At times he formulated his principle in what seems like a textbook act-consequentialist sense:

> A *practical Proposition* is, sometimes, thus express'd. "This possible human Action" (universal Benevolence; for *instance*) "Will chiefly, beyond any other Action at the same time possible, conduce to my Happiness, and that of all others, either as an essential part thereof, or as a Cause, which will, some time or other, effect a principle part thereof." It is sometimes express'd, in the *Form* of a *Command*. "Let that Action, which is in thy Power, and which will most effectually, of all those which thou can'st exert, promote the common Good in the present Circumstances, be exerted"; often also in the *Form* of a *Gerund*; "Such an Action ought to be done." In my Opinion, *these several Forms* of Speech, relating to the Law of Nature, mean the *same thing*, whether the Understanding *judges this best* to be done, or *commands* it, or tells me in the *Form of a Gerund*, that I am bound to do it. (Cumberland, 4.1, 483)

Here Cumberland portrayed the Law of Nature as commanding us to promote the greatest good on an act-by-act basis and argued that various ways of formulating it carry equivalent obligation.

At other times, Cumberland gave the impression that we choose the correct action by conforming to a socially beneficial rule. When Cumberland described the benefits of deriving the various laws of nature from a single principle, he gave several reasons: one principle requires only one proof, a single rule is easier to remember than many, and a single principle gives us greater moral clarity in our judgments. His final reason was that "from this Fountain is to be deriv'd that *Order* among the particular Laws of Nature, according to which a former, in some measure, limits a latter" (Cumberland, Introduction.24, 276). He then gave the

example that respecting property rights takes priority over keeping promises, and that keeping promises takes priority over bestowing benefits. His
rationale was that "it conduces more to the common Good, that the
principal special Law of Nature, concerning dividing and preserving
Property, should not be violated by the Invasion of another's Right, than
that any one should stand to such a Promise, as could not be perform'd,
without invading another's Right" (Cumberland, Introduction.24, 276).
The law of nature instructs us to break a promise rather than keep it if
keeping it will require violating someone's property rights. It also instructs
us to give what we have promised even if we could create more good by
using or transferring the property in some other way. Here we see
a paradigm example of rule-consequentialist logic: we follow laws that
are themselves justified by the fact that following them will maximize the
overall good. Where rules conflict, we ask which rule, if given priority,
leads to better consequences.

In the twentieth century, the next step in such an argument would have
been to clarify the tension between the two passages, perhaps by explaining
that the priority of some moral rules over others is just an epistemic shortcut,
not a binding rule. In other words, if we imagine an extreme case where
breaking a promise in order to help a person in need is the good-maximizing
option, it may still be done. Alternatively, one could clarify that the best
possible action, quoted above (4.1, 483), must be understood as the action
that conforms to the corresponding rule. Cumberland never clarified this.
There are more passages that lend themselves to the second interpretation
than the first. Cumberland often talked about the tendencies of actions,
implying that we choose based on the generalization rather than the facts of
the specific case.[4] He also made various rule-like pronouncements about
what may not be done. As noted above, "no innocent Person is to be hurt, to
procure to our selves any Advantage" (Cumberland, 1.22, 324).[5] When
differentiating natural good from moral good, he explained that the moral
"is ascrib'd only to such *Actions* and *Habits* of rational Agents, as are *agreeable
to Laws*, whether *Natural* or *Civil*, and is ultimately resolv'd into the *natural
common Good*, to the Preservation and Increase of which alone all the Laws
of Nature, and all just civil Laws, do direct us" (3.1, 463).

God figures in this equation in several ways. One way God alters our
moral conclusions is by his presence as part of the calculus. Cumberland

---

[4] See, for example, 1.2, 290; 1.24, 328; 2.11, 387–8; 5.3, 503–5; 5.5, 508; 5.40, 591–2; 5.58, 643; 7.9, 676;
8.12, 703–4.
[5] See also 7.10, 679; 9.3, 710.

used the phrase "*whole System of Rationals*" to include the good of both God and human beings. God, in fact, has primary place within this moral community (Introduction.15, 262). Piety, for example, is mentioned in passing among the moral virtues (8.5, 691). God is also the source of moral obligation. According to Cumberland, we are able to infer the existence of God from the need for a first cause (2.9, 385; 5.41, 596). From this basis we can know that since God willed to create human beings, he desires their preservation as well (5.21, 540). Perhaps most interestingly, the pains and pleasures that are naturally attached to virtues and vices can be thought of as rewards and punishments sanctioned by God (Cumberland, 5.22–4, 542–8). Similarly, the just punishments human beings mete out against each other are also to be thought of as divine punishment (5.25, 548–51). Cumberland thus assumed that God motivates compliance with the law of nature through means other than rewards and punishments in the next life.

What has struck many of Cumberland's interpreters about this argument is that in many ways God seems less crucial to it than one might expect. Although Cumberland insisted that the will of God is necessary for obligation and that God rules, not merely because of God's power (as in Hobbes), but also because of God's wisdom and goodness (Cumberland, 7.7, 673), people with no knowledge of God, who were simply trying to determine what is good by observing which actions contribute to the greatest good of humanity, would end up both following most of the laws of nature and would have a motivation to do so independent of God's will (but isn't the principle of benevolence rooted in knowing this of God's character?). Cumberland is thus seen as a secularizing thinker since direct knowledge of God seems less necessary in order to know both the content of our duties and the obligation we have to fulfill them. Much has been written about why Cumberland did think God crucial to his account of obligation. Parkin, for example, shows that this was central to his purpose of showing that some of Hobbes' ideas could be put to more respectable purposes (105–113). The emphasis in this chapter is on the actual content of morality, not the reason morality is obligatory.

Cumberland, like Locke, rejected innate ideas (Introduction.5–6, 252–4). He was uninterested in exploring direct divine revelation as a source of moral knowledge. We simply reason from experience to an understanding of God as a wise, benevolent, creator. We infer that God desires us to promote the greatest possible good, and we deduce more specific laws of nature from the fundamental principle, prioritizing them by the fundamental principle. While there are inconsistencies in Cumberland's presentation, the above strand of argument puts most of the elements in place for a theistic rule-consequentialist theory. God is the author of rules, we follow rules rather than look at specific instances, and God's authority gives us reason to follow the rules even when we think we might produce more good by breaking them.

Curiously absent from Cumberland, but present in Locke, is concern about the misapplication of the law of nature. Cumberland affirmed what Locke would later call a "very strange doctrine," namely the idea that in a state of nature any person would be justified in punishing a wrongdoer (1.26, 335). Yet, whereas Locke proceeded directly from this to the problem of self-interested bias in the enforcement of the law of nature, Cumberland passed over the issue. The reason may have been that for Cumberland those who judge wrongly are not using right reason (2.5, 378) and are thus irrelevant to the exposition of the law of nature, which is about conforming to the dictates of reason. It is principles contrary to right reason, like Hobbes' claim that usurpers become legitimate rulers, that incite wrong behavior (9.14, 751).

It is on this crucial point that his theory is very different from Locke's and from the later formulations of morality as legislation. Cumberland did require reciprocity: whatever rights I claim for myself I must grant to others in the same circumstances (2.7, 381). The later versions of consequentialism do not merely ask us to think in terms of reciprocal rules, they ask us to think about rules in a very political, legislative sense. Moral rules are analogous to an actual legal code and, like a legal code, they must be interpreted and applied by fallible human beings. A human legislator will alter the content of the legal code in order to account for the limitations of those who will follow it in order to produce better consequences. This line of thought is absent in Cumberland who generally assumed that the perspectival shift from that of human being to God leaves the content of morality unchanged. Locke was forced to reckon with this very problem and came to a very different conclusion.

Given our concerns, many of the questions about Cumberland's relationship to utilitarianism are beside the point. Utilitarianism is a multifaceted movement and commentators differ greatly in what they see as its essential components. Some of those components are relevant to discerning whether Cumberland employed a consequentialist version of the legislative point of view. Commentators sometimes make secularism, generally, or a secular theory of moral obligation, central to utilitarianism (Kirk 1987, 24–5, 128–31; Haakonssen 2000, 41). Others emphasize how the political or intellectual aims of Cumberland compared with those of the utilitarians (Forsyth 1982, 41; Parkin 1999, 100–2, 226). While all of these factors can make for useful contrasts with Bentham, they are beside the point here since the legislative point of view can be theological and is not wedded to any particular political or intellectual project. Irwin's argument that Cumberland is not a utilitarian because, rather than summing up pleasures and pains, he instead asks us to promote a shared common good that benefits all people (Irwin 2008, 228), actually reinforces, rather than undermines, the claim that Cumberland was a consequentialist.[6] He did not, as noted above, sharply distinguish rule-based thinking from act-by-act thinking or use counterfactual claims about what rules would produce good consequences if adopted to determine what should in fact be done. For that, we must turn to Locke.

John Locke

Locke developed a full version of the legislative point of view in which God employs consequentialist reasoning in determining the content of the rules that define what is right and wrong, and where the fallibility and bias of those bound by the law also affects the content of that law. Locke did not set out to develop this position, but rather found it his best line of defense when pressed on the content of the law of nature in the debates about religious toleration. Because the clearest example of Locke's use of this frame of argument occurs in the *Third Letter Concerning Toleration*, it will be unfamiliar to many contemporary readers. We will, in the next two chapters, see various echoes of it in thinkers such as Hutcheson and Paley. The three issues to be discussed

---

[6] Irwin may not be right about Cumberland and utilitarianism. Cumberland thought that "if Religion, or the publick Welfare of Men, requires it, we be ready to part with the last drop of our Blood: And, (2.) That no innocent Person is to be hurt, to procure to our selves any Advantage" (1.22, 324). If one focuses on the second point one might think it supports Irwin's reading, but it can easily be understood as a standard example of rule-consequentialist thinking given the value of a rule against harming the innocent even when it is to one's advantage. The first point, however, seems to indicate that I have an obligation to suffer hardship in order to bring about the common good, which does seem to be an example of trading off the hardship of one for the welfare of many. This is one of Cumberland's main points throughout the book and part of his claim that Hobbes neglects altruistic duties. Cumberland also thought that the punishment of crimes is for the public good, which also clearly involves the infliction of harm on some to benefit the whole (1.26, 335). The ambiguity of Cumberland on this point is nicely captured by his definition of the common good: "I proceed, more fully to explain the [*Common*] (which also I call the Publick) *Good*. By these words I understand the Aggregate or sum of all those good things, which, either we can contribute towards, or are necessary to, the Happiness of *all* rational Beings, consider'd as collected into one Body, each in his proper order" (5.8, 513). On the one hand, the language of aggregation sounds rather quantitative, while, on the other hand, the insistence on contributing to the happiness of *all* rational beings suggests that the act or rule must benefit everyone. If one insists that utilitarians be literally quantitative along the lines of Bentham, then Cumberland was not. His examples are to what he took to be fairly obvious cases where the good of the whole is greater than the good of the part.

regarding Locke are 1) the extent to which his natural law theory can be described as consequentialist, 2) the types of laws that regulate human behavior, and 3) realistic, weakly consequentialist depictions of legislative deliberation as a heuristic to determine the content of natural law.[7]

Unfortunately, much of the literature on Locke and consequentialism is preoccupied with the more specific question of whether Locke was a utilitarian or proto-utilitarian. While this is understandable given the empiricist leanings of the English utilitarians and their importance to the history of philosophy, it can distract from our current inquiry. A specifically utilitarian understanding of the goals of the one legislating the moral law is not essential to the legislative point of view. One simply needs to assess rules and modify or reject them because of the consequences they would produce. Given this, it will be helpful to frame our discussion by looking at A. John Simmons' (1992) interpretation of Locke, which takes up this question in terms of consequentialism rather than utilitarianism.

Simmons grants that Locke's theory of natural law and natural rights was thoroughly theistic, but he goes on to note that Locke frequently adopted a rule-consequentialist style of argument where the content of natural law is derived from considering what is conducive to human preservation. In doing this Simmons helpfully separates out the question of the content of the law of nature from the question of why it is binding, where Locke's answer would have been explicitly theological. Simmons notes that Locke frequently described the preservation of human life as the "fundamental law of nature" (Locke TT, 2.6, 7, 16, 134, 135, 149, 159, 171, 183). Simmons takes Locke to mean not that this is the most important of the laws of nature, but rather that the content of other laws of nature, such as prohibitions on murder, theft, and promise breaking, can be explained by showing how these more specific rules, if followed, are conducive to human preservation (Simmons 1992, 46–59). Simmons takes Locke to be articulating the goal that as many people as possible not only survive but live reasonably comfortable lives. This is not, Simmons notes, the same thing as maximizing total happiness. Rather, according to Locke, the goal is to achieve "the good of every particular Member of that Society, as far as by common Rules, it can be provided for" (TT, 1.92; see Simmons 1992, 57). The theory is consequentialist, but it aims to maximize ("as much as possible") the number of people whose lives are comfortably preserved

[7] We know that Locke thought highly of Grotius' work based on his recommendation of it (second only to Pufendorf) for works on civil law (1996, section 186). For connections between Locke and Cumberland, see Parkin (1999, 215–22).

rather than the aggregate level of happiness. Simmons presents this as one way of interpreting Locke's position that makes it more appealing to contemporary readers who can support the rule-consequentialist aspects of Locke's theory without endorsing the theological aspects of it.

Simmons also offers a separate discussion of a Kantian aspect of Locke where, again, a portion of Locke's theory could be endorsed on Kantian grounds even if Kant and Locke would have disagreed about the theological foundations of the theory. Locke thought that we are not the property of others, made for their use (TT, 2.6). There are affinities between this position and a "respect for the dignity of equal and independent moral agents" associated with Kantianism (Simmons 1992, 58). Simmons' overall argument is that Locke's thought is overdetermined and that one could arrive at a Lockean theory of individual rights either in the theological way that Locke did or by adopting a Kantian or rule-consequentialist approach. Both secular approaches are different from what Locke himself thought, but both are still recognizably Lockean.

Critics of Simmons have questioned whether Locke was consistently rule-consequentialist regarding the content of morality. Simmons' reading does, for example, create tensions with the *Essay Concerning Human Understanding* where moral principles are based on analytic deductions rather than on empirical considerations relevant to the likely consequences of a rule (White 1978, 44). Locke's account of punishment in the *Two Treatises* does not simply say that we should punish murderers to maximize the public good, but that those who are innocent deserve greater consideration than murderers because murderers have reduced themselves to the status of wild animals. The rationale for children inheriting their parent's property is that they have title to it, not that it produces the best consequences (Mack 1999, 160–2). These sorts of examples show, at a minimum, that Sidgwick was right in claiming that Locke did not show that utilitarian considerations were the basis of his specific natural law claims (Sidgwick OHE, 177).[8]

Nonetheless, I think there are important rule-consequentialist elements to Locke's thought. It is true that Locke did not explicitly link all of his principles of natural law to a theory of benevolence in the way Cumberland did, and that there is a real tension between the "demonstrative morality" of the *Essay Concerning Human Understanding* and a rule-consequentialist interpretation of Locke. We should also remember, however, that Locke's main point in making claims about demonstrative morality

---

[8] Sidgwick did not believe Locke was a utilitarian, even a reticent one, but this is consistent with the interpretation of Locke as being substantially consequentialist even though he was not utilitarian.

(ECHU, 3.11.16, 4.3.18, 4.12.8) is primarily to say that deductive moral inferences are in principle attainable because we can define moral terms more precisely than is possible with natural substances like gold or silver. He may simply be saying that some moral arguments can be deductive rather than be trying to exemplify how one would go about developing a given moral theory. These passages are certainly not representative of how Locke actually went about developing claims for moral arguments in his other works.

The questions about punishment are not clear cut either. When Locke actually explicated his approach to how much people should be punished, he rejected standard retributive rationales (Tuckness 2010). Right after the passage about punishing murderers as one would deal with a wild animal, Locke said that for lesser breaches of the natural law punishment should be "with so much *Severity* as will suffice to make it an ill bargain to the Offender, give him cause to repent, and terrifie others from doing the like" (TT, 2.12). In the paragraphs before he describes the right of punishing as being for "restraint" and "reparation" (TT, 2.10–11). It is not hard to imagine Locke thinking that punishments that deter future crimes and make restitution to victims are promoting the outcome of comfortable preservation of human life. On this reading Locke's theory is wholly consequentialist with respect to the content of the moral rules. A more likely reading is that, for Locke, restitution was not merely a policy required by consequentialist reasoning but a distinct rationale – restitution is intrinsically good (Tuckness 2010). On this latter reading, Locke can still be weakly consequentialist, it is just that the legislator has two types of consequences that must be considered (as much as possible mankind is to be preserved and as much as possible those who have been injured must receive restitution). On the former reading, perhaps Locke thought that a strong endorsement of restitution as a rationale, and not just a policy, is justified on grounds of it promoting preservation. Again, I think the most likely interpretation is that this is an instance where Locke did not adhere rigidly to a requirement to trace every moral right back to the fundamental law of nature.

Murder may be a special case. It is possible that since the fundamental law is that as much as possible mankind be preserved, Locke simply did not include murderers as part of "mankind." In other cases, more consequentialist logic predominates. Things like preferring the lives of the innocent to the guilty and giving children rights to their parents' property have often been justified on rule-consequentialist grounds. Locke even stated specifically that in cases where there are conflicting claims to property (children's right to their parents' property versus a conqueror's right to compensation in a just war), the needier party has a claim based on the fundamental law of nature that mankind be preserved (TT, 2.183). The fact that Locke did not work through the steps of the argument does not explicitly demonstrate that he was rejecting that framework. It shows only that, as Sidgwick noted, Locke did not show his work.

Also worth noting is that we see some confirmation of the rule-consequentialist interpretation in one of Locke's journal entries dated in 1680, roughly when Locke was writing the *Two Treatises* (although the chronology of the writing of the *Two Treatises* is still very disputed). In "God's Justice," Locke considered what rationale guides God in punishing human beings. He said that we cannot suppose that God's punishment "should extend further than his goodness has need of it for the preservation of his creatures in the order and beauty of the state that he has placed each of them in." We cannot harm God, so God does not need reparations. Therefore, the "misery or destruction he brings upon them [His creatures], can be nothing else but to preserve the greater or more considerable part, and so being only for preservation, his justice is nothing but a branch of his goodness" (Locke PE, 278). While this passage is in an unpublished manuscript and thus less prominent than what Cumberland wrote, it seems to be a clear prioritization of God's benevolence among God's moral attributes. It also uses preservation of life (rather than maximal happiness or pleasure) as the consequence toward which God aims.

While granting that Locke may not have been entirely consistent in using rule-consequentialist logic throughout his corpus, and conceding that Locke did not always spell out the consequentialist reasons behind his arguments, I think that Simmons has noted something important in describing Kantian and rule-consequentialist affinities in portions of Locke's argument. Simmons, however, errs in describing Locke's thought as "overdetermined" in that one can choose among the theological, Kantian, and rule-consequentialist approaches to get to Locke's conclusion. Instead, my argument will be (as developed more fully in Part II) that if one attempts to detach the theological aspects of Locke's thought, both the Kantian and rule-consequentialist approaches are necessary to get to Locke's conclusions. To speak anachronistically, the rule-consequentialist element depends on the Kantian element to explain why we should be thinking in terms of rules rather than specific acts. A hybrid theory that depends on both Kantian and consequentialist arguments is different from an overdetermined theory where one can choose one or the other.

Before showing how Locke employed his version of the legislative point of view it will be helpful to describe Locke's view of the different types of law, as this will become important in Chapters 3–4 where his idea is significant for the explicitly utilitarian thinkers who would follow him. Locke argued in the *Essay Concerning Human Understanding* that we judge the rightness of actions according to one of three standards: "1. The *Divine* Law. 2. The *Civil* Law. 3. The Law of *Opinion* or *Reputation*, if I may so call it" (ECHU, 2.28.7). Locke included under divine law both the law of nature and law as directly revealed by God, as in the Bible. Only the divine law is a consistently reliable guide to what is right (ECHU, 2.28.8). Civil law determines what will be punished by the state, but it may be wrong (ECHU, 2.28.9). The law of opinion determines what will be praised as virtue or condemned as vice in a given community, and it may also be wrong (ECHU, 2.28.10).

Norms of virtue and vice arise from the opinions of people through an informal mechanism, not through legislation by an explicit authority.

> For though Men uniting into politick Societies, have resigned up to the publick the disposing of all their Force, so that they cannot employ it against any Fellow-Citizen, any farther than the Law of the Country directs: yet they retain still the power of Thinking well or ill; approving or disapproving of the actions of those whom they live amongst, and converse with: And by this approbation and dislike they establish amongst themselves, what they will call *Vertue* and *Vice*. (Locke ECHU, 2.28.10)

Interestingly, Locke thought that people will normally converge on the correct principles of virtue and vice:

> 'tis no Wonder, that Esteem and Discredit, Vertue and Vice, should in a great measure every-where correspond with the unchangeable Rule of Right and Wrong, which the Law of God hath established; there being nothing, that so directly, and visibly secures, and advances the general Good of Mankind in this World, as Obedience to the Laws, he has set them, and nothing that breeds such Mischiefs and Confusion, as the neglect of them. And therefore Men, without renouncing all Sense and Reason, and their own Interest, which they are so constantly true to, could not generally mistake, in placing their Commendation and Blame on that side, that really deserved it not. (ECHU, 2.28.11)

Locke did not specify the exact mechanism, as his successors would, but there may be reasons why opinions about moral right tend to converge with natural law. If we frame questions of praise and blame in terms of general principles, we have a self-interested reason for choosing principles that promote the common good. We will return to this idea in the next chapter in the thought of David Hume.

The law of opinion is often the most powerful law influencing human behavior:

The Penalties that attend the breach of God's Laws, some, nay, perhaps, most Men seldom seriously reflect on: and amongst those that do, many, whilst they break the Law, entertain Thoughts of future reconciliation, and making their Peace for such Breaches. And as to the Punishments, due from the Laws of the Commonwealth, they frequently flatter themselves with the hopes of Impunity. But no Man scapes the Punishment of their Censure and Dislike, who offends against the Fashion and Opinion of the Company he keeps, and would recommend himself to. Nor is there one of ten thousand, who is stiff and insensible enough, to bear up under the constant Dislike, and Condemnation of his own Club. (Locke ECHU, 2.28.12)

We will see the importance of this line of thought in subsequent chapters. People, in their everyday lives, have access to a powerful form of legislation simply by the opinions they express about what is right and wrong, virtuous and vicious. This alternative form of legislation is available in theories that deny the existence of divine law and can be paired with civil laws to try to shape human behavior to produce better consequences. Once people come to understand that they have choices about what to affirm as right and good, that they can choose to affirm principles because of the beneficial consequences of those principles, and that claims about what is right that are formulated as general principles are often more persuasive to fellow citizens, a framework exists in which a secular version of the legislative point of view can take hold in which the standard of right is no longer determined by God's use of the legislative point of view.

We can now turn to our third main point about Locke, which is that Locke did in fact use the legislative point of view to determine the content of natural law. We see Locke's willingness to do this in the later *Letters Concerning Toleration*. Locke's most famous argument for toleration was not the one that Locke himself ultimately thought was his strongest argument. While he is famous for arguing that force should not be used to bring people to the true religion because force is unable to bring about sincere belief, Locke in his later writings on toleration gradually abandoned this argument. His critic, Jonas Proast, pointed out that force might in fact indirectly influence our beliefs by changing the arguments to which we are exposed. We will not be led astray by heretics we never hear and moderate force might lead people to listen to arguments they would otherwise ignore. Proast claimed that force, wisely applied, would be beneficial because it would bring more people to the true religion.[9]

---

[9] I argue for these claims in more detail in Tuckness 2008. The following section draws on this work as well as Tuckness 2002.

As the debate between the two progressed, Locke argued that it was not enough to show that force was beneficial, one also had to show that one had the authority to employ it, authority that might come from God through either scripture or the law of nature. God also permits people to authorize force through their own consent. Locke argued that there was no authorization for religious persecution from any of these sources. It was at this point that Proast made an argument that led Locke to formulate a rule-consequentialist response with affinities to the modern versions of rule-consequentialism. Proast argued:

> 'Tis true indeed, *the Author and Finisher of our Faith* has given the Magistrate no new Power, or Commission: nor was there any need that he should, (if he himself had any Temporal Power to give:) For he found him [the magistrate] already, even by the *Law of Nature*, the *Minister of God to the People for good*, and *bearing the Sword not in vain, i.e.* invested with Coactive Power, and obliged to use it for all the good purposes which it might serve, and for which it should be found needful; even for the restraining of false and corrupt Religion. (Proast 1691, 31)

In a sense, what Proast does in this passage is take the law of nature to include an open-ended authorization to do as much good as can be done. In doing so, the law of nature becomes analogous to act-consequentialism, which instructs the king to act in the way that produces the best consequences. If force may be used "for all the good purposes it might serve," then showing that a given specific act of coercion produces good consequences (for example, conversion to the true religion) is enough to authorize it.

Locke's response to this argument made the move that would become characteristic of legislative rule-consequentialism. He insisted that one could not take the law of nature to be the sort of principle that directs us to maximize the good on an act-by-act basis. Rather, the law of nature provides a standard by which other proposed rules can be assessed to determine whether they are morally obligatory. Locke wrote:

> [Y]ou have recourse to the general law of nature; and what is that? The law of reason, whereby every one is commissioned to do good. And the propagating the true religion for the salvation of men's souls being doing good, you say, the civil sovereigns are commissioned and required by that law to use their force for those ends. But since by this law all civil sovereigns are commissioned and obliged alike to use their coactive power for the propagating of the true religion, and the salvation of souls; and it is not possible for them to execute such a commission, or obey that law, but by using force to bring men to that religion which they judge the true; by which use of

force much more harm than good would be done towards the propagating the true religion in the world, as I have showed elsewhere: therefore no such commission, whose execution would do more harm than good, more hinder than promote the end for which it is supposed given, can be a commission from God by the law of nature. (Locke Works, 6:213)

The first thing to notice about this passage is that the law of nature is not, for Locke, a generic admonition to bring about as much good as one can. Rather it consists of more specific rules. He took Proast to be claiming that "Magistrates should use force to bring people to the true religion" is one of those rules. The characteristic two-level structure is thus present: a specific act of persecution must be justified by a specific rule (level 1) directing people to use force in certain settings and the rule is justified by its contribution to bringing about a better consequence (level 2).

Second, and even more importantly, Locke was not merely saying that we must look at the consequences of a class of actions rather than a specific act. He was also pressing very hard on the metaphor of legislation. Proast did not say that all magistrates should promote the religion they think true, but rather that magistrates should promote the religion that actually is true. Locke's argument is intended to thwart this move. A human legislature promulgates its law to all those under its jurisdiction and must recognize the fallibility of those who will interpret and apply the law as written. One could abolish the criminal code and replace it with "imprison people for as long as is beneficial," but such a code would have to be interpreted by fallible people who would frequently imprison the wrong people for the wrong amount of time while giving little guidance to citizens as to how to avoid being imprisoned. Locke insisted that there be specific written laws and impartial adjudication (TT, 2.142). In doing this, human legislators are setting up laws to provide additional incentives so that people will act in ways that promote the common good. Within this framework there is a close parallel for Locke between human legislation and divine legislation. It is not merely, as Locke explicitly stated, that good laws will track with the law of nature. Rather, as we have seen, the content of natural law itself is also determined by thinking of it as analogous to human legislation.

Third, Locke's argument is framed in broadly consequentialist terms rather than utilitarian terms. Though both he and Proast would no doubt have agreed that getting more people into heaven was the pleasure- and happiness-maximizing outcome, the argument is not put in terms of happiness or pleasure. Rather, it is open-endedly consequentialist. It simply assumes that there is a morally valuable goal that the legislator has formulated, in this case bringing people to the true religion, and then asks which more specific rules are admissible and rejects those whose consequences undermine the original goal.

Fourth, if there is a way Locke's argument differs from standard rule-consequentialism it is that Locke did not explicitly use a maximization test. In the case at hand there are only two possible rules under consideration: persecution and toleration. He thought one undermines the goal of the legislator and the other doesn't and so clearly a rational legislator would choose the one that does not undermine the legislator's goal. Locke did not expressly deal with the situation where there is more than one principle that would further the legislator's goal and claim that the legislator must choose the one that does so to the greatest extent. It would not be hard to draw that conclusion from Locke's argument, at least in cases where all other factors are equal, but Locke did not draw it himself. Nonetheless, Locke's argument is at least weakly consequentialist and a counterfactual, realistic depiction of the legislative point of view. It may also be a direct application of the fundamental law of nature: God desires human life to be preserved, and all human beings face death, eventually, unless they receive eternal life from Jesus. Adopting the rule that increases (or maximizes) the number of people who experience eternal life would seem to be an extension of Locke's fundamental law of nature.

Locke's toleration argument depends upon the fact that since the law of nature is received via human reason, it must apply to all human beings, unlike scripture that could be addressed only to some.[10] Whatever specific rule the law of nature includes regarding religious persecution, the rule applies to and thus should be followed by all governments everywhere. Since so many of the world's magistrates reject what both Locke and Proast affirmed, that the Church of England is the true church, the result of everyone acting on this principle would be bad consequences not good consequences. For this reason, the proposed rule is rejected and replaced by a rule commanding religious toleration, which produces better consequences when all magistrates everywhere in the world attempt to interpret and apply it.

Conclusion

We thus see in Grotius, Cumberland, and Locke the early versions of what would become the characteristic rule-consequentialist way of thinking

---

[10] Locke, for example, claims the Old Testament law is binding only on the Jewish people because it was they who were named in "*Hear, O Israel.*" See Letter, 44.

about morality. In Grotius' version of the argument, the legislative point of view was expressed more clearly in the law of nations than the law of nature. Those who are in a position to influence the former are in a legislative context factually, and the deliberative frame they use is factual, rather than counterfactual, in cases where there is an already established norm. Grotius did not press the counterfactual perspective by claiming that one must act on rules that had not been adopted yet on grounds that, if they were adopted, they would be beneficial. Cumberland was more consistent than Grotius or Locke in placing benevolence at the center of his theory and using the language of pursuing the good of all. While there are questions about whether he was a utilitarian or a common-good consequentialist and about whether he articulated a consistently rule-based approach to the above goals, the ambiguities in his work were sufficient to provide material for later thinkers. What does clearly seem to be missing from Cumberland is explicit recognition of the way that the dictates of rationality from a situated perspective and a legislative perspective can pull apart. Cumberland normally assumed a harmony between these two for those who are appropriately altruistic.

It was Locke who came closest to the contemporary rule-consequentialist argument. Locke was less consistently consequentialist in his overall thought than Cumberland. Although he did declare the preservation of mankind as the fundamental law of nature, its place was not highlighted to the same degree that Cumberland's principle of benevolence is. Nor did Locke explicitly try to derive all of his specific moral principles from it, as Cumberland did with benevolence. In this sense, the standard interpretations of Locke that view him as having affinities with later utilitarian thought while not consciously being a utilitarian are correct. Nonetheless, when pressed in the area of religious toleration, Locke formulated what would become the crucial argumentative strategy for saving consequentialist theories from the undesirable conclusions to which the act-based perspective leads. In Locke's theory, the consequentialist ethic assumes a God who is greatly interested in producing good consequences and who desires to direct human behavior by means of generally applicable rules. Locke, while not specifically endorsing maximization, assumed that the legislator, in setting the content of the rules, must account for the selfishness, bias, and general fallibility of those who will attempt to abide by the rules. Importantly, one discovers the content of these rules not by turning directly to the Bible but rather by asking oneself what would be rational from God's point of view.

CHAPTER 2

Legislators, Architects, and Spectators
The Path to Hume

Locke's development of the legislative point of view was published in one of his less prominent writings, the *Third Letter Concerning Toleration*. Some of the uses of the legislative point of view in the eighteenth century may have been inspired by George Berkeley's use of the argument in a sermon published in 1712 rather than by Locke's version. Berkeley is famous, in part, as a critic of Locke's argument in *An Essay Concerning Human Understanding* (ECHU), so it is possible that he was familiar with Locke's writings on toleration as well. Interestingly, Berkeley used exactly the same legislative frame that Locke had used on toleration to argue against Locke's main contention in the *Two Treatises* about the right of the people to revolt, a politically charged issue in the decades after the Glorious Revolution. We will see in this chapter, from Berkeley, that one option was simply to use the argument the way Locke had, where the legislative metaphor helps us discern what God has decreed. But that was not the only option. Another critic of Locke, the Third Earl of Shaftesbury, pursued a different line of thought that focused more on God as architect. In this second metaphor, the world, including human nature, is the result of God's benevolent design and so an impulse to act virtuously is built in to our nature. In the architectural metaphor, God's law is, in a sense, within us, but we know it naturally because of how the divine architect designed us rather than by consciously trying to imitate legislative thinking.

Francis Hutcheson attempted to synthesize these two perspectives while adding a third metaphor, that of the spectator. If the divine architect has designed us with a "moral sense" that is corrupted by self-interest, then the moral pronouncements of a large number of impartial spectators will accurately track the divine moral order. He tried to combine this with a legislative understanding of specific moral principles. Hutcheson's attempted synthesis, however, proved unpersuasive to many. Joseph Butler worried about the arrogance of us attempting the legislative calculations that only God had the wisdom to make and thought it safer to place the architectural metaphor at the center, while also noting the counterintuitive conclusions that a focus on act-by-act benevolence would bring with it. Most importantly, Hume developed an account of human moral judgments that utilized the spectator metaphor without requiring God as either legislator or architect. Hume attempted to show how, in practice, justice might be very "law-like" in the way it functions as a set of general rules that are beneficial in the aggregate though not in each specific case. The legislation can emerge gradually and through the mechanism of a spectator without requiring an actual divine legislator or people consciously trying to mimic the divine legislator's thinking. By the time of Hume, we have a legislative view of justice that does not depend on the existence of a God who consciously employs the legislative point of view.

George Berkeley

Berkeley's use of the legislative perspective occurred in the context of debates about whether there is a duty of passive obedience when the laws or actions of the government are thought to be unjust or tyrannical. Locke had argued in the *Two Treatises* that people may actively resist an unjust government that fails to protect the rights of the people or promote the common good. Berkeley in his sermon used a very Lockean framework to argue for the opposite conclusion, that though we may refuse to obey an unjust law (passively resisting), we may not actively resist an unjust government. Berkeley was, of course, not thinking only of Locke, and there were other more recent people who had made similar arguments (Berman 1994, 83–94). Nonetheless, with the parallels between Locke's thought and Berkeley's description of his opponents' position, it seems very likely that Locke is one of the opponents in view (Berkeley, 23, 37 and Locke TT, 2.6, 2.23).

Berkeley began by agreeing with Locke about the origins of our knowledge and about human desire. Locke rejected innate ideas and he thought we were motivated by our desire for happiness (with caveats that we must be "uneasy" about our future in order to be so motivated). Berkeley similarly argued that

> Self-Love being a principle of all others the most universal, and the most deeply engraven in our hearts, it is natural for us to regard things as they are fitted to augment or impair our own happiness; and accordingly we denominate them *good* or *evil*. Our judgment is ever employed in distinguishing between these two; and it is the whole business of our lives to endeavour, by a proper

> application of our faculties, to procure the one and avoid the other. At our first coming into the world, we are entirely guided by the impressions of sense; sensible pleasure being the infallible characteristic of present good, as pain is of evil. (Berkeley, 5)

In keeping with this Lockean start he took the next step to show that it is rational to act according to God's will:

> And, since it is a truth, evident by the light of nature, that there is a sovereign omniscient Spirit, who alone can make us for ever happy, or for ever miserable; it plainly follows that a conformity to His will, and not any prospect of temporal advantage, is the sole rule whereby every man who acts up to the principles of reason, must govern and square his actions. (Berkeley, 6)

That God's will is our standard leaves open the question of how God expresses that will. Berkeley claimed that God does so through law: "He is, therefore, with the most undoubted right, the great legislator of the world; and mankind are, by all the ties of duty, no less than interest, bound to obey His laws" (Berkeley, 6).

Berkeley has thus set up the basic parameters for the legislative point of view, claiming that right and wrong are defined for us by God's acts of legislation that we can discover through reason. Next, Berkeley filled in the details regarding God's moral purposes so that we can use the legislative perspective to discover God's will.

> For, laws being rules directive of our actions to the end intended by the legislator, in order to attain the knowledge of God's laws, we ought first to enquire what that end is which He designs should be carried on by human actions. Now, as God is a being of infinite goodness, it is plain the end He proposes is good. But, God enjoying in Himself all possible perfection, it follows that it is not His own good, but that of His creatures. (Berkeley, 7)

Berkeley, by claiming that God's overriding motive is the good of his creatures (which, based on the earlier stages of the argument, implies pleasure), thus ensures that the legislative perspective will be substantially consequentialist.

To this point Berkeley has assumed that God governs us by law, but he must take up the question of whether God does so through one simple law such as "promote happiness as best you can in each instance" or if God adopts more specific rules that humans must obey even when breaking them might produce good consequences. Berkeley made the distinction very clear:

The well-being of mankind must necessarily be carried on in one of these two ways:– Either, first, without the injunction of any certain universal rules of morality only by obliging every one, upon each particular occasion, to consult the public good, and always to do that which to him shall seem, in the present time and circumstances, most to conduce to it: or, secondly, by enjoining the observation of some determinate, established laws, which, if universally practised, have, from the nature of things, an essential fitness to procure the well-being of mankind. (Berkeley, 8)

He then highlighted two arguments against the first option and in favor of the idea that God adopts more specific rules for us to obey. First, Berkeley thought it "far more easy to judge with certainty, whether such or such an action be a transgression of this or that precept, than whether it will be attended with more good or ill consequences" (Berkeley, 9). It is simply too difficult to try to calculate all the effects of each action. Second, we will not have enough certainty when judging the actions of others.

For, since the measure and rule of every good man's actions is supposed to be nothing else, but his own private disinterested opinion of what makes most for the public good at that juncture; and, since this opinion must unavoidably in different men, from their particular views and circumstances, be very different: it is impossible to know, whether any one instance of parricide or perjury, for example, be criminal. The man may have had his reasons for it; and that which in me would have been a heinous sin may be in him a duty. Every man's particular rule is buried in his own breast, invisible to all but himself, who therefore can only tell whether he observes it or no. And, since that rule is fitted to particular occasions, it must ever change as they do: hence it is not only various in different men, but in one and the same man at different times. (Berkeley, 9)

Given the confusion and uncertainty that act-by-act assessment would create, Berkeley concluded that the second option is correct:

It follows, therefore, that the great end to which God requires the concurrence of human actions must of necessity be carried on by the second method proposed, namely, the observation of certain, universal, determinate rules or moral precepts, which, in their own nature, have a necessary tendency to promote the well-being of the sum of mankind, taking in all nations and ages, from the beginning to the end of the world. (Berkeley, 10)

We now have a full version of the legislative point of view that repeats all the elements in Locke's version from the previous chapter. We can infer from the good consequences of a rule that it is commanded by God. Berkeley stated, "whatsoever practical proposition doth to right reason evidently appear to have a necessary connexion with the Universal well-being included in it, is to be looked upon as enjoined by the will of God" (Berkeley, 11). Again, "it is plain this cannot be determined by computing the public good which in that particular case it is attended with, but only by comparing it with the Eternal Law of Reason" (Berkeley, 13).

What is different is that Berkeley took Locke's framework to argue against Locke's substantive position. After using what for his audience would have been less controversial examples, such as that one must never commit adultery (given the specific law prohibiting it) even if doing so has net positive consequences in a particular case (Berkeley, 15), he turned to his argument for passive obedience and against a right to resist the government. His argument proceeded in steps. "First, then, submission to government is a point important enough to be established by a moral rule. Things of insignificant and trifling concern are, for that very reason, exempted from the rules of morality" (Berkeley, 17). "Secondly, obedience to government is a case universal enough to fall under the direction of a law of nature" (Berkeley, 18). The problem of obedience to government is not unique to a particular people or place, but a recurring universal problem and therefore it is appropriate for there to be a universal law of nature addressing it. Third, and crucially, this is the sort of case where the consequences are worse if we leave it to the "judgment and determination of each private person" (Berkeley, 19). The average person lacks both the "parts, leisure, and liberal education, as well as disinterestedness and thorough knowledge in the particular state of a kingdom" to make such a judgment (Berkeley, 9). Two human limitations are noted: lack of knowledge and lack of impartiality. In the same way that Locke used this framework to show that in practice rulers would wrongly apply the principle "use force to promote the true religion," Berkeley now argued that authorizing revolution means in practice authorizing fallible men to rebel when they think it for the public good. This, he thought, leads to chaos (Berkeley, 20).

Berkeley did allow for a few means of redress that made his position less extreme than it initially seems. If a king orders evil actions, those who work for the king should refuse to comply with them (Berkeley, 49). He also argued that the ban on resistance does not apply to usurpers or "madmen" who happen to hold the office of king (Berkeley, 52). Both of these exceptions require contestable judgments of the sort that Locke's theory does ("is the monarch insane?" and "is the government led by a usurper?"

are both contestable questions), but Berkeley can say that they differ greatly in impact when a person interprets the principle wrongly. There is much less harm done by incorrect judgments if people merely refrain from carrying out an act than if they try to actively overthrow the government. Moreover, contestation is a matter of degree. "Usurper" and "madman" are much more specific and less contestable than simply allowing people to make a judgment about whether resisting the government promotes the common good. The position is thus quite different from Locke's who came to the opposite conclusion, allowing overthrow of the government by the people if the government was not seeking the public good, which is a much broader permission.

In Berkeley we have a particularly clear restatement of Locke's legislative framework and use of the legislative perspective to assess the question of what is right or wrong. We also see that two people using the legislative perspective can reasonably come to different conclusions about what principles are endorsed from that perspective. Berkeley added to the discussion explicit criteria for establishing whether a proposed rule is part of the law of nature. Namely that it must be 1) a matter of great significance, 2) a universal problem rather than one specific to a particular country, and 3) a case where a general rule yields better consequences than allowing fallible people to make case-by-case judgments. Locke thought the problem of toleration met all these criteria but did not lay them out as general criteria as did Berkeley. The story we are sketching is not, however, one where people simply followed Locke's approach with minor clarifications. Instead, the legislative metaphor was challenged by competing metaphors and to those challenges we now turn.

The Third Earl of Shaftesbury

The Third Earl of Shaftesbury, grandson of Locke's patron Anthony Ashley Cooper, had been educated by Locke as a youth but came to disagree with him at a fundamental level. In his major work, *Characteristics of Men, Manners, Opinions, Times*, he rejected the legislative approach to morality that Locke had offered. In Locke's account, right and wrong are externally motivated. Shaftesbury wrote that "the principle of fear of future punishment and hope of future reward, how mercenary or servile soever it may be accounted, is yet in many circumstances a great advantage, security and support to virtue" (Shaftesbury, 185). In other words, it is "mercenary or servile" to think, as Locke had, that our future expectations of reward and punishment are our proper motive to virtue, yet these mercenary motives may have some benefit given the moral deficiencies of human beings. One of Shaftesbury's main claims is that while we do seek our own good, a disposition to pursue the good of all is a key part of our happiness and excessive self-interest is a recipe for misery (Shaftesbury, 21, 200–25). There is no need for an external moral authority or sanctions in the next life, since our own interest gives us sufficient reason to pursue virtue. He thought an approach such as Locke's, which emphasizes the rewards and punishments of an external legislator, cultivates vice rather than virtue (Voitle 1984, 120–1). While external punishments are sometimes necessary, the path of virtue comes with realizing that acting for others is good for both us and them.

In making this case, he still assumed a theistic theory in that he posited a providential ordering of the universe. He rejected, however, the idea that the moral order itself is chosen by God. Rather, he thought that we must have a standard of good independent of God's will in order to meaningfully call God's actions good (Shaftesbury, 181). Moreover, since expectations of future rewards and punishments are unnecessary (and potentially harmful) to true virtue and since the primary expression of virtue is seeking the good of others, Shaftesbury did not think belief in God was necessary for virtue (Gill 2006, 85). God plays a role, but it is the role of an architect rather than the role of a legislator. The providential order of the universe, including the composition of human nature, ensures that our interests and virtue coincide. We seek the good of the system as a whole and God has ordered the whole in a beautiful way, increasing our desire to act rightly.

In making this case, Shaftesbury took aim at another foundational part of Locke's theory. "The root of Locke's philosophical failure, as Shaftesbury saw it, was his denial of innate ideas" (Gill 2006, 81). Lacking innate ideas of virtue and vice, Locke was forced to use our experiences of pain and pleasure since these could be accounted for in his empiricist approach. Shaftesbury disagreed. "*Sense of right and wrong* therefore being as natural to us as natural affection itself, and being a first principle in our constitution and make, there is no speculative opinion, persuasion or belief which is capable immediately or directly to exclude or destroy it" (Shaftesbury, 179). Thus we are guided in our moral decisions not by speculating about what laws a benevolent deity might have chosen but by following the nature that the benevolent deity has given us. Our natural affective disposition to do good is the key to virtue. Our wrong moral thinking is learned, not innate (Shaftesbury, 179–80).

Darwall rightly notes that Shaftesbury's position "stands the legislative model on its head" because it makes moral assessment wholly dependent on the affections (such as benevolence or malice) that motivated the act rather than the status of the act itself (Darwall 1995a, 182–3). Darwall's point is that in the earlier natural law tradition it was assumed that the divine law was necessary for moral obligation and that Shaftesbury was rejecting this idea of moral obligation in favor of one that is internalized. Shaftesbury's discussion of obligation contained no "reference to the idea of law or to related notions of accountability, punishment, or blame" (Darwall 1995a, 193). What matters is not so much the act you committed as the motives that led to the action. Normally, treatments of Shaftesbury focus either on his preference for internal over external sanctions as a matter of moral motivation or his more naturalistic, affective account of our sense of moral obligation (as in Darwall). In this chapter the emphasis is on a different aspect of his theory, namely the shift away from the legislative perspective. Even if we agree that our sense of obligation is internal rather than external and that acting virtuously is its own reward, there is a third question about the relevance of rule-based thinking for determining what the right action is. Locke and Berkeley depended on a legislative perspectival shift not just to explain why doing the right thing was obligatory but to determine the right action in contested cases. Shaftesbury's architect-based rejection of the legislative approach was a challenge to that way of thinking. If God has created us such that we have direct access to God's will by way of the moral affections that are part of our nature, and we are therefore engrained with knowledge of the good, there is no need to evaluate a moral system by engaging in legislative deliberation about what general rule would have good consequences if adopted for fallible people.

Francis Hutcheson

Francis Hutcheson attempted to synthesize the perspectives of Locke and Shaftesbury. The result was a theory that, like Shaftesbury's, placed considerable emphasis on our natural knowledge of right and wrong (our moral sense) and on our natural motives to act on it. Our moral sense is instilled in us by the divine architect. Yet the natural impulse toward the greater good was not sufficient for knowing what to do and Hutcheson continued to use the legislative perspective. As with Locke and Berkeley, Hutcheson still accepted an empiricist epistemology and the use of a legislative perspective for deliberation about difficult moral questions. He accepted a legitimate place, as Locke had, for divine sanctions. He also explicitly treated the problem of exceptions to rules from within the legislative framework, arguing that exceptions are justifiable only as public exceptions that, in effect, become a more complex rule. Thus, even exceptions to rules are defined from a legislative perspective. A third metaphor, that of the spectator, appears in his theory, but not as an alternative to God. Rather the spectator is useful for explaining why our moral sense is trustworthy in general even though it may be wrong in specific cases. This third metaphor would later become primary in the work of Hume.

To understand Hutcheson, it is helpful to know that his first book was written as a defense of Shaftesbury against the criticisms of Bernard Mandeville (Leidhold 2008, xiii). Mandeville's *Fable of the Bees or Private Vices, Public Benefits* attacked Shaftesbury's optimistic account of human virtue (Kaye 1988, lxxii–lxxv). Mandeville said that Shaftesbury "calls every Action perform'd with regard to the Publick Good, Virtuous; and all Selfishness, wholly excluding such a Regard, Vice" (Mandeville, 1:324). Mandeville thought the opposite, that actions that appear to regard the public good are, using the strict definition of virtue, vices because they are ultimately self-interested. Nonetheless, these vices are in a way commendable because of the benefits that we derive from them. His approach was to argue that motives such as pride, greed, fear, and vanity are indispensable incentives for many actions that are publicly beneficial (Mandeville, 1:333–69).[1]

Hutcheson's synthesis affirms, with Shaftesbury, a natural approval of actions that spring from affections oriented toward the public good and sees this as evidence of God's benevolent design. Hutcheson argued that we can know of the existence of God by observing evidence of design in the world (Inquiry, 1.5, 46–60).[2] On the basis of this, he thought we can also infer that various aspects of our affections, responses, and evaluations are part of that design. Thus parents' concern for their children is in accord with nature's benevolent design (Inquiry, 2.5, 149). Similarly, he saw God's benevolent design in our love of honor since this helps us learn to act rightly (Hutcheson System, 1.2.6, 26). Most importantly, our moral sense is an element of God's design. If we examine our hearts, we know that our conscience, or moral sense, distinguishes right from wrong and was designed to guide us (Hutcheson PMIC, 50).

The moral sense was Hutcheson's way of synthesizing Locke and Shaftesbury. Lockean empiricism relied on our sensory inputs of pleasure

[1] For a helpful discussion of Mandeville and the implications of his approach to private vices and public benefits, see Parrish 2007, 203–31.
[2] More argumentation for the existence of God is found in Hutcheson System, 1.9, 168–208.

and pain to ground our notion of good, but this was what Shaftesbury found unacceptable. Hutcheson could stay within the empiricist framework by postulating an additional sense that approves of beauty, including moral beauty. This moral sense is, following Shaftesbury, not reducible to self-interest. We do not, for example, praise those whose treachery benefits our country (Hutcheson Inquiry, 2.5, 153). Similarly, we use the moral sense to perceive that the laws of God are good and to know about the rights and duties we have (Inquiry, 2.7, 182–3). We can use our moral sense to measure the "dignity" of a pleasure and not just its duration (Hutcheson System, 1.7.1, 119).

Our moral sense approves of those actions that are conducive to the public good.

> That *End* is called most *reasonable*, which our Reason discovers to contain a greater Quantity of *publick Good* than any other in our power. If he discovers this Truth, that 'his constant pursuit of *public Good* is the most probable way of promoting his *own Happiness*,' then his pursuit is truly reasonable and constant; thus both Affections are at once gratify'd, and he is consistent with himself. (Illustrations, 143)

The pursuit of our own good and the public good are complementary rather than contradictory. Justice consists in the "*generous calm determination*" to promote "the most universal happiness in our power" without interfering with any "more extensive interest of the system" (System, 1.11.2, 222).[3]

Hutcheson's theory was more acceptable to religious belief at the time than Shaftesbury's because he acknowledged a legitimate place for divine sanctions even though he agreed that other motives for moral behavior were possible. "The desires of glory, or even of rewards in a future state, were they supposed to be the sole affections moving an agent in the most beneficial services, without any love to God, esteem of his moral excellencies, gratitude to him, or goodwill to men, would not obtain our approbation as morally good dispositions" (Hutcheson System, 1.4.7, 63). Nonetheless, such a belief might effectively motivate moral actions. Hutcheson, trying to mediate between Locke and Shaftesbury, thought it wrong to think *only* of rewards and punishments as motives for right

---

[3] "This therefore is the sum of all social virtues, that with an extensive affection toward all, we exert our powers vigorously for the common interest, and at the same time cherish all the tender affections in the several narrower relations, which contribute toward [the utility and] the prosperity of individuals, as far as the common interest will allow it" (Hutcheson PMIC, 82). Loving God and neighbor are the "sum of the law delivered to us" (System, 2.1.1, 228). The moral sense approves affections that "are most useful and efficacious for the publick interest" (System, 2.2.2, 239).

behavior, claiming that we should be moved by the fact that God and his laws are perfectly benevolent (System, 2.1.5, 235). Within this framework, God's rewards and punishments are still beneficial because they provide additional incentives for less virtuous people.

Hutcheson's belief in a moral sense is crucial to understanding his use of the idea of the "spectator," which became increasingly important in the thought of Hume and Adam Smith. In those latter theories, the spectator provided a secular alternative to an impartial God who judges our actions. In Hutcheson's version, because our moral sense is part of God's design, it is trustworthy when prejudice or bias do not influence it. It is, therefore, unlikely that most men's moral sense, when unaffected by prejudice, would be wrong (Illustrations, 176, 179). The figure of the spectator is a way of framing this assessment of our actions. Hutcheson frequently makes use of a two-level approach, talking about our moral sense where we can describe the perspective of the actor or that of spectators. A person may be obliged by his own sense of what will be conducive to his happiness or, in another sense, he is obliged if *"every Spectator, or he himself upon Reflection, must approve his action, and disapprove his ommitting it, if he considers fully all its Circumstances"* (Hutcheson Illustrations, 146).[4] The spectator is also important for avoiding the objection that our moral sense is self-interest in disguise. If we try to reduce our sense of beauty to "some real or apparent usefulness," we can't explain the approval of the spectator who "gets no benefit" (System, 1.2.1, 18). "[W]e do not say that it is beautiful because we reap some little pleasure in viewing it, but we are pleased in viewing it because it is antecedently beautiful" (Hutcheson System, 1.4.1, 54). The causal arrow goes the other way. "Actions are conceived rewardable because they are good, not good because they are rewarded" (System, 1.4.2, 55).

Within this framework, Hutcheson avoided the extreme voluntarism to which Shaftesbury objected and agreed that there is a fixed standard of right and wrong other than God's arbitrary will.

> None can hope for Rewards from God without owning that some actions are acceptable to God in their own nature; nor dread divine punishment except upon the supposition of a natural *demerit* in evil actions. When we praise the divine Laws as holy, just and good, 'tis plainly on this account, that we believe they require what is antecedently conceived as morally good, and prohibit the contrary. (Hutcheson PMIC, 37)[5]

---

[4] He uses a similar two-level structure to describe the reason a superior would reward conduct and the reasons a spectator would approve of it (Illustrations, 182–5).
[5] See also PMIC, 38 and System, 1.4.3–10, 56–68 and 2.3.7, 265–7.

Hutcheson assumed that our moral sense tracks with something inherent in the order of the universe and that the law of God is not arbitrary. This is an important claim and actually coincides with Locke. Since they are both working within an empiricist framework, if the content of the moral law is arbitrary there is no way to discover its content by way of reason alone.

One might think that since we have an inborn moral sense, we do not need to reason legislatively to our moral conclusions, we intuitively know them. This was not, however, Hutcheson's position. We have to reason to conclusions about the content of natural law in order to know what we should do. What we reason to are general rules, not specific perceptions. Hutcheson framed his analysis of natural law in terms of rules rather than assume we simply look at particular acts and perceive them as right and wrong separate from our knowledge of rules. We reason to those rules based on a probabilistic assessment of the tendencies of different types of actions. It is here that we see how Hutcheson managed to retain the legislative perspective within his moral sense framework. He wrote:

> The laws of nature are inferences we make, by reflecting upon our inward constitution, and by reasoning upon human affairs, concerning that conduct which our hearts naturally must approve, as tending either to the general good, or to that of individuals consistently with it. These inferences we express in general precepts: they are discovered to us sometimes immediately, sometimes by induction, when we see what conduct ordinarily tends to good. (Hutcheson System, 2.17.2, 119; see also 2.17.6, 128)

An important question to ask is whether these are authoritative rules or merely rules of thumb. Can one depart from the rule if in a particular case it appears that doing so would better promote the public good?

> We form our general rule or precept from what we see tends to good in all ordinary cases. But should we see that in some rarer cases a different conduct would in the whole of its effects do greater good than the following the ordinary rule in these cases also, we then have as good a law of nature preceptive or permissive to recede from the ordinary rule in those rarer cases, as we have to follow it in ordinary cases. These exceptions are part of the law, as well as the general rule. (Hutcheson System, 2.17.2, 120)

This is a crucial claim for seeing how Hutcheson assumed a legislative perspective. He recognized that a general rule may in some cases fail to achieve the purpose for which the rule was enacted (the intent of the legislator) and he concluded that one may depart from that general rule in order to achieve the rule's original purpose (the greater good). Are these rules better understood as summaries of what would normally produce good rather than authoritative guides to conduct? No, because Hutcheson claimed that the exceptions are not a departure from the rule but part of the rule. He wrote, "the same reason and observation which discovers the ordinary general rule, discovers also the exception, which are therefore parts of the law" (System, 2.3.12, 279).

The key for Hutcheson was that he assumed one must look not just at the effects of breaking the rule in a specific case but also at the effects of a publicly known exception to the rule. "There are innumerable cases in which if we only consider the immediate effect, it were better to recede from the common rule; and yet the allowing a liberty to recede from it in all like cases would occasion much more evil by its remote effects, than the particular evils in adhering to the ordinary rule" (Hutcheson System, 2.17.3, 120). Hutcheson repeated this requirement of considering the consequences if others acted on the principle multiple times (Hutcheson PMIC, 207, 220). He recognized that a publicly known exception to a law is not a departure from the law but a more complex specification of the law itself. "No killing except in self-defense" is just as much of a rule as "No killing."

Hutcheson was aware that this way of talking about the law of nature would raise concerns. It is a far cry from the view of natural law that is rooted in immutability to say that it is an inductive inference made on the basis of probabilistic judgments and subject to revision in light of new evidence about whether a more complex specification of the rule would be better in terms of the public good. Hutcheson wholeheartedly embraced the conclusion that natural law relies on probabilistic reasoning. He wrote: "If we are no competent judges of future tendencies, we are no judges about the ordinary natural laws; which are no otherways discovered than by our reasoning upon the tendencies of certain methods of action, as they appear conducive to the publick interest or detrimental" (Hutcheson PMIC, 208).[6]

To see how thoroughly Hutcheson adopted the legislative perspective, let us recall its key features. The more we make the moral code analogous to legislation, the more the judgments of the divine lawgiver will follow the legislative rationality of a human legislator. The divine lawgiver will decide the content of that code considering things like the way the code might be misapplied or misinterpreted and the difficulty of gaining voluntary compliance. He argued that the fact that people occasionally make mistakes when claiming exceptions does not prove that one shouldn't make

---

[6] See also System, 2.17.3, 122; 2.17.6, 129 and Illustrations, 178.

exceptions (Hutcheson System, 2.17.8, 134–5). His rationale was that "In computing the advantages and disadvantages of receding from any ordinary rule, we must consider not only the immediate effects, but even the most remote, of allowing this liberty in all like cases; and even the dangers from the mistakes of others in using the like plea in unlike cases" (System, 2.17.9, 137). We can do a cost–benefit analysis of whether the harms of the potential future mistakes outweigh the good of the exception (System, 2.17.9, 137–8).

Hutcheson used this framework repeatedly to explain the content of natural law. Property rights and rules of bequest are as they are because of limitations of wisdom and altruism on the part of both human beings generally and magistrates specifically (Hutcheson System, 2.6.6, 322; 2.7.7, 352). Here the legislator adjusts the content of the code to account for the natural motive to provide for oneself, one's family, and one's posterity and the difficulty of operationalizing a principle that would redistribute property toward the most virtuous (see also Hutcheson PMIC, 136–9, 151). He also used this framework to explain why some rights are perfect while others are imperfect and not subject to human enforcement. Imperfect rights "may be very sacred: yet they are of such a nature that greater evils would ensue in society from making them matters of compulsion, than from leaving them free to each one's honor and conscience to comply with them or not" (PMIC, 113, see also Hutcheson System, 2.3.3, 257–8). He used the term "external right" to describe instances where a general practice of granting a right is beneficial even though in a particular case it is not beneficial, as in the property rights that allow a miser to be miserly (Hutcheson Inquiry, 2.7, 185–8; System, 2.3.3, 259; PMIC, 114). Hutcheson did not think the miser blameless but did think that he could not be forced into generosity. He also used the doctrine of external right to explain religious toleration. The marks of wisdom are sufficiently ambiguous and contested that claiming superior wisdom is insufficient for claiming power over a man without his consent, and this includes directing another in his religion (PMIC, 129–31). Hutcheson was thus using the legislative perspective to arrive at the same conclusion as Locke did on religion, which suggests the possibility that he was directly familiar with Locke's later writings on toleration. Hutcheson also claimed that treaties cannot be voided by claiming they were entered into under the pressure of unjust force, since almost any treaty could plausibly be ended on these grounds and this would render peace treaties futile (System 3.10.6, 354–5).

In the same way that Locke allowed the magistrate to break the law for the public good if authorized to do so by natural law via the doctrine of prerogative, so did Hutcheson. "There's beside all these a certain *extraordinary right* in the supreme governors of any people, in great exigencies, to incroach upon those rights of the subjects which for ordinary are to be religiously maintained to them" (Hutcheson PMIC, 244). People will praise the one who departs from the ordinary law rarely in cases of great magnitude and with integrity (Hutcheson System, 2.17.8, 135). What is interesting to note is that, based on the framework we have constructed, the magistrate may not merely note that in a particular case deviating from the rule is for the public good. Rather, the magistrate must ask whether a general exemption applying to other cases and other magistrates would have positive consequences.

In Hutcheson we have a thorough explication of the legislative point of view that is still within the traditional divine natural law framework. The moral law is still understood to be the law of God. Yet Hutcheson's approach contains materials out of which Hume's secular theory can be constructed. Because there is a built-in predisposition to approve of things that promote the public good there is no longer a necessity of divine rewards and punishments. Our motives for moral actions can come from within us. Because of his rejection of voluntarism, we can know directly what is morally good and bad in a general way (though rules are needed to determine specific actions specified by natural law). Most interestingly, the way we actually determine the law of nature is by reasoning from experience about what general rules and general exceptions would be most conducive to the public good. We discern God's rules by figuring them out ourselves. We can easily imagine someone who goes through the same thought process without mentioning God and who instead just asks what moral code would be best for us. That person, however, would have to justify the legislative shift. Why should we think as if we were legislators when we are not? Hutcheson did not think he needed to answer this question since he assumed that our being governed by general laws was part of God's providential design.

Joseph Butler

Before proceeding to Hume, I will briefly discuss one other important figure, Joseph Butler. Butler was not only important in the debates about the competing metaphors but also as an early critic of the counterintuitive conclusions to which morality, focused on act-by-act benevolence, leads. Butler's ideas influenced Hume and provide a striking example of the "God as architect" theme and hesitations about the divine legislator heuristic. Butler takes benevolence to be an essential aspect of God's character. He stops short, however, of endorsing the legislative point of view, as Hutcheson had, as the normative structure for ethical deliberation. Like Hutcheson, Butler wanted to emphasize that a natural desire to act benevolently is not the same thing as a moral obligation to act benevolently (Darwall 1995a, 244–5). Butler claimed that Shaftesbury did not present an adequate account of the authority of conscience (Butler, 2.xv–xviii). This, Butler notes in Sermon 2, is the defining aspect of our conscience, that it speaks to us with a unique authority about what should or should not be done. Butler thought that conscience had to approve of things other than benevolence in order to avoid unacceptable moral conclusions.

For our purposes, what is of most interest is Butler's critique of the benevolence-based legislative ethic that Hutcheson defended. In 1737 Butler published his dissertation *Of the Nature of Virtue* and specifically criticized a person of "great and distinguished merit" who gives the impression of imagining "the whole of virtue to consist in singly aiming, according to the best of their judgment, at promoting the happiness of mankind in the present state" (Butler, 1.279). William Scott argues that this person is Hutcheson (Scott 1900, 97) and, based on the above analysis, this seems likely. The problem with the legislative approach, according to Butler, is that even if we accepted that God is solely motivated by benevolence (and "solely" is controversial), "we are constituted so as to condemn falsehood, unprovoked violence, injustice, and to approve of benevolence to some preferably to others, abstracted from all consideration which conduct is likeliest to produce an overbalance of happiness or misery" (Butler, 1.278). In other words, Butler, like Hutcheson, takes our natural moral judgments as evidence of God's design, but notices that we are not designed such that we approve and disapprove morally merely on the basis of judgments about probable aggregate happiness. Benevolence is a part of human virtue, but not the whole of human virtue. Our moral sense is designed to condemn falsehood and injustice as such, not just because they are harmful.

Even if one grants the supposition that God is motivated by benevolence, it does not follow that we human beings should try to aim at it directly. Instead, we should think that a benevolent God, "giving us the above-mentioned approbation of benevolence to some persons rather than others, and disapprobation of falsehood, unprovoked violence, and injustice, must be, that he foresaw this constitution of our nature would produce more happiness than forming us with a temper of mere general benevolence" (Butler, 1.278). Here we see Butler previewing what would become an increasingly important strategy, the claim that our pursuit of happiness (whether individual or collective) must be indirect. Butler was not, however, arguing for a theological version of rule-utilitarianism. Rather, Butler was arguing that God has benevolently created human beings with a tendency to approve not only benevolence but also justice and veracity (1.272). Acting on the combination of these produces better actions than trying to act directly on benevolence alone.

A key part of Butler's argument is to show that if we appeal to benevolence alone there will be particular cases where that moral system leads to unacceptable conclusions. "For it is certain, that some of the most shocking instances of injustice, adultery, murder, perjury, and even of persecution, may, in many supposable cases, not have the appearance of being likely to produce an overbalance of misery in the present state" (1.279). Notice that Butler says that it will do so "in many supposable cases" rather than stating that a general rule would sanction such actions. As noted above, Butler had said that an author "of great and distinguished merit" gives the incorrect impression that virtue is merely about promoting happiness in the present state. This implies that the author in question (Hutcheson) does not really say this but could be thought to say it. One way of understanding Butler is that he is aware that Hutcheson is not proceeding on an act-by-act basis and so Hutcheson, rightly interpreted, need not defend the cases of murder and perjury that Butler lists. Nonetheless, Butler worries that people will simply equate virtue with act-by-act benevolence, leading to morally unacceptable consequences. If this is right, he interestingly makes a point similar to the one W. D. Ross would make in the twentieth century.

In any case, Butler thinks that there is a better alternative to Hutcheson's position even if we interpret it on a rule basis. Whereas Hutcheson made much of our ability to form probabilistic judgments about future consequences, Butler was more skeptical. "The happiness of the world is the concern of him who is the Lord and the Proprietor of it; nor do we know what we are about, when we endeavour to promote the good of mankind in any ways but those which he has directed; that is, indeed, in all ways not contrary to veracity and justice" (Butler, 1.279). Butler thought that we should simply follow our consciences, which disapprove of injustice and falsehood even in cases where we think an unjust action or a falsehood will produce greater good, because doing otherwise would be encroaching upon a legislative responsibility that belongs to God. God's role is as architect, designing our moral sense. We do not deviate from the dictates of that implanted moral sense on the basis of our own judgments about what God as legislator would have wanted.

While this might seem like a case of stark opposition, in fact Butler's position may be closer to Hutcheson's than is obvious from the above commentary. We have seen that Hutcheson himself agreed that one should only make exceptions in publicly generalizable cases and that, in a sense, we have to decide what counts as an injustice. When Butler considered this position in a sermon on love of neighbor, he again considered the supposition that all of virtue rests on benevolence. While not affirming the presupposition (in that he still thinks that, practically speaking, conscience cannot be so reduced), he did find considerable common ground. He noted that "when benevolence is said to be the sum of virtue" there is an assumption that there will be significant rational reflection on the "distant consequences" of an act. We will see the utility of our natural preference for helping our friends and family and affirm that preference as conducive to the greatest good.

> And as there are numberless cases, in which, notwithstanding appearances, we are not competent judges, whether a particular action will upon the whole do good or harm; reason in the same way will teach us to be cautious how we act in these cases of uncertainty. It will suggest to our consideration, which is the safer side; how liable we are to be led wrong by passion and private interest; and what regard is due to laws, and the judgment of mankind. All these things must come into consideration, were it only to determine which way of acting is likely to produce the greatest good. (Butler, 2.141–2)

This perspective is quite similar to Hutcheson's. The legislative shift was Hutcheson's mechanism for helping us to be cautious about straying from normal moral practices. The precondition of imagining a publicly known exception and of accounting for the foreseeable "passions and private interest" that would affect judgment and behavior was intended to produce the required caution.

Hutcheson and Butler clearly differed in that the former, but not the latter, was willing to explicitly use a consequentialist legislative framework as a normative strategy. Butler, by contrast, preferred to see the dictates of conscience as authoritative even though some of those dictates were grounded independently of benevolence or utility. Both of them moved away from the idea that future rewards and punishments were needed to motivate moral behavior, finding instead an internal motivation in human nature. Neither of them were theological voluntarists, but both of them relied upon the claim that our moral sense is part of God's design.[7] Butler's conscience is a kind of internalized legislator given to us by the divine architect and our confidence in its legislation is closely linked to the idea that this is the faculty God has given us to guide our decision-making. He

---

[7] On the importance of theological teleology for Butler see Hebblethwaite 1992 and Millar 1992.

thought of it as an important source of moral guidance because the problematic conclusions of act-by-act benevolence were already apparent well before the days of Jeremy Bentham. In the next section, we see how Hume shifted to the metaphor of the spectator while trying to retain a legislative understanding of justice.

David Hume

Hume was very aware of the fact that the rules of justice are valuable as general practices but, in particular cases, contrary to the public good. He could see that we are better off if we can imagine rules of justice that function like laws and that eventually may be supported by laws. These law-like principles of justice account for the tendencies and limitations of those who will attempt to obey and enforce them. They are also justified by the fact that the rule, on the whole, is beneficial, and they are also designed to keep us from noting the utility of breaking the rule in particular cases. What is important about Hume is that he imagines a system that attempts to account for the law-like nature of justice without invoking God as a legislator. This is obviously an important step in explaining the transition from the older theories like Locke's where God as legislator is central to later theories like Bentham's where God is notably absent.[8] Hume's approach uses the metaphor of the spectator to explain our support for these law-like principles of justice. The spectator is different from the legislator or architect. The first two are active in that they bring laws or designs into existence. The spectator must rely on rules and practices that somehow already exist and then respond with approval or disapproval. Because human beings have a natural tendency to judge by general rules and practices, and because of the benefits that rules of justice bring, the spectator will approve of these principles. In Hutcheson's version, our trust in our moral sense is rooted in the idea that God designed us to approve of right action and the metaphor of the spectator is a way to differentiate unbiased responses from biased ones. In Hume's theory the religious aspect receded and he argued that it just happens that human nature, such as it is, will approve of useful practices, including the principles of justice, and that norms of justice can slowly emerge without a conscious decision by a legislator to enact a rule.

For the sake of brevity, what follows will sketch Hume's account from the later and more succinct account of justice in the *Enquiry* (E) with some

---

[8] On the secular shift in Hume in comparison with his earlier predecessors, see Forbes 1975, chapters 1–2.

citations to parallel passages in the *Treatise* (T). Hume regarded the *Enquiry* as the better work (although posterity has not always agreed) and it is the more helpful of the two texts for seeing how Hume interacted with the legislative point of view. Hume agreed with his eighteenth-century predecessors that human beings have both self-love and sympathy. The latter sentiment is crucial to explaining virtues like benevolence. We are motivated to prevent suffering in others, although we are even more motivated to prevent our own. This, however, creates a puzzle when we think about justice. There are many specific cases where justice instructs us to act contrary to benevolence. Hume's explanation is that justice is an artificial virtue and it is on the construction of that artificial virtue that we now focus.

Hume boldly claimed that "public utility is the *sole* origin of justice, and that reflections on the beneficial consequences of this virtue are the *sole* foundation of its merit" (E, 3.1, 83; see also T, 3.3.6, 618). Statements like this lead some to see Hume as a utilitarian (Rosen 2003, 29–57). Rosen argues that the reasons often given for denying this depend on an overly strict definition of utilitarianism and glossing over passages where Hume said that utility is the measure not only of character but also of specific actions.[9] Part of the difficulty comes from the fact that Hume's project prioritized the descriptive over the prescriptive, explaining psychologically (and socially) how we come to have the moral sentiments and beliefs we in fact have. This is a rather different project from utilitarianism conceived as a normative theory. Hardin thinks that Hume was a "psychological utilitarian" but that he did not believe in an impersonal perspective from which one could rank some distributions better than others (Hardin 2007, 155). Hardin also thinks Hume was an "institutional utilitarian" in that we want our social institutions to bring us utility (155–6).[10] However Hume is classified, the argument that follows gives further support to the claim that his ideas were an important source for consequentialists after him.

The virtue of justice was of special interest to Hume and created a unique problem for his theory. He believed that our moral judgments flow from our sentiments and that, as a matter of human psychology, we praise things because they are useful. It is easy to see why we would find the benevolence of others useful and thus to explain why we would praise this character attribute. Justice, however, is different. Hume wrote:

---

[9] For an example of using this factor as a reason to deny Hume is a utilitarian see J. Harrison 1981, 85–8.

[10] Darwall 1995b, for example, argues that Hume is important in the history of utilitarianism because he advanced a conception of the moral good that is grounded in the natural good. Baier notes differences between Hume and Bentham's understandings of utility (Baier 2010, 231–2). Such claims are not the focus here.

> For if it be allowed (what is, indeed, evident) that the particular conse-
> quences of a particular act of justice may be hurtful to the public as well as to
> individuals; it follows, that every man, in embracing that virtue, must have
> an eye to the whole plan or system, and must expect the concurrence of his
> fellows in the same conduct and behaviour. (E, Appx. 3, 172; see also T,
> 3.2.2, 497–8; 3.3.1, 579)

Hume, like Hutcheson, was aware of the way the laws of property may
grant a large inheritance to a selfish miser rather than to someone who
would use the wealth benevolently (E, Appx. 3, 171). If we look only at the
particular case, our sentiments would lead us to approve of taking wealth
from the miser and giving it to another since this would be more useful.
Justice requires a social convention and derives its utility from being
accepted as a social convention (see also T, 3.2.1, 480–4). Justice is more
like a "vault" than a wall in that it requires coordination with others in
order to be useful (E, Appx. 3, 171). Justice is only beneficial when we obey
the general rule (E, Appx. 1, 157).

The key question is how this convention comes about. Theistic theories
might posit the existence of a benevolent lawgiver who sees that the rules of
justice would be beneficial for human beings and who then enacts corresponding laws. Hume took a different approach. He began by noting
a general tendency human beings have toward thinking in terms of rules.[11]
We are not born into a lawless state of nature, but rather a child is born to
parents who train him in a "rule of conduct" (E, 3.1, 88). Hume assumed that
the virtue of justice is expressed through rules aimed at the "good of
mankind" (E, 3.1, 90). The reason for this rule-based thinking is related to
the constraints within which we articulate moral praise and blame.

> Every man's interest is peculiar to himself, and the aversions and desires,
> which result from it, cannot be supposed to affect others in a like degree.
> General language, therefore, being formed for general use, must be moulded
> on some more general views, and must affix the epithets of praise or blame,
> in conformity to sentiments, which arise from the general interests of the
> community. (E, 5.2, 115–16)

If I want to persuade you that something is good or bad, I cannot appeal to
reasons that are specific to my situated position. "X is a virtue because it
benefits me" will not be a very effective argument, while "X is a virtue
because it benefits us" is. When using moral language, a person must
"depart from his private and particular situation, and must choose

---

[11] The influence of general rules is a prominent theme in the *Treatise* as well, see Hume T, 2.1.10, 309;
2.2.5, 362; 2.2.7, 371; 2.2.8, 374; 3.2.2, 499; 3.2.6, 531–3; 3.2.9, 551; 3.2.12, 572; 3.3.2, 598.

a point of view, common to him with others" (E, 9.1, 148).[12] Hume did not need to claim that we consciously think this when making moral claims. We might instead just have an unconscious sense about what sorts of arguments are appropriate.

If we want our statements of moral approval and disapproval to be persuasive to others, we must move from our own situated view and our own interests and take up a more general point of view. Here Hume used the idea of the spectator that Hutcheson had developed (E, 5.1, 104; 5.2, 117; 6.1, 119; 7, 134–7; 9.1, 151).[13] Given the importance of the figure of the spectator, it is worth thinking about how this metaphor relates to the figure of the legislator. A convention of justice, as it emerges, will be praiseworthy from the spectator's point of view because the rules of justice, in aggregate, produce better results than uncoordinated acts of benevolence. The spectator provides a way of approximating the impartiality of God's legislative perspective in the following sense: a legislator looking at a previous law would want to consider whether or not the practice as a whole is working for the good of the people and might revise the law in light of information about how people with their characteristic biases and limited altruism behave. The spectators that Hume had in mind are not directly interested parties and thus are in a better position to approve or disapprove based on the system as a whole. Because they look at the actions of others and think about the system as a whole (at least in some cases), they can approve of things that are valuable as rules because of the way they account for human fallibility, bias, etc. Hume gave examples of rules that spectators approve of for the same reasons that a legislator would have passed them.

The difference is that a legislator is active in a way a spectator is not. The legislator is consciously trying to maximize the good through law, but for Hume there was no claim that either the actor or the spectator is under an obligation to maximize utility (Whelan 1985, 185, 213). The legislator feels empowered to try to change the rules when this will be desirable while the spectator merely observes and approves or disapproves. Yet, as we will see, the situation is not that simple because we actually experience ourselves as having choices regarding what we will praise and thus choices about what criteria will guide our praise.

[12] See also Hume T, 3.3.1, 591 and Cohon 2008, 126–57. One way of thinking about the spectator is that moral judgments are statements about the moral sentiments that we believe would be experienced by spectators who observe from this common point of view.

[13] Hume noted in the *Treatise* that certain virtues will be approved anywhere in the world by a "judicious spectator," T, 3.3.1, 581. See Stewart 1992, 133–6.

Hume was not claiming that our overriding desire for the good of others leads us to act justly, but rather that we have the capacity to view systems of justice as systems and to evaluate them as such and that we tend to be pleased with systems that produce useful outcomes (Hardin 2007, 168). The belief that we are pleased with utility-producing institutions is not the same as a full-on act- or rule-utilitarian position. The rules of justice are expressed in terms of general rules, but one need not be a rule-utilitarian to see the value of general rules. When asking the question "should I support this institution?" The act- and rule-utilitarian can agree that a beneficial institution should be supported. The harder question arises when we face dilemmas as individuals about whether to follow those conventions.

Let us consider a specific example. Hume noted that, in the past, the practice of tyrannicide was frequently extolled because it was a way to free human beings from oppressive rulers. More recently it has been discovered that the "practice" of tyrannicide "encreases the jealousy and cruelty of princes" (Hume E, 2.2, 81). There is danger on both sides – danger in denying the right to remove a tyrant and danger in affirming it. Hume argued in his essay "Of Passive Obedience" that "when the execution of justice would be attended with very pernicious consequences, that virtue must be suspended, and give place to public utility, in such extraordinary and such pressing emergencies" (Hume PW, 182). Hume claimed that the stakes under tyranny are so high that we will in fact approve of the removal of a tyrant but that the dangers of this being misapplied provide good reasons for strictly interpreting the conditions under which one may resist the government.[14] In making this argument, we have a partial statement of the legislative view: different principles are compared and the consequences for fallible people of the adoption of each principle are compared. His argument here may be a reply to Berkeley defending Locke's position within a legislative framework.

Nonetheless, this does not actually answer the question of what I should do when deciding whether or not to join a resistance movement. The above argument tells me that if I join and we (the resistance) win and make the people better off they will, *ex post*, approve of our actions. If, however, I enjoy the patronage of the tyrant and have much to lose by joining the opposition, Hume has not given a moral argument for why I must.

Hume made a related point in the *Enquiry*, noting that public laws are also subject to exceptions:

---

[14] See also Hume T, 3.2.10, 563.

Does any one scruple, in extraordinary cases, to violate all regard to the private property of individuals, and sacrifice to public interest a distinction, which had been established for the sake of that interest? The safety of the people is the supreme law: All other particular laws are subordinate to it, and dependent on it: And if, in the *common* course of things, they be followed and regarded; it is only because the public safety and interest *commonly* demand so equal and impartial an administration. (E, 2.3, 92)

What is important to notice here is that the principles of justice are expressed as social rules and are justified by their utility as rules that hold even in cases where they do not produce ultimate rules. Nonetheless, there are some cases so extreme where the prior commitment to utility is more powerful than the commitment to justice and we set justice aside in the name of benevolence (Sobel 2009, 181–2). Hutcheson would not have disagreed on this point, but he would have framed it as appealing to the true will of the legislator (God) in deviating from the rule in the specific case. In Hume's version, if there is a something analogous to a legislator, it is the general sense of the public that the rules of justice exist for our good and can be set aside occasionally when they are not.

Conclusion

In Locke and Berkeley's theory we assume a legislative God who considers human nature and human limitations when deciding what rules of justice will best preserve human life. We must reason to our moral beliefs, at least if we want to avoid the normal course of merely accepting the norms of our culture uncritically. The divine legislator both defines what is right in this legislative manner and motivates compliance through supernatural sanctions. Hutcheson also used this framework but situated it in a theory that gave greater emphasis to our moral reactions and to the way those moral reactions might be validated by an impartial spectator. In Hume's theory, principles of justice emerge as a solution to the problems that arise when beings of limited altruism interact in conditions of limited scarcity. Justice still has the law-like features it had before in that it operates by general rules that must account for the limitations of those who follow them, but the artificial convention arises, in a sense, naturally rather than via a divine intermediary. In place of the divine legislator we have human spectators. Through sympathy with the spectators we can approve of principles of justice that are beneficial in the aggregate.

In the next chapter we turn to Bentham and Paley and to the great divide between theistic and secular approaches to the legislative point of view.

Paley rejected Hume's approach and attempted to vindicate a more Lockean point of view using a psychology that was less sophisticated than Hume's, in that it overlooked the central role of sympathy. Paley insisted upon the need for God as a way to provide appropriate moral motivations for otherwise self-interested persons. He also contended that God directs us via rules. Bentham, by contrast, chose the secular approach that Hume had begun. Bentham took Hume's descriptive account of human beings pleased by utility and transformed it into an unrelentingly normative program of social reform. In the next chapter we look at two contrasting approaches to using the legislative point of view to determine what is right and what is wrong.

CHAPTER 3

The Great Divide
Bentham and Paley

The authors surveyed in the previous chapters had set all the basic elements in place for the great division between William Paley and Jeremy Bentham over whether to retain God as legislator in consequentialist ethical systems. Hume had provided a plausible psychological account of how a system based on rules of justice could arise without the need for people to be conscious of a divine legislator. If one set aside claims about the existence of God there were still questions about why we are obligated to act morally and whether we have sufficient psychological motivation to act morally when doing so is against our interests. While these questions have been discussed above and by others, there was also an explicit awareness that act-by-act consequentialism could lead to morally shocking and troubling conclusions. The influential Joseph Butler, as we have seen, had made the argument that any wicked act, if benefiting the common good, could in principle be morally right given such a framework (O'Flaherty 2019, 87). This third concern is of primary interest because it allows us to see a way in which the alternative strategies of Paley and Bentham preview the later debates between act- and rule-utilitarians.

Paley sought to promote a utilitarian outlook by presenting a rule-based theory that was sufficiently similar to prevailing beliefs to be taken seriously, an endeavor that was largely successful. His rule-based approach avoided what were taken by most people to be decisive counterexamples where act-by-act utilitarianism yielded immoral results. The twentieth-century rule-utilitarians would make the same move, but with their arguments transposed into a secular key. Bentham, by contrast, saw that the counterfactual use of the legislative point of view made little sense in a secular theory and was much more committed to secularism than to arriving at moral conclusions that his contemporaries would find palatable. Rather than deny that act-by-act utilitarianism would lead to those troubling conclusions or explicitly draw attention to them, Bentham strategically shifted his attention away from the counterfactual contexts where we are not legislating and focused his attention on cases where our contexts were plausibly legislative. In these contexts, Bentham could deploy a secular legislative point of view without paradox and without drawing attention to the counterintuitive conclusions. This chapter will explore Paley and Bentham's conflicting strategies that preview twentieth-century debates while foregrounding the theological dimensions that were largely absent from those later debates.

William Paley

While Jeremy Bentham is far more famous now, William Paley's version of consequentialism received a much warmer reception in the closing years of the eighteenth century. William Whewell, in his *Lectures on the History of Moral Philosophy in England*, wrote of Paley's book, *The Principles of Moral and Political Philosophy* (Paley 1785), that "It was very favorably received by the public, and was almost immediately adopted into the course of teaching in this University [Cambridge]" (Whewell 1852, 165). Paley's book continued to be the standard text on morals and politics at Cambridge for more than two decades. Paley was also a prominent proponent of natural religion, having authored a book titled *Natural Theology* that explored what could be known about God by reason alone (Paley 1802). John Stuart Mill (CW, 10:53–7) thought that much of Paley's appeal was due to the fact that his version of utilitarianism was more congenial to the political and religious status quo. Bentham's radicalism was absent.

Paley is interesting in that he is so like Bentham in some ways and yet so unlike him in others. Like Bentham, he argued that the good is defined in terms of consequences. His theory of human motivation, like Bentham's, claimed that we always act for our perceived self-interest. Like Bentham, he was skeptical, or at least noncommittal, about whether human beings had an innate moral sense. Like Bentham, he thought that rather than consulting our moral sense we needed to calculate the expected consequences of different types of actions. The principles of morality that most people accept are understood as a summation of principles that society has found beneficial and therefore affirmed. Our focus here is on his emphasis of a rule-based approach to consequences based on the ideas that we are obligated to obey God and that God governs the world through general rules that aim at happiness.

Early on, Paley made clear the central role that God plays in his argument. "Virtue is '*the doing good to mankind, in obedience to the will of God, and for the sake of everlasting happiness*'" (Paley, 25). Here we see a utilitarian criterion of right as "doing good" and a self-interested conception of human motivation (our future rewards in heaven motivate our virtuous action). In between is his claim that virtue is "obedience to the will of God," and this is the principal source of his divergence from Bentham. The disagreement is not primarily about motivation. Paley's concept of obligation, like Bentham's, is primarily about our response to positive and negative incentives. For both Paley and Bentham, I can be obligated by a robber's threat as much as by a just law. Rather, the difference between Paley and Bentham stems from God's use of general rules.

Paley argued that the Bible is incomplete in that it does not answer all our moral questions. Moreover, it does not give new rules, but gives better sanctions and certainty to old ones in that it reaffirms what reason and conscience reveal to us (Paley, 5). The word "rules" is important. Paley assumed that whether through reason or revelation, God reveals his will by general rules. "The method of coming at the will of God, concerning any action, by the light of nature, is to inquire into 'the tendency of the action to promote or diminish the general happiness'" (Paley, 39). By "tendency" Paley did not mean the probable effects of a particular action; he meant the effects of a whole class of actions that are permitted, required, or forbidden by a general rule. Once we discover which rules lead to beneficial outcomes, we know God's will. He claimed that "what promotes the general happiness, is required by the will of God" (Paley, 33).

That God rules the world through general rules is crucial to his argument. He stated that while the benefits of general rules are well known in human government, there is some disagreement about whether God also governs by general rules. His answer is "that general rules are necessary to every moral government" (Paley, 44) including that of God. Without general rules, those governed cannot know what is expected of them and rewards and punishments cannot serve their intended purpose of modifying our conduct. There are several different ways we might think about "general tendencies." First, we might note that an action, in addition to its immediate effects, may also affect a person's character. When considering the temptation to gain attention from a fairly harmless white lie, a person should reflect on how the habit of truthfulness has been valuable and how a new habit of lying might lead to trouble (Paley, 28–9; see also 109). This is a form of argument that John Stuart Mill would use later (RBP, 10:7–8). Second, we might think about how other people's actions might be influenced by our own action. A full accounting of the consequences of a particular act should include how others will view us if they discover we have committed it, whether they will be likely to imitate the behavior, and so on. Neither of these arguments require recourse to a counterfactual legislative point of view. They only require a more thorough examination of the likely future effects of a particular act.

The third form of "tendency," and the one that is our concern, is explained in the following example. In many cases, a person may think that an action that should not be performed if it were to be publicly known may be performed if the action can be kept secret. One might think that people who plan their own suicides so that it will look like an accident can set aside the objection that they will encourage others to commit suicide or that their families will be harmed by knowing that they died by suicide rather than accidentally. Paley replies that "those who reason in this manner do not observe, that they are setting up a general rule, of all others the least to be endured; namely, that secrecy, whenever secrecy is practicable, will justify any action" (Paley, 45). Notice that the person in question is no longer considering the direct and indirect consequences of a particular action. Instead, the person is contemplating whether a generally known rule would be beneficial. If the only things that mattered were the actual consequences of the act, then secrecy, by changing the consequences, could change the moral permissibility of the act. Paley denied this.

A crucial point is whether one must follow the rule even when it seems like breaking the rule would produce better consequences. Paley did occasionally admit that the benefits of breaking a rule might sometimes outweigh the costs. He considered the principle "let us not violate a general rule, for the sake of any particular good consequence we may expect." His comment on it was that it "is for the most part a salutary caution, the advantage seldom compensating for the violation of the rule" (Paley, 49). His qualification "for the most part" gives the impression that this is not an absolute principle. There are several things Paley might have meant here. He might have meant that, as in act-utilitarianism, rules are only a heuristic shortcut and can be violated whenever one is sufficiently confident one can produce better consequences. This would contradict his whole framework and the way he deploys his principle in the cases discussed elsewhere. A second interpretation is that we have to compare the good produced by breaking the rule not with the good of following the rule in this particular case, but with all the good produced by the rule in aggregate. A third interpretation is that Paley was envisioning cases where a rule that includes an exception produces better results than one without an exception and so some rules should have escape clauses built into them.

The third interpretation is closest to Paley's original meaning. The clearest example of Paley's endorsement of exceptions is in the area of international law. He followed Hume in finding international agreements less binding than normal promises. In Hume's example, the obligation to keep our promises is a function of the benefits of that practice (Hume E, 2.4, 99–103; Hume T, 3.2.11, 567–9). Since nations are more self-sufficient than individuals, they have less to lose by breaking faith with other nations than individuals do by breaking faith with other individuals. Moreover, the stakes may be much higher and nations may have far more to lose by keeping an unfavorable agreement. Paley made a similar point, arguing that a nation might break a particularly burdensome treaty (Paley, 457–8). This seems to be closer to interpretation three than two. In Hume's example, a prince is not likely to think that all treaties in the world will become void if he breaks a burdensome one, which is what would happen if violation of the particular instance were compared with the value of the entire practice. Instead, what both Hume and Paley seem to have had in mind is a known, tacit exception that is part of the rule. When countries enter into treaties with each other, they know the other party is likely to back out if it becomes too onerous and the parties account for this in making their agreements. This way of framing it allowed Paley to think of the exceptions as a kind of generalizable, universally understood rule.

A crucial feature of the legislative point of view is imagining morality as a code highly analogous to a legal code such that one must consider effectiveness of sanctions, fallibility and bias in enforcement, likelihood of popular acceptance, and so on. These features of Paley's consequential-ism were fully articulated in the late eighteenth century. In what follows, we will examine seven different examples of this sort of argument in Paley. These examples both illustrate how much he relied upon counterfactual use of the legislative metaphor and also show how, by using this frame-work, he was able to defend positions that made his theory attractive given the prevailing moral opinions of his time. Some of those judgments are much less widely shared today, so the claim is not that present readers will agree that in each case Paley's views lead to morally superior conclusions than an act-by-act approach would have. Instead, it is to suggest a parallel: although various moral opinions changed from the eighteenth century to the twentieth century, in each century the legislative approach would have more closely aligned with people's considered moral judgments. Here we explore the eighteenth-century examples and in Chapter 5 we will look at the twentieth-century version of this same strategy.

First, Paley agreed that, as a matter of moral right, the poor sometimes have a just claim on some of the property of the rich. He denied, however, that they should be able to take property by force because a general rule allowing them to do so would be misapplied and resisted (Paley, 54). On the other hand, in cases of truly dire necessity, he does think the poor can take property without permission so long as they aim to make restitution in due course (Paley, 61). In the case of a typical beggar, allowing him to take alms by force would, as a general practice, cause too many problems. Genuine life and death cases are rarer and we gain more by allowing an exception. Paley's position here is in line with many of his predecessors who also thought that extreme need could override property rights, but he frames his position in such a way as to avoid radically undermining the institution of private property. By denying the poor the right to take property by force and by requiring restitution, he assigns a high priority to protecting the system of rules that constitute private property.

A second example comes from divorce laws. Given the fact that there are cases where the law might prevent a divorce that both parties believe would make them better off, Paley pursued two lines of argument. First, he argued that some causes for divorce are such that a general rule permitting them is advisable. He gave examples such as adultery, desertion, "outrageous cruelty," and insanity. He rejected as causes dislike, coldness, severity, peevishness, and jealousy. His reason was "not that these reasons are trivial, but because such objections may always be alleged, and are impossible by testimony to be ascertained; so that to allow implicit credit to them, and to dissolve marriages whenever either party thought fit to pretend them, would lead in its effect to all the licentiousness of arbitrary divorces" (Paley, 189). This would be uninteresting if he were talking about actual divorce legislation, but the paragraph begins by making clear that what he was addressing was whether "the law of nature admits of an exception in favour of the injured party" in cases of divorce. The difficulties of differentiating true from false claims impact both how the law of nature and civil laws are understood. His second line of argument takes up the objection that in cases where both parties want a divorce it must be in their best interest to allow it. Again, he reverted to the framework of a legal code and stipulated that the divorcing couple must be told that "the same permission, as a general rule, would produce libertinism, dissension, and misery, amongst thousands, who are now virtuous, and quiet, and happy, in their condition" (Paley, 190). Even so, it is wrong to assume that Paley always accepted the status quo without revision. For his day, this position still represents a liberalization of divorce laws. Foreseeing the opposition this would likely create, the rule-based approach provides him with a strong response to the critic who says that a utilitarian must approve of divorce under any circumstances where the affected parties would be happier.

A third example addresses the worry that an obligation to promote the greatest good would be overwhelming. Paley, discussing the special obligations of parents to their own children, said that

> the good order and happiness of the world are better upholden whilst each man applies himself to his own concerns and the care of his own family, to which he is present, than if every man, from an excess of mistaken generosity, should leave his own business, to undertake his neighbour's, which he must always manage with less knowledge, conveniency, and success. (Paley, 197)

Paley's logic is that we are more effective at promoting happiness where we have more knowledge and that we have much more knowledge about what will benefit those close to us than we do for strangers. This justifies parents focusing on the well-being of their own children. Such a rule produces more happiness than if all parents regarded all children as equally deserving of their assistance. Though Paley did not say so explicitly in the passage, he likely took as given that the natural concern of parents for their children is part of the calculation of the best rule. His goal was to put it within proper boundaries so that it is not excessive. This is one example that closely parallels later debates. A persistent worry about utilitarianism has been that its strong claims of impartiality would be unacceptable and burdensome given the normal tendency to show special concern for one's family and friends. Most utilitarians employ some sort of indirect strategy to avoid this counterintuitive conclusion. Paley's rule-based strategy provided a very straightforward way to do this.

A fourth example relates to self-defense. Some argue that self-defense can be used to justify killing whenever any of our rights are threatened, no matter how insignificant the right. Paley instead argued that if we think about general rules that would have better and worse consequences, lethal force should only be permissible in the cases of attempted rape or attempted murder. Even here, if one can escape harm some other way, one should do so (Paley, 217–8). Paley weighed the harm inflicted by the attacks against the harm done by the responses. His conclusion is more restrictive than Locke's, given that Locke allowed lethal force in cases of attempted robbery. Here I think it is fair to characterize Paley's position as reformist without being radical. He did not have to say that in each case one may use whatever level of force is utility-maximizing in the particular case.

A fifth example is another argument related to suicide. If the goal is human happiness, it would seem that there are at least some cases where a person's estimate that his remaining life will be unhappy or painful would justify suicide. Paley argued that we would reject a rule authorizing suicide in such cases because people who are "melancholy" wrongly calculate the consequences of suicide (Paley, 225–6). Put in modern terms, people with clinical depression are not good estimators of their likely future happiness. Paley further noted that added worry by third parties about whether others will commit suicide would be an additional harm incurred due to the rule (Paley, 227). Paley relied on the assumption that any rule will be publicly promulgated and that we will worry that people, knowing suicide is permitted, will make use of the permission. Given prevailing opposition to suicide in Paley's day, an act-by-act application of utility to this question would have been a major problem for his theory and the rule-based account provided Paley with a way to justify a suicide prohibition that would otherwise be rejected.

Paley's general principle for evaluating rules was that "uniformity is of more importance than equity, in proportion as a general uncertainty would be a greater evil than particular injustice" (Paley, 362). A sixth example shows that in some cases uncertainty is worth the costs. He considered the question of whether persons may take up arms against a bad government. He allowed them to do so if they think it expedient based on the overall costs and benefits that revolt will likely bring. To those who objected that it is too dangerous to allow individual persons to make such a judgment, Paley responded that "The danger of error and abuse is no objection to the rule of expediency, because every other rule is liable to the same or greater" (Paley, 299). Here Paley was likely following Locke who thought that the alternative of letting the government judge whether the government should continue in power was unacceptable and that the threat of revolution might deter some bad behavior by government. Writing not long after the American Revolution, Paley gave this practical illustration: the Americans should have reasoned about whether a rule allowing all colonies to separate was good for the whole empire, not just whether America separating from England would be beneficial (Paley, 303). In his own day, this is one of the better examples of Paley trying hard to find neutral ground on a volatile topic (O'Flaherty 2019, 194–5). Being able to affirm Locke's general conclusions (and thus the permissibility of the Glorious Revolution) while raising doubts about the justification of revolution in the American case was helpful for Paley. The rule-based approach allowed him to differentiate the cases by showing that only in the first case was there a principle that would be approved from a legislative point of view.

Lastly, let us look at his views on religious toleration and establishment. His argument here closely followed Locke's argument from the *Third Letter Concerning Toleration* discussed in Chapter 1. In principle, Paley said, religion is not exempt from political regulation (Paley, 407–8). Governments exist to promote the good and promoting religion might be one way to accomplish this. It does not follow that rulers should force people to their religion even if they think this is the greatest possible good for them. This is mistaken because we must look at the "general tendency."

> It obliges the magistrate to reflect, not only whether the religion which he wishes to propagate amongst his subjects be that which will best secure their eternal welfare; not only, whether the methods he employs be likely to effectuate the establishment of that religion; but also upon this farther question: Whether the kind of interference which he is about to exercise, if it were adopted as a common maxim amongst states and princes, or received as a general rule for the conduct of government in matters of religion, would, upon the whole, and in the mass of instances in which his example might be imitated, conduce to the fartherence of human salvation. (Paley, 409–10)

This is exactly Locke's argument from the *Third Letter*. The extraordinary degree of similarity between the two arguments provides evidence for the claim that this approach to thinking about the generalized consequences of rules when applied by fallible human actors was one taken from Locke.

Paley's argument left open room for religious establishment. Although Locke did not discuss it as explicitly, as a member of the Church of England he likely thought that religious establishment was permissible so long as dissenters were free to worship in other peaceful churches. Paley agreed with this conclusion and was willing to state a general rule such that if a religious minority persuaded enough people to join its ranks and thus become a majority, that group would then be allowed to change which church received public support (Paley, 416). Both authors, seeing general value in belief in God, were willing to use state power to discourage atheism. In Paley's treatment of religion, we see many of the elements of the legislative point of view in play. God as the author of general rules must consider how a rule allowing religious persecution would be used not just in London, but also in Paris and Constantinople. The likely wrong applications provide an additional and decisive reason for toleration. On the other hand, atheism (which Locke would also have criminalized) poses a threat to public order. This helps justify public funding for a national church and even fines for those who don't attend any church (Paley, 246). The legislative framework allowed Paley to defend the permissibility of religious establishment alongside religious toleration.

The perception of Paley as a simple apologist for the status quo is unfair. Paley may have strategically taken less radical positions so that the general utilitarian framework he proposed would be more widely adopted, trusting that others could draw their own conclusions once they became adept at using the framework (O'Flaherty 2019, 173–7, 192–5). This general tendency did not keep him from taking some strongly reformist stands, such as being an early opponent of the African slave trade (O'Flaherty 2019, 275–7). We have noted other reformist elements of his theory above. On the whole though, the legislative approach made his thought appealing to his contemporaries on two levels. First, the prominent role of God as legislator was reassuring to an audience that still expected morality to be grounded in religious beliefs and found outright rejection of God scandalous. Second, the rule-based framework yielded more acceptable conclusions than an act-by-act approach would have. Bentham's view would be more controversial on both counts.

Jeremy Bentham

While Bentham is sometimes known as the father of utilitarianism, Ernest Albee was closer to the mark more than a hundred years ago by identifying him as the father of *secular* utilitarianism. Most distinctive of Bentham was his secularism and anticlericalism that fed into his eagerness to upend commonly held beliefs.[1] Among his most deeply held convictions was that religious belief and practice were a detriment, rather than benefit, to human happiness. It promoted a pointless asceticism, depriving people of pleasures and subjecting them to needless pains. To this particular enterprise, Bentham brought an amazing talent for classifying phenomena in very detailed taxonomies. Bentham's rejection of the claim that God plays any meaningful or constructive role in utilitarian ethics was a very conscious decision, yet he drew little attention to the way the content of a utilitarian ethic changes when one eliminates the counterfactual perspectival shift. This helps account for some peculiar features of Bentham's theory. Bentham focused primarily on giving advice to human legislators, thus obviating the need for a divine motivation for private individuals to take on the legislative point of view in nonlegislative contexts. When discussing our private moral evaluations of the actions of individuals, Bentham reframed moral praise and blame as a kind of moral legislation, following Locke's lead.

We have seen that Paley was part of a long tradition of viewing God as the author of a morally binding code who promulgated his will through

---

[1] For a book-length account of the importance of secularism to Bentham's philosophical project, see Crimmins 1990.

rationally discoverable general rules. Bentham challenged this both implicitly and explicitly. He challenged it implicitly by simply leaving God out of his writings. For example, in his most famous work, *An Introduction to the Principles of Morals and Legislation*, there is no hint that it is helpful to ask what God would legislate in deciding what human beings should legislate. To Bentham, this was an unnecessary assumption. Religion did enter in but only in a descriptive way. Bentham famously began Chapter 2 of that book by stating that "Nature has placed mankind under the governance of two sovereign masters, *pain* and *pleasure*. It is for them alone to point out what we ought to do, as well as to determine what we shall do" (Bentham PML, 1). These sentences include one of the biggest problems with Bentham's theory. If, in fact, human beings are motivated by their own pleasures and pains, they will do what maximizes their own utility whether it maximizes the good of the greatest number or not. Bentham seems to hold up a criterion for good, namely the greatest good for the greatest number, that is contrary to the way human motivation actually works.

In this early work, Bentham's strategy was to focus on the perspective of human legislators; hence, the *Introduction* is primarily a guide to legislation. One role for a writer is to help people see more clearly what is in their interests so they will be motivated to do it. The incentives that human legislation brings with it are, however, only one of the factors that influences human behavior. Physical sanctions relate to the normal cause and effect of our actions. Drunkenness, for example, has the physical sanction of a hangover. Political sanctions are additional rewards or punishments administered by governments. Moral sanctions are the sanctions of praise and blame we get from other people (Locke's law of opinion or reputation). Religious sanctions are rewards or punishments given out directly by God. Framing human motivation this way allowed Bentham to take the religious sanction as an empirical psychological question. If people believe that God will punish something, that gives them a reason not to do it, whether or not God actually exists and whether or not God would actually punish the action in question. What matters is the belief. From there, Bentham framed the rest of the book in this way: his goal was to give advice to the legislator of political sanctions, but such a legislator must be aware of the way beliefs about moral or religious sanctions will either help or hinder human laws (PML, 27–8).

The focus on human legislators was only a partial solution for Bentham. If it is true that human beings are governed by hedonistic motivation, then altering the political sanctions can alter their behavior in ways that will create more overall good. This, however, only shifts the problem up one level. What will prompt legislators to legislate for the common good rather than their own good? Eventually Bentham thought democracy was a solution to this problem as it would give legislators an incentive, in theory, to pursue the good of the majority (Harrison 1983, 195–224). Moreover, Bentham's egoistic hedonism must apply, not just to legislators, but to Bentham himself. If the ethicists must only write what will bring them pleasure or lessen their pain, can we rely on the fact that there will be a convergence of the interests of ethicists and the public? Thomas Rawson Birks, a nineteenth-century critic of Bentham (and utilitarianism more generally) argued: "But while the herd of mankind are left under this necessity of pure selfishness, the moralist and the legislator, we are taught, must rise above it" (Birks 1874, 27). For Bentham and his original audience, this seemed to have been the most important problem to solve, namely how his theory of motivation and his ethical theory fit together. More specifically, would removing God deprive ethics of a necessary moral motivation?

Bentham took up this issue in his scathing attack on natural religion. Paley had written an entire book titled *Natural Theology* in which he argued on the basis of nature and science that the Earth contained evidence of "contrivance," or design. From this we could then infer various characteristics of God, importantly including God's benevolence. This was crucial to Paley's argument and those of his predecessors who argued that belief in a benevolent legislator, God, was both available by reason and beneficial to humanity. Bentham rejected both claims, vehemently, in his book *Analysis of the Influence of Natural Religion on the Temporal Happiness of Mankind.*

This daring and incredibly polemical book was published under the pseudonym Philip Beauchamp in 1822. Bentham, as was common for him, had worked on the book in manuscript but left it incomplete. A friend took the papers and put them into their present form. We have every reason to think that what we have represents Bentham's own views (McKown 2004, 19–20). Bentham took the radical position that whether or not natural religion was true, it was certainly harmful rather than beneficial. Given the incendiary claim, Bentham carefully framed his argument so that, in the event that his authorship was discovered, he could say he was only describing natural religion, not revealed religion. He could thus claim that his book was not an attack on religion in general or Christianity in particular, only on those who promoted natural religion. Nonetheless, the actual content includes any number of claims that clearly are attacks on religion generally and Christianity specifically. When combined with his other works in which he attacked the Bible as authentic revelation (he had particular contempt for the Apostle Paul), it shows Bentham consciously advancing, in the early nineteenth century, a radically secular agenda. Bentham's religious writings were sufficiently controversial that the editor of his collected works chose to omit them, thus obscuring for many readers in later generations this aspect of his thought (Crimmins 1990, 3–4).

In the *Analysis of the Influence of Natural Religion*, Bentham argued first that on the basis of reason we know next to nothing about what God wants us to do and how punishments and rewards will be distributed in the next life. He stated "that natural religion communicates to mankind no rule of guidance" (Bentham Analysis, 10). The result is that natural religion leads us to think that human beings find themselves under the power of a God who is capricious and terrifying, hardly a situation beneficial to our temporal happiness. To this he added an argument that we know those in positions of weakness tend to use praise and commendation when they seek to influence others while those in positions of strength use condemnation and punishment. It is therefore reasonable to think that God, who is incomparably powerful, uses condemnation and punishment to influence human behavior. Humans, from our position of weakness, can respond only with flattery: "mere natural religion invariably leads its votaries to ascribe to their Deity a character of caprice and tyranny, while they apply to him, at the same moment, all those epithets of eulogy and reverence which their language comprises" (Bentham Analysis, 16).

Not only that, but Bentham found religious sanctions from natural religion to be unhelpful. Religion and legislation work at cross purposes, with the former advocating things contrary to the human happiness that the latter seeks. "It is altogether impossible, therefore, that the mandates of natural religion can be directed to the promotion of temporal happiness, since they diverge so strikingly from the decrees of the legislators" (Bentham Analysis, 40). In fact, where people claim that we need divine sanctions to motivate people to behave differently, what we should instead do is solve the problem through better human legislation. "To affirm therefore the necessity of a recurrence to a super-human agency for the repression of any definable mode of conduct, is merely to say that human laws are defective and require amendment" (Analysis, 43).

We can see the convergence of these lines of thought in Bentham's *Deontology*. This work, also left uncompleted by Bentham, was published by his editor in the collected works such that it was more of a paraphrase than a work by Bentham himself. More recently, a critical edition based on

Bentham's original manuscripts has become available. The work is important in that it is the only work where Bentham puts morals rather than legislation at the center of the endeavor. It is also a very strange book. One might think a principal issue in deontology is explaining why someone should fulfill their duty when it conflicts with their interest. Bentham opened the chapter "of deontology in general" (likely intended to be the first chapter of the book) by writing:

> That a man ought to sacrifice his interest to his duty is a very common position … But when both interest and duty are considered in their broadest sense, it will be seen that in the general tenor of life the act of sacrifice is neither possible nor so much as desirable; that it can not have place, and that if it were to have place, the sum total of the happiness of mankind would not be augmented by it. (Bentham Deontology, 121)

He was, therefore, dismissive of ethicists who go around telling people what they ought or ought not to do (Bentham Deontology, 206–7). Bentham himself had sometimes used this very language, something critics were quick to point out. Nonetheless, Bentham in the *Deontology* was trying to follow his own advice. The topics he took up are more in the form of an advice column than a lecture on duty. He was helping people see which course of action is in their best interests in areas for which the law has not seen fit to prescribe rules.

The broadsides against religion continued in *Deontology*, without the qualification that he was only talking about natural religion. "Religion is misapplied – how can it be otherwise? – in proportion as it is applied to any part of the field of morals" (Bentham Deontology, 166). While the religious claim that God is benevolent, the God they describe is not. Bentham was thus very consciously stripping the consequentialist tradition of its theological underpinnings. He was aware that in doing so he raised the question of what would motivate human beings to act for the good of all when their own interests were in conflict. Bentham's solution to this problem was human legislation in two forms. The first and most prominent is governmental legislation: where additional incentives were needed human law could provide them. It is in the area of individual ethics, however, that the objections we have focused on in this book are found. There is no question about whether to have a law permitting us to hang innocent people (we should not), the problem is what to do in individual cases where hanging an innocent person (who is thought to be guilty) might produce better consequences than the available alternatives, despite the illegality of the act. Granting that the law may say that I should not commit perjury, what if I am confident my perjury will not be discovered and that it will be in my interests? Perhaps it will even be in the interest of all who are affected. What is the ethical thing to do?

It is at this point that Bentham shifted the question and introduced the legislative perspective in a second, indirect way: the act of giving out praise and blame becomes a form of legislation. Human legislators are, by their position, forced to take on a legislative point of view. Since the legislator will implement general rules, the legislator must take into account problems of insufficient motivation, biased interpretation, and faulty enforcement. Given Bentham's view of human motivation, we will do whatever we think is in our interests, "oughts" notwithstanding. Nonetheless, since there are many issues where the law cannot reach, our natural desire for praise and esteem can be harnessed as a powerful motivator. We will be told that perjury is always wrong because truth-telling in court is so valuable and important. If I am caught out in my lie, I can expect to be condemned for it. But that need not mean I actually did anything wrong. In Bentham's view, calling something wrong is just another sort of act that one does for one's own benefit (since every action is so motivated). We praise things we want other people to do and condemn things we want other people not to do. As with Hume, Bentham thought we are more effective in influencing the behavior of others if we frame our praises and condemnations as if they were general rules that applied to us as well. The nature of effective praising and blaming pushes us to make general statements about what everyone must do and to then use our praise and blame as the enforcement of those rules. This, in a sense, pushes us as individuals toward taking on the legislative point of view in a way that is not counterfactual. When I make general public statements about what should be praised or blamed, I am acting in a legislative capacity, and when I apply those principles to specific cases I affirm the rule and enforce its sanctions (praise or blame).

This interpretation of Bentham is borne out in many places, but one is in his treatment of religion. Throughout, he treated religious praise and blame as the self-interested actions of religious people. Since he thought religious duties were onerous, hypocrisy was perfectly rational. I can gain favor with God by getting other people to obey him while avoiding costly obedience whenever I can. What is interesting is that Bentham's objection was not really to hypocrisy, but to the fact that a powerful tool was being used in a way that diminishes rather than increases human happiness. All moral speech will lead to precisely the phenomenon of sometimes condemning as wrong actions that, in the specific case, actually increased utility. Utilitarians must condemn these utility-maximizing acts because of the utility of people thinking there is a general rule that outweighs it.

Schultz argues that these indirect strategies for motivating compliance with utility are crucial to Bentham's response to the objection that his egoism prevents him from taking utility as a true normative principle. The "obvious answer is that it is of course possible for people to find their best interest in serving the interest of all, just as Bentham himself did" (Schultz 2017, 105). Laws and moral opinions can shape us to make this eventuality more likely. In any case, Bentham thought a system relying on both legal and moral sanctions would be more effective than one that simply urged us to be altruistically disinterested because the former worked with our dominant motive.

For our purposes, what is important is to juxtapose these alternative forms of human legislation alongside Bentham's conspicuous silence on the sorts of counterexamples that those before and after him had wrestled with extensively. I have reconstructed how Bentham could answer the question involving a case where perjury appears to be utility-maximizing. Bentham explained the reasons why both law and social norms would inflict punishment in this type of case even though the action is utility-maximizing. He also explained why we might educate people so that their consciences would also inflict pain on them if they committed perjury in such a case. All of this is true, yet it is striking that Bentham himself did not spend time addressing questions like this one, questions where the difference between a situated perspective and a legislative perspective would be central to determining what is right and wrong in a particular case. Given how extraordinarily voluminous Bentham's writings were, it seems unlikely that his lack of interest in these questions is because he never had time to write about them.

The following are plausible reasons for Bentham's silence on this issue. First, Bentham, like Paley, was calculating. Bentham gave considerable thought to how his words (and even his body after his death) might be deployed to maximize happiness (Schultz 2017, 62–6, 69–72). Bentham strategically withheld some works from publication and published others anonymously so that they would detract less from the plausibility of his overall theory. The works cited above that show the depths of his animosity toward religion were not published in his lifetime under his name, and several were omitted from his collected works by his editors after his death because of their controversial nature. Bentham wanted to see utilitarianism adopted as the principle to guide legislation and it would have only made it more difficult to bring that about if he had highlighted the ways in which utilitarianism would justify individuals breaking moral rules that were widely endorsed in his day. It was better to simply set those topics aside. Second, having extracted God from his theory, Bentham likely saw counterfactual questions as pointless. Given that there is no God who is legislating a system of rules based on utility, why spend time speculating about what God would have legislated when one can instead make practical proposals about what sorts of laws and moral norms should be adopted, laws and norms that would have beneficial effects? The second reason is probably more fundamental than the first. Although Bentham was strategic about which of his works he published, he clearly had no qualms about writing things in his unpublished work that would have been incredibly controversial. One can, after all, find defenses of animal rights and homosexuality in his writings. But those controversial opinions were geared toward actual legislative questions: what the laws or norms of our society should be.

Conclusion

In Paley and Bentham, we see two contemporaries charting two very different paths forward for consequentialist thinking. Paley's view was religious and built rule-based deliberation into the foundations of moral deliberation. Bentham's view was secular and viewed rules instrumentally. Paley's strategy won over more adherents in his day, but as the discipline of philosophy turned in an increasingly secular direction, Bentham's approach became the more important one for tracing the future history of this line of thought. Perhaps the last important proponent of Paley's style of consequentialism was John Austin. In Lecture II of *The Province of Jurisprudence Determined*, Austin argued that divine laws are different from human laws in having God as their author and that God can legislate by directly revealing his law or through other means. Austin wrote of these laws of God that are not directly revealed:

> These laws are binding upon us (who have access to the truths of Revelation), in so far as the revealed law has left our duties undetermined. For, though his express declarations are the clearest evidence of his will, we must look for many of the duties, which God has imposed upon us, to the marks or signs of his pleasure which are styled the *light of nature*. Paley and other divines have proved beyond a doubt, that it was not the purpose of Revelation to disclose the *whole* of those duties. (Austin, 39)

Austin's religious views lent themselves toward Unitarianism, something that distinguished him from his sometime friend John Stuart Mill (Morison 1982, 36–8). While Austin had ties to the Bentham camp, his decision to situate himself alongside Paley is noteworthy. He adopted the older view of a literal divine lawgiver whose will can be known apart from special revelation.

Austin rejected appeals to a moral sense (Austin, 40–1). He instead argued that "God designs the happiness of all his sentient creatures" and that God intends that we promote that happiness (Austin, 41). After arguing that we assess utility by looking at the tendencies of acts, Austin stated

> if the tendencies of actions be the index to the will of God, it follows that most of his commands are general or universal. The useful acts which he enjoins, and the pernicious acts which he prohibits, he enjoins or prohibits, for the most part, not singly, but by classes: not by commands which are particular, or directed to insulated cases; but by laws or rules which are general, and commonly inflexible. (Austin, 43)

Austin's work, published in 1832, shows that while Paley continued to have disciples for another generation, his influence was decreasing. By contrast, Austin's counterpart, John Stuart Mill, pursued a strategy closer to Bentham's. It is the line of thought leading from Bentham to Mill and Sidgwick that would come to be known as the paradigmatic utilitarian position. Bentham's successors, however, had to grapple directly with the implications of the secular break. We will see in the next chapter that they talked more explicitly about the implications for individual moral action if we think of moral expression as a kind of legislation. Rather than ignoring the individual level problem in order to focus on genuinely legislative situations, Mill and Sidgwick tried to work out a theory of right and wrong from the perspective of the individual who has accepted utilitarianism to be correct. They both grappled with the differences between deliberation about right and wrong from the legislative perspective and that of the situated perspective of a given individual. In exposing the implications of Bentham's thought, they would set in place the conditions for the twentieth-century debates about act- and rule-consequentialism.

CHAPTER 4

Moral Expression as Legislation
Mill and Sidgwick

John Stuart Mill was the most important successor to Bentham's legacy. Bentham had taken a utilitarian approach to morality and legislation and pushed it in a decisively secular direction, in contrast to William Paley who stood in the line of theological consequentialists (or quasi-consequentialists) that included Cumberland, Locke, and Hutcheson. Whereas Bentham had been raised in a religious home and came to reject the claims of religion, John Stuart Mill was raised by Bentham's close friend James Mill in a thoroughly secular, even atheistic environment. As Mill famously stated in his autobiography, "I am thus one of the very few examples, in this country, of one who has, not thrown off religious belief, but never had it" (Mill CW, 1:44). It was Mill and Henry Sidgwick who would grapple more fully with the consequences of the secularization of utilitarianism. Bentham, Mill, and Sidgwick were very cognizant of the religious (or anti-religious) implications of their thought. Most prominent for them was the relationship between atheism and hedonistic psychology. If human beings were under the sovereign power of pleasure and pain and incapable of acting other than for what they thought would bring them pleasure or help them avoid pain, there was a clear possibility of a disjunction between what is best for the individual (egoism) and what is best for all (utilitarianism). In earlier theological theories, like Locke's or Paley's, divine sanctions in the next life could reconcile egoism with moral duty, but this solution was unavailable to the secularists. While this issue preoccupied them (and ultimately led Sidgwick to reject Bentham's hedonistic psychology), I have been making the case in this book that there was a second and less noticeable shift also taking place, namely that it became harder to justify the shift to a legislative point of view in situations where we are not, literally, legislators. Mill and Sidgwick grappled more directly and explicitly with the implications of Bentham's shift.

This chapter will explore these themes in the works of Mill and Sidgwick. A major theme in their work, and a major point of scholarly debate on Mill specifically, has been the role of secondary moral rules, such as prohibitions on lying or punishing the innocent, within a utilitarian framework. Mill and Sidgwick both thought secondary rules extremely important as a way to make utilitarianism practically feasible and as a way to diffuse some of the worries about the way it might undermine moral beliefs that were regarded as foundational. They also saw both law and public opinion as important sources of sanctions that could shape human behavior and help align self-interest with behavior that increased overall happiness. They pushed further down the path Bentham had begun in conceptualizing public moral expression as a form of legislation. Rather than making moral judgments by thinking God's legislative thoughts after him and then publicly expressing what God has decreed, public moral expression is now recast as a legislative activity. Instead of merely expressing my views about whether something is right or wrong, I am actually making a kind of legislative proposal for a new public norm and I must attend to the same sorts of questions as a legislator prior to making public statements. What are the chances of the proposed norm being widely accepted? How will others interpret and apply the norm differently than I might? How should a recognition of the fallibility and limited altruism of human beings shape the content of the norms I propose?

This legislative turn in moral expression led to some surprising tensions, some well-known, some less so. One underappreciated tension for Mill, we shall see, is the way the legislative approach to moral expression potentially conflicts with the rationale for freedom of expression in *On Liberty*. That rationale celebrates free expression oriented toward the discovery of truth and greater realization of individuality. The legislative perspective, however, will often require people to voluntarily withhold their beliefs about what is actually true. If one thinks of the lives of actual legislators, it is hardly one of unfettered individuality but rather of constant calculation about which public positions to take and when to change those positions. In Mill's view, we are all legislators. Mill himself consciously restricted his statements in a legislative manner long before he became an actual legislator in Parliament.

While Mill was Bentham's most famous successor, it was Henry Sidgwick who faced up to the appropriate attitude toward moral rules for a thoroughly secular utilitarian theory with the greatest precision, clarity, and candor. Sidgwick noted that what is right to do and what is right to praise or blame (including moral praise and blame) are very different questions. He followed the argument to its logical conclusion, that utilitarianism would sometimes lead one person to act rightly while at the same time dictate that other people punish that person (whether through opinion or governmental punishment). Sidgwick famously argued that even this truth might need to be concealed from most people so that an esoteric morality might only be known and practiced by a few enlightened persons. This troubling conclusion would make Rawls' publicity-laden theory of justice, which requires that the principles of justice be publicly known, more attractive to many people. It can be seen as part of the outworking of the secular shift and the need to move the legislative burden from God to human beings. Sidgwick presented, arguably, the most consistent secular version of the legislative point of view, but only by defending claims to which, in the twentieth century, many people would object.

Mill, Utilitarianism, and Legislative Rules

One of the most prominent debates about Mill's philosophy, since the 1950s, has been about whether or not Mill was a "rule-utilitarian." We will turn to the twentieth-century thinkers who consciously identified themselves as such in the next chapter. The term itself is not one that any nineteenth-century thinker used. Nonetheless, there are important analogies between it and the theistic consequentialism of the seventeenth and eighteenth centuries. In both cases one is limited in one's ability to justify deviation from a rule that has beneficial consequences even though one thinks that, in the specific case at hand, one can produce even better consequences by breaking the rule. Rule-utilitarianism requires its practitioners to assume a legislative perspective in order to arrive at the content of morality. A number of commentators think we risk (or commit) anachronism by trying to force Mill into categories (act v. rule) that he himself did not use.[1] In this section I review the debates about the role of moral rules in Mill's theory and proceed from those debates to a different set of categories. Whereas in the standard act versus rule debate the question turns on whether publicly known utility-maximizing moral rules are definitive of what is actually right, our inquiry in the following section is whether Mill used the legislative point of view and, if so, whether he used it counterfactually in nonlegislative contexts. To be sure, this is also a question that Mill would not have formulated in these terms. Nonetheless, it is worth exploring since one of the major claims of this book is that authors who

---

[1] On this point, see Schultz 2017, 60; Donner 1998; Gray 1996; Rosen 2003; and Skorupski 1989. Others simply conclude that Mill's theory is confused: Dale Miller 2011; Eggleston 2011; and Ryan 1974.

consciously chose secular approaches noticed some, but not all, of the implications of that shift. The tensions in Mill that give rise to the debates about the role of rules in his theory are, in part, because Mill is both attracted to the legislative perspective and straining to cope with the implications of adopting it in a purely secular theory.

James Opie Urmson, in an influential article (1953), argued that in Mill's theory, one determines the rightness of actions not by applying the principle of utility directly to the act but by "showing that it is in accord with some moral rule" and that the "moral rule is shown to be correct by showing that the recognition of that rule promotes the ultimate end" (35). Fuchs (2006) provides a helpful overview of how Mill developed these ideas. Mill began by giving the impression that the doctrine of utility applies directly to actions. "The creed which accepts as the foundation of morals, Utility, or the Greatest Happiness Principle, holds that actions are right in proportion as they tend to promote happiness, wrong as they tend to produce the reverse of happiness" (Mill U, 10:210). On the other hand, as the work unfolds, the place of rules became increasingly prominent. Mill wrote, "But to consider the rules of morality as improvable, is one thing; to pass over the intermediate generalizations entirely, and endeavor to test each individual action directly by the first principle, is another. It is a strange notion that the acknowledgment of a first principle is inconsistent with the admission of secondary ones" (U, 10:224). Here Mill makes it clear that one will often be guiding one's action by secondary rules and that over time one hopes those rules will improve.

Mill's most detailed application of this idea, in the context of whether a person should lie, is found in *Utilitarianism* and will be quoted at length:

> But inasmuch as the cultivation in ourselves of a sensitive feeling on the subject of veracity, is one of the most useful, and the enfeeblement of that feeling one of the most hurtful, things to which our conduct can be instrumental; and inasmuch as any, even unintentional, deviation from truth, does that much towards weakening the trustworthiness of human assertion, which is not only the principal support of all present social well-being, but the insufficiency of which does more than any one thing that can be named to keep back civilization, virtue, everything on which human happiness on the largest scale depends; we feel that the violation, for a present advantage, of a rule of such transcendent expediency, is not expedient, and that he who, for the sake of a convenience to himself or to some other individual, does what depends on him to deprive mankind of the good, and inflict upon them the evil, involved in the greater or less reliance which they can place in each other's word, acts the part of one of their worst enemies. (U, 10:223)

Mill here was making a point that he had made earlier in his 1833 *Remarks on Bentham's Philosophy* where he criticized Bentham for not accounting for the way the decision to act shapes one's character and thereby influences future decisions (Mill RBP, 10:7–8).[2] He was also emphasizing that what was at stake is not merely the undermined confidence of the person being lied to, but also the loss of confidence in a socially beneficial general rule.[3] Mill then continued in *Utilitarianism*:

> Yet that even this rule, sacred as it is, admits of possible exceptions, is acknowledged by all moralists; the chief of which is when the withholding of some fact (as of information from a malefactor, or of bad news from a person dangerously ill) would preserve some one (especially a person other than oneself) from great and unmerited evil, and when the withholding can only be effected by denial. But in order that the exception may not extend itself beyond the need, and may have the least possible effect in weakening reliance on veracity, it ought to be recognized, and, if possible, its limits defined; and if the principle of utility is good for anything, it must be good for weighing these conflicting utilities against one another, and marking out the region within which one or the other preponderates. (U 10:223)

Here Mill argues that we need more complex rules than simply "don't deceive" but that we should make these more complex rules publicly known and we should use the principle of utility to judge between competing rules.[4] As we saw in Chapter 2, there is a long history of viewing publicly known exceptions to rules as more complex specifications of the rules, so allowing exceptions in this sense does not show that Mill is an act-utilitarian. The qualification "if possible," however, indicates that the

---

[2] Interestingly, Mill takes Bentham to have been very interested in the general consequences that would come from a class of actions. Bentham, he thinks, "confounded the principle of Utility with the principle of specific consequences, and has habitually made up his estimate of the approbation or blame due to a particular kind of action, from a calculation solely of the consequences to which that very action, if practised generally, would itself lead." Bentham's failure was not in lack of generalization, but lack of attention to the effects on character. Likewise, Mill said Paley was concerned with "the probable *consequences* of that particular kind of act, supposing it to be generally practised" (RBP, 10:7). Mill thought Paley, unlike Bentham, was determined to use utility to justify the status quo. See CW, 10:54–6 and CW, 10:173.

[3] "Rules are necessary, because mankind would have no security for any of the things which they value, for anything which gives them pleasure or shields them from pain, unless they could rely on one another for doing, and in particular for abstaining from, certain acts" (Mill CW, 10:192).

[4] He makes a similar point about the rule against murdering in his response to Whewell: "At all events, the existence of exceptions to moral rules is no stumbling-block peculiar to the principle of utility. The essential is, that the exception should be itself a general rule; so that, being of definite extent, and not leaving the expediencies to the partial judgment of the agent in the individual case, it may not shake the stability of the wider rule in the cases to which the reason of the exception does not extend" (Mill CW, 10:183).

publicity requirement may itself be subject to exceptions, which suggests a more act-utilitarian reading.

Applying utility to adjudicate conflicts between incompatible secondary rules is a major theme in Mill's important discussion of justice in chapter 5 of *Utilitarianism*. The desire to punish, though it may start with an amoral sentiment of resentment, can be moralized into a part of justice if a person "does feel that he is asserting a rule which is for the benefit of others as well as for his own" (U, 10:249). The problem, he explains, is that we have conflicting principles of justice, sometimes tied to desert, sometimes to law, sometimes to equality, and so forth. When deciding which one is appropriate in a given context: "Social utility alone can decide the preference" (U, 10:254).[5] Thus far we have an argument for secondary rules that emphasizes 1) the need to simplify decision-making that would otherwise be beyond our capabilities, 2) the need for common rules on which we can mutually rely, and 3) the importance of maintaining and nurturing desirable character qualities.

Some take the above as evidence that Mill was, in fact, a rule-utilitarian. Others claim that a sophisticated act-utilitarian, and such they take Mill to be, can still acknowledge the value of rules for all three of the above reasons. A third interpretation of Mill must also be noted, namely that he is actually a sanction-utilitarianism. This position is thought by many to be closer to the rule position than the act position but is nonetheless distinct. The key passage is found in *Utilitarianism*, chapter 5: "We do not call anything wrong, unless we mean to imply that a person ought to be punished in some way or other for doing it; if not by law, by the opinion of his fellow creatures; if not by opinion, by the reproaches of his own conscience" (U, 10:246). David Lyons (1976) drew attention to this passage, noting that it does not mean that any act that fails to maximize utility is wrong, nor does it mean that any act that fails to conform to a rule which would maximize utility if everyone were to follow it is wrong. Rather, wrongness exists only when, from a utilitarian point of view, some form of punishment is beneficial (whether governmental punishment, public opinion, or internalized conscience). This approach receives further support from Mill's

---

[5] Mill makes a similar point in *Bentham*:

"Those who adopt utility as a standard can seldom apply it truly except through the secondary principles; those who reject it, generally do no more than erect those secondary principles into first principles. It is when two or more of the secondary principles conflict, that a direct appeal to some first principle becomes necessary; and then commences the practical importance of the utilitarian controversy; which is, in other respects, a question of arrangement and logical subordination rather than of practice; important principally in a purely scientific point of view, for the sake of the systematic unity and coherency of ethical philosophy" (CW, 10:111).

statements at the end of *System of Logic* (S, 8:949–52) about "the art of life." The idea is that there are three distinct realms (Morality, Prudence or Policy, and Aesthetics) and that the principle of utility governs all three. Suppose I am deciding whether or not to give away half of my wealth since I would still be, by global standards, very well off, and I could help many people in dire poverty. On one interpretation, the principle of prudence or expediency would say that I should, since doing so would maximize overall happiness. Morality, however, would not require this of me because a general principle that would punish people (even if only in feeling a perpetually guilty conscience) for failing to give at this level would not be utility-maximizing given the limited altruism of most people.[6] People may simply reject moral claims they find too burdensome. The sanction view has ties to the earlier theological theories in that it links "what would be punished by a beneficial rule" directly with what is actually wrong.

Some scholars, influenced by Lyons, argue that these considerations actually lead to the conclusion that Mill is a rule-utilitarian. Miller (2010), for example, arrives at this conclusion first by noting that Mill particularly emphasizes the sanction of conscience and feelings of guilt, and second by noting that feelings of guilt are conceptually related to breaking moral rules that we have internalized (86–8). Donner (2009), also influenced by Lyons and the sanction view (37–8), concurs with Miller that the form of rule-utilitarianism that Mill adopts is an ideal-code version where right and wrong are determined by the moral code that would be best for society to internalize (52). This position is also sometimes called the ideal-conscience view since right and wrong are determined by the set of rules that would best regulate feelings of guilt in a person's conscience, where best is defined in terms of the utility produced by having internalized such a conscience.

I will not deal with the sanction or ideal-conscience interpretation separately from the rule-utilitarian interpretation because it may, as Donner and Miller claim, reduce to the latter and, more importantly, because my goal here is not to definitively establish which reading of Mill is correct but to note Mill's reliance on the legislative point of view. The sanction interpretation will, from that standpoint, present similar problems. One is that it is still counterfactual to move from the question "what conscience should I try to bring about in myself that will produce the greatest happiness?" to "what conscience would be best if adopted by everyone?" given that I am not in a position to actually bring about

---

[6] Donner 2011 supports the idea that morality is restricted to the sphere where sanctions are appropriate (148–9) and a benefit in restricting its scope is more room for individuality.

widespread change in the consciences of other people. I might be able to produce more utility by developing a different conscience in myself than what would be best in everyone. We thus still have to ask if, on consequentialist grounds alone, I can justify the switch to the legislative point of view. A second problem is that even bringing about a change in my own conscience to conform to the ideal may be psychologically difficult given the knowledge that in following my ideal conscience I will sometimes be acting irrationally in the sense that I will be producing less utility than I otherwise might. This is particularly difficult if I think that utility is the ultimate source of all value.[7]

Act-utilitarian interpretations of Mill agree that he does not think we must always use the principle of utility as a decision procedure. Rather, they argue that act-utilitarianism is compatible with indirect forms of utilitarianism. Mill himself clearly believed that the direct pursuit of happiness could be self-defeating. Mill wrote in his *Autobiography* about his return to utilitarianism after a crisis: "I never, indeed, wavered in the conviction that happiness is the test of all rules of conduct, and the end of life. But I now thought that this end was only to be attained by not making it the direct end" (CW, 1:145). In *Utilitarianism* he decided that utility, the standard of morals, need not also be the motive for acting morally (U, 10:219–22). Moreover "in this condition of the world, paradoxical as the assertion may be, the conscious ability to do without happiness gives the best prospect of realizing such happiness as is attainable" (U, 10:217). An act-utilitarian can choose a different decision procedure, proponents of this reading argue, if doing so yields better outcomes (Crisp 1997). They also point to the following letter to John Venn in which Mill seems to reject the rule-utilitarian position.

> I agree with you that the right way of testing actions by their consequences, is to test them by the natural consequences of the particular action, and not by those which would follow if every one did the same. But, for the most part, the consideration of what would happen if every one did the same, is the only means we have of discovering the tendency of the act in the particular case. (CW, 17:1881)

He then gives the example of someone contemplating not paying taxes and assessing the harms of the specific act by considering the consequences of the general act. Brink (2013), defending the act-utilitarian interpretation,

---

[7] Miller 2011, 107–12 says that Mill's account is incoherent in this sense and that his account opens the door to an "individual" version of rule-utilitarianism where the binding code for one individual could be different than for another person.

notes that while Mill does seem drawn to the sanction position at times, even this can be reconciled with his preferred interpretation since one could say that an action is wrong if, in this particular case, it will produce more happiness to punish it in some way.[8]

Against this, defenders of the rule interpretation can argue that the above view does not give adequate weight to the role rules are playing in Mill's thought (Fuchs 2006). They can point to a letter of their own, this one to Henry Brandreth: "The duty of truth as a positive duty is also to be considered on the ground of whether more good or harm would follow to mankind in general if it were generally disregarded and not merely whether good or harm would follow in a particular case" (CW, 16:1234). Even in the above example about paying taxes, a person who thinks they can underpay their taxes completely undetected and give the money to a worthy cause might come to a different conclusion if allowed to reason only about the specific action.

We can now take the above debate and reframe it in terms of whether and to what extent Mill made use of the legislative point of view. In one sense, the legislative nature of Mill's position is straightforward in that he thinks the principle of utility ought to be a guide to those who form laws that will have an important impact both through threatening sanctions and by fulfilling an educative function. As we have already seen and will explore in more detail below, Mill thought this included not just the laws of governments but also internalized beliefs about right and wrong that are substantially shaped by public opinion and education. Mill understood these to be very important and believed that utilitarianism should shape how those who legislate think about the content of the legislation. Mill was thus very comfortable using the legislative point of view in contexts that could be described as legislative.

The more difficult questions are those cases where the shift to a legislative perspective is counterfactual. Suppose that I have the opportunity to break a widely held moral rule with very little chance of anyone finding out. Suppose, to use Mill's own example, I have income that I am supposed to report on my taxes but about which the government has no possibility of knowing. Suppose also that others are very unlikely to know that I underreported my income on my taxes. I want to give the resulting tax savings to a charity that I have very good reason to believe will help

---

[8] Ten (1980, 50) argues that the sanction view in practice comes to similar conclusions as act-utilitarianism since act-utilitarianism differentiates between what is wrong and what should be praised and blamed and punished.

people more efficiently than the government. Should a utilitarian, in such a case, underreport income? Mill's letter to Venn seems to indicate that the answer is no. One explanation is that faced with this dilemma one unreflectively follows the norm (don't cheat on your taxes) because it would be too time-consuming to work out the competing utilities. Suppose, however, that the person has time and inclination to think about it more deeply. We might imagine them engaging in the following counterfactual reasoning: if there were a generalized exemption such that no one paid taxes on hard-to-verify income, what would the consequences be? Berger (1984, 112) would object that in practice Mill didn't engage in this sort of reasoning, where one imagines that one has powers to enact any new rule that would have good generalized consequences. Instead, it is crucial in a case like this that there is already an established rule and that we use the principle of utility to critically examine that rule. Even if Berger is right that Mill always started from formerly received rules, the question of what rule I think should be publicly adopted does not actually answer the question of whether I should follow that rule or whether that rule defines what is morally right.

The best example of Mill using the legislative point of view counterfactually is in his rejection of paternalism. Mill argued that a man

> cannot rightfully be compelled to do or forbear because it will be better for him to do so, because it will make him happier, because, in the opinions of others, to do so would be wise, or even right. These are good reasons for remonstrating with him, or reasoning with him, or persuading him, or entreating him, but not for compelling him, or visiting him with any evil in case he do otherwise. (OL, 18:223–4)

The claim that one may "remonstrate" him but not visit him "with any evil" raises an interesting tension that we will explore in the next section. For present purposes, the main point is that this complete rejection of paternalistic coercion is a notoriously difficult position for Mill to defend from an act-utilitarian perspective because, if utility is the ultimate standard of right, it is implausible that in every case paternalism decreases utility. Even if most paternalistic laws and policies are bad on utilitarian grounds, why not just set a very high threshold and allow paternalistic laws in the small number of cases where they increase utility?

Mill's solution to this problem is recourse to the legislative point of view. He adopted the perspective of deciding whether a general rule authorizing paternalism should be affirmed, rather than whether specific examples of paternalistic laws should be affirmed. In doing so, his use of the legislative perspective was realistic in the sense that he took the mistakes and moral limitations of those who will interpret the law as relevant to deciding what the content of the law should be. We see this first in his appeal to the general tendency of people to impose their beliefs on others whenever they can:

> The disposition of mankind, whether as rulers or as fellow-citizens, to impose their own opinions and inclinations as a rule of conduct on others, is so energetically supported by some of the best and by some of the worst feelings incident to human nature, that it is hardly ever kept under restraint by anything but want of power; and as the power is not declining, but growing, unless a strong barrier of moral conviction can be raised against the mischief, we must expect, in the present circumstances of the world, to see it increase. (Mill OL, 18:227)

Mill, like a good legislator, considered the disposition of those who will be empowered to make moral judgments that constrain others, whether formally or informally. It is also interesting that his proposed solution to this problem is raising up "a strong barrier of moral conviction." He is envisioning a general anti-paternalistic moral rule of the sort he just articulated that would restrain this impulse.

Later, when Mill considered more directly the claim that there are still some specific cases where paternalistic laws promote utility, his argument leans even more strongly on counterfactual use of the legislative point of view: "But the strongest of all the arguments against the interference of the public with purely personal conduct, is that when it does interfere, the odds are that it interferes wrongly, and in the wrong place" (OL, 18:283). This is exactly Locke's legislative argument for religious toleration (most rulers will promote the wrong religion) but posed in secular terms. If Mill were reasoning from a situated perspective, looking only at the effects of one particular paternalistic intervention, he might be forced to admit that occasionally paternalism increases happiness. Instead, from a legislative perspective, he noted that a general rule authorizing paternalistic interventions would, on balance, be bad because of the natural human tendency to intervene too often. Given that Mill's commitment to free speech would prevent him from using governmental power to silence paternalists, he is best understood here as proposing a norm, to be enforced through public opinion, about the sorts of moral expression that are and are not permissible. Mill then went on to compare the two norms, one that allows paternalism in a small number of cases and one that, from the legislative point of view, does not:

> It is easy for any one to imagine an ideal public, which leaves the freedom and choice of individuals in all uncertain matters undisturbed, and only requires them to abstain from modes of conduct which universal experience has condemned. But where has there been seen a public which set any such limit to its censorship? or when does the public trouble itself about universal experience? (OL, 18:283–4)

In this argument, Mill assumed the position of a constitutional framer who must set down a rule for future legislators to follow and who rejected giving them broad powers based on his estimates of how fallible legislators would likely use those powers. To reject this perspective is to "adopt the logic of persecutors, and to say that we may persecute others because we are right, and that they must not persecute us because they are wrong" (OL, 18:285). The persecutor refuses to adopt the legislative perspective and proceeds directly to consider the rule only as they would apply it, not as others would.

From one angle, this is a clearly counterfactual use of the legislative perspective. Even though Mill's antipaternalistic principle had not yet become a widely accepted norm, Mill thought that a legislator should vote against paternalistic legislation because an antipaternalistic super norm would be beneficial if it were adopted. This seems to hold even if there were a particular paternalistic law that would be beneficial. There is, however, a different way of interpreting Mill's argument. If we think about what Mill himself did in writing *On Liberty*, it is fair to say that his goal was precisely to convince people to adopt a strong norm of nonpaternalism. When we remember that moral opinion can be a form of legislation, Mill's support of a new norm in *On Liberty* is not actually counterfactual. As a person who actually could influence the moral opinions of others, he thought legislatively about what moral principles he wanted them to hold. Mill, in his capacity as legislator of moral norms, may face different calculations than he would as Member of Parliament, and even there Mill would have to think about how a paternalistic vote would undermine his advocacy for the antipaternalistic super norm. The next section explores the way that Mill's emphasis on moral opinion as a type of law and moral expression as a type of legislation creates complications for his commitment to individual expression and antipaternalism.

Mill and Moral Expression as Legislation

Mill is famous for his vigorous defense of freedom of expression and the value of individuality. In chapter 2 of *On Liberty* Mill made the case for unfettered free speech rights, rights that are only moderately curtailed at the end of the book when he conceded the right to restrict fraudulent commercial speech and incitement to violence. In chapter 3 he stressed the value of individuality, particularly of those who will live and speak differently from the ways of life that dominate a society of conformist people who "like in crowds" (OL, 18:265). He justified both as ways to enable us to get closer to the truth. "All silencing of discussion is an assumption of infallibility" (OL, 18:229). Allowing free criticism makes it possible to recognize and correct our mistakes, to get closer to the truth. Allowing "experiments in living" (OL, 18:281, 306) will help us make new discoveries about the best possible lives to lead. In one of Mill's most overly optimistic statements, he claimed free expression will lead us to converge at the truth: "As mankind improve, the number of doctrines which are no longer disputed or doubted will be constantly on the increase: and the well-being of mankind may almost be measured by the number and gravity of the truths which have reached the point of being uncontested" (OL, 18: 250). Mill thus gave a truth-infused defense of free expression and liberty with an assumption that truth and happiness will go hand in hand.

Alongside this defense of free expression and individuality, Mill is also famous for his emphasis on the way that public opinion can stifle individuality even if the public does not use the government to impose its will through traditional legal channels. In fact, public opinion is actually the more powerful form of social control.

> For a long time past, the chief mischief of the legal penalties is that they strengthen the social stigma. It is that stigma which is really effective, and so effective is it, that the profession of opinions which are under the ban of society is much less common in England, than is, in many other countries, the avowal of those which incur risk of judicial punishment. In respect to all persons but those whose pecuniary circumstances make them independent of the good will of other people, opinion, on this subject, is as efficacious as law; men might as well be imprisoned, as excluded from the means of earning their bread. (OL, 18:241)

While it is the economically vulnerable who experience public opinion at its most coercive, Mill thought that it is a powerful sanction for members of every social class. "In our times, from the highest class of society down to the lowest, every one lives as under the eye of a hostile and dreaded censorship" (OL, 18:264). Opposed to this, Mill wanted to promote a society where people can live and speak in ways that challenge conventional norms.

At the same time, Mill was clear that the law of opinion should be thought of in legislative terms. He claimed that "for such actions as are prejudicial to the interests of others, the individual is accountable, and may be subjected either to social or to legal punishment, if society is of opinion that the one or the other is requisite for its protection" (OL, 18:292). Mill assumes that people consciously decide whether inflicting informal reputational sanctions or formal legal sanctions (or both) is the best way to keep people from engaging in behaviors that actually harm others. The ideal, in keeping with his antipaternalism, is that this coercive power of opinion only be used in cases where the condemned behavior harms others.

As we move to the level of everyday moral judgments, Mill struggled with how to reconcile his legislative approach to moral expression with his commitments to free expression, the greatest happiness, and truth. How am I to respond if I see others engaging in activities that I think are degrading to them or harmful to them but that do not directly harm others? How should I think about false religious beliefs that do not directly harm others? Mill wrote:

> It would be a great misunderstanding of this doctrine to suppose that it is one of selfish indifference, which pretends that human beings have no business with each other's conduct in life, and that they should not concern themselves about the well-doing or well-being of one another, unless their own interest is involved. Instead of any diminution, there is need of a great increase of disinterested exertion to promote the good of others. But disinterested benevolence can find other instruments to persuade people to their good, than whips and scourges, either of the literal or the metaphorical sort. (OL, 18:276–7)

In this passage Mill seemed to indicate that it is laudable to express our moral opinions so long as we do so to persuade rather than punish.

Mill was aware that the strict antipaternalism of his theory was potentially very restricting of free expression. In the subsequent pages he repeatedly tried to separate moral expression from the infliction of social penalties.

> Though doing no wrong to any one, a person may so act as to compel us to judge him, and feel to him, as a fool, or as a being of an inferior order: and since this judgment and feeling are a fact which he would prefer to avoid, it is doing him a service to warn him of it beforehand, as of any other disagreeable consequence to which he exposes himself. It would be well, indeed, if this good office were much more freely rendered than the common notions of politeness at present permit, and if one person could

honestly point out to another that he thinks him in fault, without being considered unmannerly or presuming. (OL, 18:278)

Mill here seemed to be proposing that a new social norm allowing people greater freedom to criticize each other would be a significant improvement as it would speed the rate at which we learn from each other and better ourselves. Yet even in this passage it looks rather like we are giving an offender their "warning" that "judgment" is coming unless they change course. When we tell people they are making a mistake with their lives or that they are acting wrongly (even though the wrong is to themselves alone) they will characteristically feel this as a kind of sanction, one that is more powerful the more widespread the condemnation. To recall the passage from the previous section, our "remonstrances" of others may be experienced by them as "evils." In some cases our appeals may succeed and the person will regard our criticism as indeed benevolent, but often this is not the case.

Mill attempted to navigate this tension by indicating that it matters whether that sense of condemnation is intentionally inflicted or is a byproduct of our own free expression.

> In these various modes a person may suffer very severe penalties at the hands of others, for faults which directly concern only himself; but he suffers these penalties only in so far as they are the natural, and, as it were, the spontaneous consequences of the faults themselves, not because they are purposely inflicted on him for the sake of punishment. (OL, 18:278)

Here the contrast seems to be between simply speaking one's mind as a private individual and having as one's goal the infliction of social sanctions on another to change that person's behavior, the desire to punish. Even if our intentions are wholly benevolent rather than punitive in expressing our moral corrections, lack of punitive intent does not ensure lack of punitive effect, and, in the end, consequences are what count for utilitarians.

Here we see the nature of the tension, namely that if I am supposed to look at moral expression as legislation, I must be very aware of the punishments my judgments will inflict. This is rather different than simply expressing my views and letting others experience my low opinion of them as what Mill previously termed "a spontaneous consequence of the faults themselves." It is hard to see, in practice, how the two viewpoints can coexist simultaneously. If we take seriously the idea that moral expression shapes the law of public opinion, the most powerful coercive instrument in society, it will be hard to think of the effects of our judgments as spontaneous consequences. Now admittedly, in modern culture, people may join in online condemnation without thinking of themselves as trying to punish those they condemn. They might view their statements of moral outrage as "spontaneous consequences" rather than intentional legislative activity. This might well be true descriptively, but on Mill's logic it would seem that behavior of this sort is normatively questionable. It amounts to wielding legislative power via public opinion while denying that one is doing so. Mill's commitment to free speech would likely provide legal protection for such statements, but it would still seem to violate a moral norm.

There are other ways in which our moral expression mirrors legislation. We noted in the previous section Mill's strong emphasis on the use of secondary rules to guide moral conduct and, presumably, moral expression. Given the rule-grounded way in which we must justify our moral positions we will have to speculate about the consequences a new moral rule would have when we consider expressing it in hopes that others will adopt it as well. Not only that, but we must think about the way others, perhaps less enlightened than ourselves, might use the principle we articulate for ill purposes. Mill's justification for antipaternalism relies on this logic and there is no good ground for restricting it to super norms only. Finally, we must also consider the chances of getting our legislation "passed." We might have to compromise on some issues in order to advance others that we care more strongly about.

Mill's own example is instructive here. It seems clear that at various points he consciously restrained from correcting the religious errors of others. Though he believed these religious errors caused harm, he worried that stating his heterodox religious views more clearly might jeopardize his goals of making utilitarianism widely accepted and consequently hinder political causes like women's rights. Mill had witnessed the tension between what his father thought true and what his father thought utility allowed one to express in the area of religion specifically. His father advised him to keep his religious views largely secret when he was a child (CW 1:45–6). In the next paragraph Mill remarked:

> The great advance in liberty of discussion, which is one of the points of difference between the present time and that of my childhood, has greatly altered the moralities of this question; and I think that few men of my father's intellect and public spirit, holding with such intensity of moral conviction as he did, unpopular opinions on religion or on any other of the great subjects of thought, would now either practise or inculcate the withholding of them from the world; unless in the cases, becoming rarer

every day, in which frankness on these subjects would either risk the loss of means of subsistence . . . or would amount to exclusion from some sphere of usefulness peculiarly suitable to the capacities of the individual. (CW 1:46–7; see also 89)

What is interesting is that Mill argued not that his father's application of utilitarianism to public expression was wrong but that times had changed enough that the calculations that justified keeping one's actual views secret occurred less frequently. Mill's exceptions still leave plenty of room for silence. Mill was, of course, willing to take highly controversial stands, but it seems also the case that, as above, he was assessing the times to figure out which of his views could be promoted profitably and vigorously. To elaborate on the analogy, Mill showed a second way in which legislative thinking might constrain moral speech. One might refrain from making a moral statement because, while it is an appropriate response to a particular case, it fails as a generalizable public norm for reasons we have discussed previously (vague terms that lead to contested applications, difficulty of accurate and effective enforcement, difficulties of obtaining sufficient consensus, etc.). All these relate to the quality of the norm assessed legislatively. The worry that one might lose one's job with the East India Company if one said all one really thought (coupled with a belief that that job provides income and a platform making possible one's other civic activities) is similar, instead, to the way legislative speech is constrained by the need to get reelected. Actual legislators often censor their true beliefs, calculating that exposing their entire perspective would cause them to lose their position and ability to exert influence on other issues. Mill and those who follow him are constrained in this way as well.

It is hardly unique to Mill's position that a person may face hard decisions about which of their moral views to make public, and Mill was certainly not alone in thinking that sometimes one has a moral duty to refrain from saying all that one thinks. What is interesting about this is the particular metaphor through which these decisions are to be made. It is not merely that I must ask whether speaking in a particular way might violate some right of yours or cause more harm in the specific case than benefit. It is rather that I must think legislatively, considering my words as a proposal for a new public rule that, if successful, will have coercive power. The harder one presses on this metaphor the further apart one's legislative acts of moral expression and one's actual beliefs about moral truth may be. Since thinking legislatively involves a separate action that is, in principle, subject to its own utilitarian calculation, it may not be sufficient to merely keep silent. I can even imagine situations where as a legislator I am compelled to uphold a salutary rule though I know that, in this case, the violation of that rule is justified. Mill's position thus points to the need for an esoteric morality. Sidgwick understood the full implications of the position Mill and Bentham had taken and addressed the issue more clearly, and provocatively, than his predecessors.

Sidgwick, Esoteric Morality, and Legislation

Henry Sidgwick is famous for defending "the self-evident principle that the good of any one individual is of no more importance, from the point of view (if I may say so) of the Universe, than the good of any other" (Methods, 3.13.3, 382; see also 4.2, 420). Such an approach certainly has analogies to looking at things from God's point of view, but Sidgwick was clear that recourse to God was unhelpful in ethics. If his tombstone is to be believed, he died with at least some belief in God,[9] but he was skeptical of the claims of those who thought they had access by revelation to moral knowledge. As he wrote in the second edition of *The Methods of Ethics*, "I cannot fall back on the resource of thinking myself under a moral necessity to regard all my duties *as if they were* commandments of God, although not entitled to hold speculatively that any such Supreme Being really exists."[10]

Interestingly, we get an early glimpse of Sidgwick thinking in terms of the legislative point of view as he was deciding whether or not to continue subscribing to the Thirty-Nine Articles of the Church of England, as was required at the time for those holding fellowships at Oxford and Cambridge. Schultz discusses Sidgwick anguishing over how much of his religious skepticism it was appropriate to share with the world (Schultz 2017, 245–6). Sidgwick knew that many academics did not believe all of the articles yet signed anyway. He imagined what would happen if everyone who had skeptical thoughts refused to sign. Here Schultz quotes from one of Sidgwick's letters to a friend explaining his decision to resign his fellowship since he could not in good conscience subscribe to the articles:

> I am obeying a sound general rule – I feel very strongly the importance of "providing things honest in the sight of all men." It is surely a great good that one's moral position should be one that simple-minded people can

---

[9] Sidgwick had desired that these words be said at his funeral: "Let us commend to the love of God with silent prayer the soul of a sinful man who partly tried to do his duty. It is by his wish that I say over his grave these words and no more." His tombstone read "In Thy Light Shall He See Light" (Schultz 2004, 720).

[10] Quoted in Schultz 2017, 295–6.

understand. I happen to care very little what men in general think of me individually: but I care very much about what they think of human nature. I dread doing anything to support the plausible suspicion that men in general, even those who profess lofty aspirations, are secretly swayed by material interests. After all, it is odd to be finding subtle reasons for an act of mere honesty: but I am reduced to that by the refusal of my friends to recognise it as such. (Schultz 2017, 246)

Sidgwick was aware that many people were skeptical of academics who subscribed to things they did not believe in and he thought it important to justify his decision in terms of which general rule he would want to be widely adopted. Interestingly, he was in a sufficiently influential position that his decision to resign contributed to the abolition of religious tests for faculty two years later. His decision actually did contribute to both changing a norm and changing a law.

Sidgwick is important because of the clarity with which he defended the use of the legislative perspective when staking out public moral principles while also holding a consistently act-utilitarian position – that the right action is the one that produces the best consequences. In a sense, with Sidgwick, there is no counterfactual shift to the legislative point of view. One uses it when one is actually legislating. This is a frequent occurrence since more or less all of our public moral statements become examples of legislating. Those statements then become important considerations that influence how ethical individuals make specific choices. As in the above example, he as an individual must think about how his actions might undermine a public rule that he deems valuable.

Sidgwick thought that skepticism about religion was one of the main problems for philosophy to address. His *Outlines of the History of Ethics* shows his deep awareness of the larger tradition, including theistic tradition, of which he was a part. He saw the chief contribution of Christianity as being the idea that morality is primarily legal in character with God as the legislator (OHE, 111–13). He made a similar point in *Methods*: Christians view "the process of conscience as analogous to one of jural reasoning, such as is conducted in a Court of Law" (Methods, 1.8.3, 100). Sidgwick wrote "jural" rather than legislative because in the cases he is considering God's will is known to be law through revelation and human beings simply obey that law. He discussed the shift from Cumberland and Hutcheson to Hume in a note at the end of 1.8 (Methods, 104). His point seems to be that these other thinkers were moving further and further away from traditional Christian ethics and it was not until Hume that people realized how far they had strayed. Interestingly, when Sidgwick discussed the changes in thought during that time period, he did not emphasize the legislative shift. What is important about Locke's theism is his use of divine sanctions (OHE, 175–6) to reconcile psychological hedonism and duty.[11] Sidgwick valued Butler primarily for his important contribution to the motive issue, namely his rejection of egoism (OHE, 196). In general, Sidgwick thought the main issue in Butler's ethical thought was the tension between intuitionism and utility (OHE, 199–200).

The sanction problem also loomed large in the book as a whole. Sidgwick believed that there was no necessary connection between virtue and the individual's own happiness (Methods, 2.5.4, 174–5). The last chapter of *Methods* famously ends discussing the religious utilitarians (Methods, conclusion, 504). He emphasized their solution to the motivational problem, not the perspectival problem. This is because he was haunted by the fact that there seemed to be no decisive argument through which he could compel an egoist to abandon egoism. He concluded that ethics contains two irreconcilable views, egoism and utilitarianism (Methods, conclusion, 509). As we have seen in previous chapters, theology was serving a greater purpose in these earlier theories than reconciling egoism with duty, it was justifying a particular perspective from which moral questions should be answered, a legislative perspective. Sidgwick was not unaware of this problem and his proposed solution was controversial to say the least.

Sidgwick's approach allows a place for indirect utilitarianism. "By Utilitarianism is here meant the ethical theory, that the conduct which, under any given circumstances, is objectively right, is that which will produce the greatest amount of happiness on the whole; that is, taking into account all whose happiness is affected by the conduct" (Methods, 4.1.1, 411). Universal happiness is the "ultimate *standard*" but that doesn't mean "Universal Benevolence is the only right or always best *motive* of action" (Methods, 4.1.1, 413). "Thus the very acceptance of Pleasure as the ultimate end of conduct involves the practical rule that it is not always to be made the conscious end" (Methods, 3.14.5, 403; see also 405). Utilitarianism can direct us to inculcate, in ourselves and others, motives other than promoting utility, since, for reasons similar to those of Mill, we will be happier if we do.

Sidgwick then took this indirect approach to its logical conclusion. Praising and blaming are public acts and subject to their own calculation.

---

[11] See also Methods, 3.1.2, 205.

> From a Utilitarian point of view, as has been before said, we must mean by
> calling a quality 'deserving of praise' that it is expedient to praise it, with
> a view to its future production: accordingly, in distributing our praise of
> human qualities, on utilitarian principles, we have to consider primarily not
> the usefulness of the quality, but the usefulness of the praise. (Methods,
> 4.3.2, 428)

This has momentous implications. What is expedient to do and what is
expedient to praise can differ.

When we engage in public moral expression, we are to think of ourselves
as contributing to the formulation of general social rules. Sidgwick
described "the *ensemble* of rules imposed by common opinion in any
society, which form a kind of unwritten legislation, supplementary to
Law proper, and enforced by the penalties of social disfavor and contempt." After explicitly connecting the rules of common opinion to
legislation he makes it equally clear that when we make moral statements
we act as legislators. "Any change in it [the unwritten legislation] must
therefore result from the private action of individuals, whether determined
by Utilitarian considerations or otherwise" (Methods, 4.5.2, 480).

In his discussion of intuitionism he gave several examples of how the
implicit requirement of a legislative point of view expresses itself in
common moral claims. Our views about justice regarding property can
be thought of as arising when we who are grateful for the productive labor
of others develop the idea that there is a duty of gratitude to those who
provide benefits. If we "*universalize* this impulse and conviction, we get the
element in the common view of Justice, which we are now trying to
define." This, after several steps, can help explain property rights based
on a universalized sense that people are best rewarded for their efforts if
property rights are recognized (Methods, 3.5.5, 279–80). He claimed that
our belief that people's labor deserves reward is patterned on common
views about divine justice (which, as we have seen, is thought to be jural).
In discussing our duty to tell the truth he focused on the exceptions that are
commonly allowed and generally he shows how common morality
includes principles that sometimes conflict with each other. These conflicts
of rules can be dealt with by appeal to utility (Methods, 4.3.1, 426).

When I claim that there should be a general exception to a publicly
known rule, what I am really doing is proposing an amendment to that rule
that will make it a more complex rule (Methods, 4.5.3, 485). In proposing
a new rule or a change to an old one, all the typical legislative considerations apply (Crisp 2015, 224–6). Schneewind (1977, 339–40) notes that
Sidgwick thought we should not propose a new rule unless that rule could

be adopted and applied with good consequences by the ordinary person. This will limit the complexity, demandingness, and number of exceptions. In general, too many exceptions will help to rationalize bad behavior, decrease shared expectations, and undermine support for the code. Many of the principles will not be held on consciously utilitarian grounds. In some cases, we allow an exception because we have nonmoral grounds for thinking that few will use the exception (the general practice of celibacy would be catastrophic but is highly unlikely). It is more difficult to inhibit the action when we depend on a moral belief.

Here we enter into Sidgwick's esoteric morality. The person thinking about whether to lie will sometimes confront cases where he has "(1) the knowledge that his maxim is not universally accepted, and (2) a reasoned conviction that his act will not tend to make it so, to any important extent" (Methods, 3.7.3, 319). Sidgwick acknowledged what is obviously true, that there are many times where we can act without actually having any appreciable effect on the general rule we think valuable and where we think we can justify an exception in our case but where we deny that a public general exception would be valuable.

Sidgwick discussed this idea in great depth in *Methods* 4.5.3:

> We have, however, to consider another kind of exception, differing fundamentally from this, which Utilitarianism seems to admit; where the agent does not think it expedient that the rule on which he himself acts should be universally adopted, and yet maintains that his individual act is right, as producing a greater balance of pleasure over pain than any other conduct open to him would produce. (486)

He gave as an example that it hardly follows that because an army walking over a bridge would destroy it, that a single person should not walk over it. The most difficult cases are those where we rely on a common moral judgment to shape behavior "because a moral sentiment is inseparable from the conviction that the conduct to which it prompts is objectively right" (488). From here Sidgwick drew the paradoxical conclusion:

> Thus, on Utilitarian principles, it may be right to do and privately recommend, under certain circumstances, what it would not be right to advocate openly; it may be right to teach openly to one set of persons what it would be wrong to teach to others; it may be conceivably right to do, if it can be done with comparative secrecy, what it would be wrong to do in the face of the world; and even, if perfect secrecy can be reasonably expected, what it would be wrong to recommend by private advice or example. These conclusions are all of a paradoxical character: there is no doubt that the moral consciousness of a plain man broadly repudiates the general notion of an esoteric

morality, differing from that popularly taught; and it would be commonly agreed that an action which would be bad if done openly is not rendered good by secrecy. (Methods, 4.5.3, 489–90)

Here we have a potentially large disjunction between what an individual believes to be right and what that individual can express as right. Even so, he held out the possibility that a future utilitarian society might not need esoteric morality (Methods, 4.5.3, 489–90).

Not only must an individual keep some beliefs secret, it may also be necessary to publicly blame utility-maximizing actions lest they set a dangerous precedent. At one point Sidgwick drew back, noting that

> it may conduce most to the general happiness that *A* should do a certain act, and at the same time that *B, C, D* should blame it. The Utilitarian of course cannot really join in the disapproval, but he may think it expedient to leave it unshaken; and at the same time may think it right, if placed in the supposed circumstances, to do the act that is generally disapproved. (491)

Here the utilitarian is apparently not required to join in with those who condemn but to remain silent while others do. It is not clear at all that this can be a universal exemption. Sidgwick may assume that in general no one will notice the utilitarian's silence in such situations, thus preserving the rule without the addition of the utilitarian's public approval. This, however, is a contingent fact and may not always be true. By his logic, it would seem necessary to sometimes condemn what we believe to be right.

Sidgwick, interestingly, was arguably breaking his own rule in defending the position, a position that still has contemporary defenders who also note the irony of publicly defending esoteric morality (Lazari-Radek and Singer, 2014). Sidgwick's decision to publicly defend esoteric morality may have been a concession to the conviction that one must speak the truth even when the legislative perspective forbids one to do so.

Conclusion

In the earlier theistic versions of the legislative perspective there was no disjunction between the legislative point of view and one's own view of moral truth, since God's will defined truth and the legislative point of view was a heuristic for discovering that truth. Given the assumptions that God is benevolent, that God expresses his moral will through universally applicable rules, and that God reveals his moral will in a way accessible to all rational human beings, one can engage in legislative reasoning, asking what rules would be beneficial if widely adopted, in order to discover what God has, in fact, willed. In the theories of Mill and Sidgwick, human beings take on this divine role and are now actually legislating what is right and wrong rather than merely unearthing it. This creates the possibility of paradoxes that did not exist in the earlier approaches. The legislative perspective is no longer constitutive of what is actually right, but rather a statement of what it is useful to praise and blame. In utilitarian thought these can diverge. The result is that Mill's theory, which begins from a commitment to individuals bravely speaking the truth on moral matters of great importance, may end with individuals who find themselves constrained by the requirements of legislative thinking when trying to express themselves. In some cases this constraint may be salutary, but it leaves open the question of why we are obligated to take on this new legislative responsibility. Suppose we just want to spontaneously express our views, noting that we never consented to having this legislative obligation placed upon us?

We also see the implications of the disjunction between what is right and what is proclaimed to be right that are caused by the counterfactual shift. A secular thinker who believes that the legislative point of view is valuable but unjustifiable in nonlegislative contexts can mitigate the problem by expanding the number of contexts that are described as legislative. If I view widely held moral norms as a kind of informal code and my public moral statements as legislative participation in the reinforcing or reforming of that code, I can continue to use the legislative perspective in shaping my statements about morality. Sidgwick, however, was right that there is still a gap that cannot be completely closed. There will be people who think they have good grounds for breaking a rule because they or their group have enlightenment that others lack. There will be people who think that they can keep their deviation from the rules secret so that confidence in the rule is unaffected by their transgression of it. In such cases the question of why we should shift to the legislative perspective when we are not, in fact, legislating remains either unanswered or, as in the case of Sidgwick, answered in the negative.

In the next chapter we will see how these tensions led to a series of twentieth-century debates about the place of rules in consequentialist thinking. The debate over rule-consequentialism (and rule-utilitarianism specifically) was largely over the question of whether a secularized consequentialist logic could make use of the legislative perspective and so avoid some of the more troubling conclusions of consequentialist thinking that proceed from the situated point of view of individual decisions and decision makers. Simple act-utilitarianism seemed to publicly sanction things that should not be sanctioned and esoteric morality was not seen as a satisfactory solution to this problem. Some utilitarians attempted to avoid this outcome within the constraints of a purely utilitarian theory, while others attempted to broaden the bounds of utilitarian orthodoxy to include deontological elements by infusing theories that utilized the legislative view in nonlegislative contexts with greater coherence.

CHAPTER 5

Secular Heterodoxy
Twentieth-Century Rule-Utilitarianism

At the end of the nineteenth century, the leading alternatives for consequentialist thinking were represented by Mill and Sidgwick. Whether or
not one considers Mill a rule-utilitarian, he was clearly eager to use rule-
based thinking to avoid some of the counterintuitive conclusions to which
act-by-act assessment using utilitarian criteria led. Sidgwick, with greater
clarity, produced a theory where there was a disjunction between what we
publicly pronounce as right and what is actually right. By turning public
moral discourse into a form of legislation, Mill and Sidgwick found one
solution to the dilemma of how to justify a counterfactual starting point
within an otherwise realistic and consequentialist theory. If my moral
expression is participation in a kind of legislative enterprise, helping to
shape the moral principles that are esteemed in my society, the legislative
perspective is no longer counterfactual.

This solution was not, however, a particularly satisfying one. The
severance of what is right from what we say is right merely threatened to
replace one set of unappealing moral conclusions with another, since this
incongruity is morally problematic for many people. Even if the disjunction is only between the decision rule I use to guide my own actions and the
standard of right, there are still real difficulties. It is psychologically ardu-
ous, though not impossible, to maintain one view about what is right and
a different view about how to practically think about moral decisions.
Another problem is that the "moral expression as legislation" strategy that
grounds this doctrine can only replicate a version of the legislative point of
view to the extent that people believe they have measurable influence over
what norms will be widely held. In many cases my ability to impact on the
prevailing norms of my society may be so small that the legislative nature of
my position seems far-fetched. If my effective influence on the strength of
norm is essentially nil, why should I run my actions through a legislative
grid instead of just performing the act that, in this case, has the best
consequences?

In the twentieth century, there were several attempts to endorse a more thoroughly legislative approach to ethics within a utilitarian framework, prompting many forceful arguments that such an approach was misguided. In this chapter I trace that debate and argue that the paradoxical status of rule-utilitarianism in much of the twentieth century emerged from the difficulties associated with justifying the shift to a legislative perspective as an underappreciated byproduct of the shift toward secular utilitarianism. Rather than an innovation, rule-utilitarianism was in some respects a more analytical and philosophically precise return to the earlier approaches from which Bentham and company had departed. The utilitarians, such as Bentham, who led the way in secularizing the approach realized that the absence of divine rewards and punishments in the afterlife posed a problem, but it was a predicament they were willing to confront in light of the complications arising from the religious account. As noted throughout the book, God played an additional role in the rule-consequentialist theories by helping to justify why right and wrong are determined from a legislative perspective. In the twentieth century it became increasingly clear that it was difficult to justify this perspectival shift in contexts that were not actually legislative. Rule-utilitarians were often accused of a kind of heterodoxy insofar as their theories seemed to require some Kantian elements to justify the legislative shift. In a number of important cases, the rule-utilitarians in question openly acknowledged non-consequentialist influences on their thought, including Kantian ones, but still saw themselves as within the utilitarian tradition. They are more charitably read not as inconsistent (heterodox) utilitarians but as advocates of hybrid approaches who were attempting to broaden the definition of utilitarianism itself. Can a theory be termed "utilitarian" if it uses utilitarian criteria to identify the moral rules that define what is right and wrong, yet employs nonutilitarian reasons to explain why the question "which rule?" takes priority over the question "which act?"

First, this chapter will trace the development of rule-utilitarianism in the early to mid-twentieth century, noting important Kantian elements in these theories and that some of the key proponents were not card-carrying utilitarians. They were stretching the boundaries of utilitarian orthodoxy. Next, it will examine battles over what constitutes utilitarian orthodoxy. On one side were those who viewed rule-utilitarianism as superstitious rule-worship or, more charitably, as making claims that were inconsistent with utilitarian foundations. In contrast, we see important examples of rule-utilitarians who continued to openly acknowledge debts to non-consequentialist sources but who still identified themselves as operating within that tradition in some meaningful way. These thinkers who stretch the boundaries of utilitarian orthodoxy introduce the hybrid approach to the legislative point of view that will be the focus of Part II of this book. The last section will summarize the historical significance of the argument thus far before transitioning to contemporary debates in Part II.

Stretching the Boundaries of Utilitarian Orthodoxy

In 1903, G. E. Moore's *Principia Ethica* took up the question of the role of moral rules in our decision-making. Moore distinguished between cases where there is a generally useful moral rule that is already well-established in a society and cases where we think a moral rule would be generally useful if it were adopted by society. The latter has to do with what we have called counterfactual use of the legislative point of view, and Moore's view was that counterfactual moral laws should not have much authority in our decision-making.

> The question whether the general observance of a rule not generally observed, would or would not be desirable, cannot much affect the question how any individual ought to act; since, on the one hand, there is a large probability that he will not, by any means, be able to bring about its general observance, and, on the other hand, the fact that its general observance would be useful could, in any case, give him no reason to conclude that he himself ought to observe it, in the absence of such general observance. (Moore, 5.98, 161)

Moore rejected counterfactual generalizations, noting that observing a law will not cause it to suddenly become the law that others observe.

Although Moore rejected counterfactual use of the legislative point of view, he interestingly held a strong commitment to following moral rules that were generally beneficial and widely accepted. He realized that these rules can only be generalizations about what is likely beneficial rather than what is beneficial in every case, and in this respect his position seems like an act-utilitarian use of rules of thumb. The interesting twist is that Moore also proposed a decision rule where I reason that since the rule is right in most cases it is improbable that the particular case I am considering, where it seems that breaking the rule would be on balance beneficial, is actually one of these cases:

> It seems, then, that with regard to any rule which is *generally* useful, we may assert that it ought *always* to be observed, not on the ground that in *every*

particular case it will be useful, but on the ground that in *any* particular case the probability of its being so is greater than that of our being likely to decide rightly that we have before us an instance of its disutility. (Moore, 5.99, 162)

We have an additional reason to follow the rule once we acknowledge that our example in breaking the rule, even if we are right to do so, will likely encourage others to break it when they shouldn't (Moore, 5.99, 163). As we have seen, these arguments rest on empirical assumptions that, unfortunately for Moore, are not assumptions that have been generally accepted. Sometimes we have a high degree of confidence that our action will not be publicly known, negating the second point. Regarding the first, people often feel that they can see exactly why in general people should follow the rule and why a particular case may be an exception.

Although this strategy of providing utilitarian reasons for adhering to existing moral rules would continue to be important, an article by C. D. Broad that appeared in 1916 is more relevant for our purposes as it focuses on the problem of counterfactual generalization. David Lyons described this article as the "earliest, pioneering study of a form of utilitarian generalization" (Lyons 1965, 8). While "largely ignored" (9) at the time, the article raised the question that will be at the center of the present discussion: "Is the goodness or badness of the consequences of admittedly false hypotheses ever relevant in deciding rightness or wrongness of a course of action; and, if so, what is the distinction between those false hypotheses whose probable consequences are relevant and those whose probable consequences are not?" (Broad 1916, 379). His answer was that while the question "What if everyone acted that way?" is based on a false hypothesis (because everyone will not act as you act), it does have some limited use. It might help to eliminate selfish actions that we can defend only on the assumption that we alone do them. The question "what would Jesus do?" is based on a false hypothesis since it is I, and not Jesus, who must now act, but Broad thinks this could conceivably help inform a person's moral judgment. But what if we are concerned about actual consequences? Broad notes that in some cases the effects of an act depend on how many other people do the same thing (walking on grass became the standard example). In other cases, one might conclude that avoiding paying one's taxes would make no noticeable difference to the government but a significant difference to oneself and decide it maximized utility not to pay. In both cases, we think it unfair for a person to act in a way that would cause harm if everyone were to do the same. The crux is that the universalization test is not identical to our concern about fairness. He concludes that false hypotheses are of limited value in settling ethical questions.

About fifteen years later, the work of W. D. Ross helped increase the interest in what we now call rule-utilitarianism. Ross' intuitionism challenged utilitarianism precisely by pointing out the counterintuitive conclusions to which it led. Ross argued that utilitarianism captured one prima facie duty, that of beneficence, but that there were other prima facie duties such as honesty and justice. Utilitarianism, Ross claimed, could not give a satisfactory account of our reluctance to break promises or punish the innocent (Ross 1930, 34–6, 56–64). As we have seen, there are strong parallels between this critique and Butler's theological version of the same position in the eighteenth century.

In 1936, R. F. Harrod wrote an article tellingly entitled "Utilitarianism Revised." As the title indicates, Harrod claimed that a new version of utilitarianism was needed to answer the objection that utilitarianism is in conflict with "common moral consciousness" (156). This article constitutes an attempt to expand the boundaries of what counts as orthodox utilitarianism. As his is the first full defense of rule-utilitarianism in the twentieth century, it will be useful to examine it in more depth so that we can then compare it with the later forms. Harrod argued that moral philosophy should account for the everyday moral intuitions of people (as Ross would have agreed) and that utilitarianism seemed vulnerable, in its crude form, to the charge that it neglects common experience. For example, there is a difference between creating happiness for yourself and creating happiness for someone else. Utilitarianism seems to indicate that if the happiness achieved in either event is the same, the acts are equally praiseworthy, but common-sense morality would assign greater approval to acts that are altruistic, all else being equal (Harrod 1936, 141). On the other hand, utilitarianism is helpful in that it can generate moral insights without depending on a mystical understanding of "the good." Harrod claimed: *"Acts are morally significant when they affect the ends of other people and they are morally good when they promote those ends"* (142). His version of utilitarianism is not about maximizing pleasure in the world (he thought it unproven that pleasure is the only desire) but rather about a greater number of people achieving their ends, with ends roughly equaling desires (146). Ends need not be judged as good or bad except in cases where the end either makes it harder for others to achieve their ends or leads to a state of affairs that the person in question does not actually desire. A foolish desire is one that, if satisfied, brings about a state of affairs one does not desire (145).

With this background we can now turn to Harrod's argument for rule-utilitarianism. He thought that certain obligations arise because there are some actions that have different effects when performed by many people than when performed once. "*There are certain acts which when performed on* n *similar occasions have consequences more than* n *times as great as those resulting from one performance*" (Harrod 1936, 148). For example, since much human interaction depends upon trustworthy communication, we should notice that the effect of 10,000 lies is likely greater than the effect of one lie multiplied by 10,000. He thought that Kant was insightful in noting that we should ask what would happen to people's ability to pursue their ends if everyone acted on a given principle. Kant's mistake was in trying to divorce this insight from consequentialism. Harrod argued that if people act on crude utilitarianism, far fewer desires will be satisfied and thus those committed to utility should act on principles that have good consequences when also employed by others.

Harrod was aware of several important counterarguments. First, in some instances what seems important is the existence of a practice. The consequences of telling a lie are different if there is already an established principle of truth-telling than if there is not. One might, therefore, make the obligation conditional on the existence of the practice. Here he showed some explicit sympathy for Hobbes' view that in the absence of practices that make reciprocation likely many moral obligations are void. Harrod did consider a different form of the calculation to be used by someone hoping to start a beneficial practice: he should consider the consequences, not of everyone acting on the principle, but only of people of moral character and good will. If the benefits of them so acting outweigh the costs, then he should try to establish the new norm.

Second, there is the problem of secrecy. What if no one will ever know that I have deviated from the moral rule and the additional negative repercussions follow only if they know? Here Harrod argued that it would still be known that morally upright people will act contrary to the rule if they can do so secretly and that this still undermines trust. Should everyone say one thing and do another? "It may be that the common interest would in fact be best served by each man acting on the principle of crude expediency himself and believing that others were following certain arbitrary rules. Such a system would certainly be an interesting one. But it is not one which the word morality is used to denote" (Harrod 1936, 153).

Harrod was here departing from Sidgwick's position that utilitarian ethics can be esoteric.

Third, what about the claim that it is impractical to try to act on behalf of all other persons? In such a case, he thought the generalization principle helps by explaining why a rule directing us to focus on a narrower set of people (perhaps to whom we are more naturally disposed to do good) might yield better results (Harrod 1936, 154–5). Fourth, exceptions can be made to principles such as "don't lie" if we can specify a rule such that lying in those situations is beneficial (149). Lastly, one must consider the difficulties involved in enacting a new system of moral approval and disapproval. Particularly complex rules may end up being counterproductive. "For if there was too great a proliferation of obligatory practice, the sanctions with which they could rationally be upheld would be weaker and the exceptions recognized as admissible more numerous. Such a state of affairs might become unstable" (154).

Harrod's argument is thoroughly grounded in claims about our moral intuitions. Act-utilitarianism is rejected because it fails to come to the right conclusions on various topics. The solution of esoteric utilitarianism is rejected because a moral theory that directs people to not act according to its own professed positions is out of step with our intuitions about morality. His argument also displays an awareness of key problems: the need for rules with some degree of complexity, the problem of secrecy (acting against a rule without your action being known), and limited altruism. There are also clear Kantian themes in Harrod's argument that suggest the heterodox nature of his revised utilitarianism. He sought to reconcile a commitment to publicly known universal rules with consequentialist criteria for selecting those rules.[1]

In the 1950s, rule-utilitarianism achieved the height of its popularity. Jonathan Harrison argued that "unmodified" utilitarianism should be rejected because it was self-defeating. Harrison claimed that there are some actions we have a duty to perform even though the particular action will not produce the best consequences. We have this duty because of the benefits that follow when many people are performing these actions. Since

---

[1] On Harrod's importance and his attempt to combine utilitarianism with Kantianism, see Scarre 1996, 122. Historically, there was another group of scholars interested in rule-utilitarianism for a different reason. Rather than trying to respond to Ross, they were worried about the relativistic implications of the discipline of anthropology. Rule-utilitarianism or rule-consequentialism seemed to provide a way of answering that challenge: the rules that exist in other cultures are accepted because the people there believe that those rules produce good consequences. See Campbell (1948), Toulmin (1950), and Macbeath (1952). I agree with Willard (2018, 230) that Toulmin is not really advocating normative rule-utilitarianism but is rather describing how moral discourse works.

there are many cases where my performing the action is not necessary to achieve the desirable consequences, act-utilitarianism cannot explain these duties. We need rules to act on, but this raises other problems. First, there are a multitude of possible descriptions of an act. How do we decide which ones are to be generalized?

> The class of actions "lies told by one-eyed, red-headed men, with warts on their right cheeks, and mermaids tattooed on their left fore-arms," is a wrong one because it can be "irrelevantly generalized"; that is to say, by subtracting characteristics such as "being an action performed by a one-eyed man" I can obtain more general classes of actions, the consequences of the general performance of which do not differ from the consequences of the general performance of actions belonging to it. (Harrison 1952–1953, 116)

The test here is whether or not some aspect would affect the implications of the action when aggregated. That a person lied to save a life might well have this effect while random characteristics of the person telling the lie would not. Whether force is used by a police officer or a vigilante citizen might have significant differences when the principle is generalized. Following Harrod, he emphasized that some actions have different effects depending on the number of people that perform them (Harrison 1952–1953, 120).

How then do we explain exceptions to rules? Harrison argued that in hard cases we should ask whether a generalized exception to the rule for those in similar circumstances would produce better outcomes than keeping the unmodified rule (Harrison 1952–1953, 121). This, Harrison thought, is a better alternative to Ross. Like Ross, he could explain why one should depart from the dictates of act-specific benevolence, but unlike Ross' approach we now have a theory that tells us how to know when to tell the truth and when to lie rather than simply relying on individual intuition. Where prima facie duties conflict, we can ask which prioritization, if followed by others in like circumstances, produces better results (Harrison 1952–1953, 123–4). Harrod had claimed that determining whether we have a duty does in some cases depend on how many others act likewise. Harrison responded that this is ceding to the opposing position. Harrison argued that we have no more reason to think others will keep the rule than they have reason to think we will. If everyone uses this mentality, too many people will perform the unjust act and the results will be bad. He was still willing to allow nonperformance if one has conclusive knowledge that others will not act likewise. His point pertains to the burden of proof, so to speak. He thought that there are a large number of cases where we do not have definitive knowledge of how others will act and where act-utilitarianism would encourage people to act in ways that lead to suboptimal outcomes (Harrison 1952–1953, 132). If one were omniscient, the act- and rule-utilitarian positions would converge.[2] Because we are often lacking in knowledge, and because morality requires generalizable principles (which seems to introduce nonconsequentialist considerations), the unmodified version must be rejected as self-defeating. Harrison's article presents a kind of hybrid Kantian/utilitarian point of view. It is Kantian in that universalization seems to be an independent requirement for a principle to be considered moral (Harrison 1952–1953, 133).

Mabbott (1953) and Ewing (1953a) also advanced views that included both Kantian and utilitarian elements. Mabbott looked to advance beyond Ross and traditional utilitarianism by proposing a synthesis of Kant and utilitarianism: we act on universal principles of legislation but do so with the end of producing happiness. He mentioned Francis Hutcheson as one who thought along similar lines (Mabbott 1953, 106).[3] These Kantian approaches provide a way of justifying the perspectival shift: the nature of morality is such that one must think as a legislator in order to articulate a moral principle. In his earlier work on punishment (Mabbott 1939) he argued for using utilitarianism to work out the content of our legal scheme of punishment but denied that we could use utilitarianism to depart from those rules in specific cases by punishing people directly on utilitarian grounds.

In 1953, A. C. Ewing published an article in *Philosophy* titled "What Would Happen If Everyone Acted Like Me?" Ewing first noted that it is odd to focus on a counterfactual set of consequences instead of the actual consequences that would flow from committing an act (Ewing 1953a, 17). His conclusion was that a universalization requirement where we think through the consequences of the counterfactual hypothesis is useful for explaining things like why one should vote, but that its justification must rest on appeals to fairness, not hedonistic utility. He claimed that one must either reject utilitarianism or opt for a hybrid "ideal utilitarianism," which broadens the definition of utility to include fairness as one aspect of what makes a state of affairs good (Ewing 1953a, 24). Ewing's ethical approach is

---

[2] He showed some awareness of the historical tradition on this topic as he quoted Joseph Butler's statement that "we are not competent judges," referring to the claim that even if God is a benevolent legislator, human beings lack the wisdom to know when departing from God's law would be net beneficial (Harrison 1952–1953, 130).

[3] The reference is to Hutcheson *Inquiry*, 2.3, 118.

an interesting example of this hybrid "ideal utilitarianism" that draws on utilitarian, Kantian, and Ross' intuitionism. In his introductory book *Ethics*, he discussed utilitarian attempts to avoid unwelcome conclusions by appealing to the negative utility of a class of actions. He concluded that

> It would be a bad thing if everybody acted like me, but why should I not do so, when it is certain that my action will not result in everybody acting like me? It seems only possible to answer such a question adequately if we say that it is *unfair* to profit by the rules governing society and yet refuse yourself to obey them. (Ewing 1953b, 40)

This, he said, is to step outside of the utilitarian conviction that everything reduces to happiness. He thought Kant could provide a better account of our intuitions about classes of actions than utilitarianism (Ewing 1953b, 56), but held that Kant should have allowed much more room for consequences to determine which principles we adopt so long as "consequences" is interpreted broadly and not reduced to pleasure and pain (Ewing 1953b, 63–4). He thought that ideal utilitarianism and Ross' intuitionism can effectively come to the same conclusions since the ideal utilitarian can admit that things like injustice or breaking promises are intrinsically bad and thus have a certain independent weight in our moral calculations (Ewing 1953b, 81–5). These hybrid approaches are, he thought, better than hedonistic utilitarianism or Kantianism. While Ewing did not encourage people to adopt the legislative point of view, his willingness to include breaking a rule that others ought to follow among the things that are unjust allows him to indirectly approximate that view. He would have been particularly at home with the approach we will describe in Part II, where statements from the legislative point of view count in favor of the rightness of actions without always being determinative of them (see also Ewing 1959, 147–9).

In 1954, P. Nowell-Smith argued that many of the objections against utilitarianism are based on a misunderstanding of what it is. Utilitarianism is not an explanation of why we obey moral rules, the reasons we give for obeying moral rules, or why we should obey rules on particular occasions. When utilitarianism attempts to be a totalizing theory, it results in the extreme, counterintuitive moral demands that Ross rejected (Nowell-Smith 1954, 232–6).[4] Instead, he claimed that utilitarianism is for legislators, not judges (236–9). This, he argued, is what the early utilitarians were actually interested in. Nowell-Smith provided yet another instance of an

---

[4] See Ross 1930, chapter 2.

author who believed utilitarianism right in part but thought it needed to be bolstered with nonutilitarian principles. His restriction of this approach to legislators is an example of what, in Part II, will be described as a "restriction of scope" approach to moral rules. If the worry is that one cannot justify the legislative perspective in counterfactual situations, one simply stipulates that it only applies to situations that are actually legislative.

John Rawls entered the debate, interestingly, as a defender of rule-utilitarianism, or at least that is how many who read his article "Two Concepts of Rules" understood his contribution at the time. Rawls argued that a rule-based approach to consequences better squares with our moral intuitions than an act-based approach. While there might be individual instances where convicting an innocent person of a crime or breaking a promise produces good consequences, we get different results if we imagine a practice authorizing the arrest and conviction of innocent people or authorizing people to lie in particular circumstances. In making this argument, he never actually stated that rule-utilitarianism is the best approach, just that it reaches better conclusions than act-utilitarianism (Rawls 1955). Clearly, in *A Theory of Justice* (1971), Rawls opted for a nonutilitarian approach. Another major contribution of the article is a clarification of different roles a rule can play in a theory. If a rule is just a heuristic shortcut, the problems of act-utilitarianism will persist. On the other hand, in some cases the rules are constitutive of the practice and acts performed within the practice. One can only strike out if one is playing baseball, and one is not allowed to persuade the umpire that four strikes would produce more utility in this case than three. On the practice conception, utilitarianism can only be applied to the selection of practices, not to setting aside the rules from within the practice. Interestingly, his point of departure here was partly H. L. A. Hart's approach to punishment, which applied utility only to the job of the legislator, not to that of the judge. It goes without saying that Rawls thought utilitarianism inadequate on its own and that in his later work the original position is a prime example of using nonconsequentialist justifications for why questions should be decided on the basis of general principles rather than simply on an act-by-act basis. We will return to Rawls briefly in Part II.

Marcus Singer (1958) argued against ethical relativism by claiming that while moral rules have exceptions and while practices can rightly differ by time and place, moral principles are more fundamental and are both categorical and universal. By "moral principles" he had in mind things like a generalization requirement, that what is right for one person must be right for others in similar circumstances. Other examples are that one should not do X if the consequences of doing X are undesirable, that one should not cause unnecessary suffering, and that if the consequences of everyone's acting in a certain way are undesirable, then one should not act in that way. His claim was that these principles do not conflict with each other and that they yield an approach that is rule-consequentialist even if some of the underlying principles are not justified by consequences alone.

An important moment for rule-utilitarians was the publication of Richard Brandt's book *Ethical Theory* in 1959. Brandt would become one of the theory's most effective proponents in the coming decades and he would modify his approach to counter the powerful criticisms that were already being expressed in the 1950s and that became even more powerful in the 1960s. Brandt argued that we test moral theories based on their impartiality and whether an informed person in a normal state of mind could consistently approve of them. Brandt argued for what he called "extended rule-utilitarianism," which we would now term rule-consequentialism. He departed from strict utilitarianism in that he took the equal distribution of welfare to have some intrinsic value. His historical account of the position was as follows:

> This theory, a product of the last decade, is not a novel one. We find statements of it in J. S. Mill and John Austin in the nineteenth century; and indeed we find at least traces of it much earlier, in discussions of the nature and function of law by the early Greeks. But in the earlier statements of it we do not find it sharply defined, as an alternative to act-utilitarianism. Clear formulations of it have been the work of the past few years. (Brandt 1959, 396)

This is largely right, in that there are parallels with Austin and perhaps Mill. It is also true that the early theological formulations didn't make precise contrasts with act-utilitarianism in the way the literature of this era had, yet we will see later that this account underestimates the similarity of Brandt's own position to the pre-Bentham authors.

Brandt's early formulation was this:

> It is obligatory overall for an agent to perform an act *A* if and only if the prescription that it be performed ["Do *A*!"] follows logically from a complete description of the agent's situation plus ideal prescriptions for his community; and ideal prescriptions for his community are that set of universal imperatives [of the form "Do *A* in circumstances *C*"] containing no proper names, which is (*a*) complete and as economical in distinct imperatives and in concepts as is compatible with completeness, and such

that (*b*) a conscientious effort to obey it, by everyone in the agent's community, would have greater net expectable utility than similar effort to obey any other set of imperatives. (Brandt 1959, 396–7)

This formulation is by far the clearest presentation from the 1950s and closest to the versions of rule-utilitarianism that will follow. Notice that it prohibited appeal directly to the principle of utility, that it considered the construction of a somewhat complex moral code that functions as the standard of evaluation, and that it assumed we are interested in the consequences if everyone makes a conscientious effort to follow the code. He thought this approach was coherent, yielded more reasonable conclusions than act-utilitarianism, and provided more guidance in hard decisions than did Ross. I discuss Brandt's later work at the end of the chapter.

The Battle over Utilitarian Orthodoxy

The heightened interest in rule-utilitarianism in the early 1950s led to increasingly strident rejections of it in the years that followed. One of the first came from A. K. Stout in his article "But Suppose Everyone Did the Same." He voiced one part of what would become the standard (purist) act-utilitarian critique. If my action will weaken a valuable practice, that negative consequence is one for which act-utilitarians can account. What is mysterious, on utilitarian grounds, is why I should desist from performing the action that will have the best consequences, even after accounting for the possibility of being wrong, the possibility of being caught, and so on. Stout's article is interesting in part because of the way he framed the argument historically. He recognized rule-utilitarianism in Austin's *Lectures on Jurisprudence* (Stout 1954, 7) and saw it presented in a theistic manner. Austin wanted to know how we can ascertain the will of God apart from revelation, reasoned that God must be a utilitarian, and deduced that therefore God's will is that we perform the action with the best consequences. Stout tellingly wrote of Austin's view:

> God is a utilitarian, and so long as we act on the principles of utility we shall be obeying his will. The only difference between this position [Austin's] and a non-theological utilitarianism is that the motive of the good man for seeking "the greatest happiness of all" is not simply the desire to do what is good (or best) for its own sake, but the desire to obey God's laws, that is, his commands. (Stout 1954, 7–8)

Stout voiced a common view among utilitarians, namely that while there is some theological language present in the works of earlier utilitarians, the only function of God in those theories was to provide an additional motive to do what it is already known should be done. The absence or removal of God from utilitarianism would have no effect on its practical recommendations.

Stout noted that in practice Austin looked at general classes of actions rather than individual actions and that he used these to explain why one should not steal from the rich or cheat on income taxes. Nonetheless, Austin included an escape clause that allows us in extreme cases to appeal directly to the consequences of the act (Stout 1954, 10). This, Stout thought, threw Austin's whole approach into disarray. He believed that a consistent utilitarian theory could not count consequences when there was no causal connection between a person's act and the positive or negative consequences that would counterfactually happen if others were to act the same way. Stout then presented an argument that sat uncomfortably with his earlier analysis of Austin. He understood Austin to claim that God foresees that if we were given permission to break rules in cases when doing so is justified on utilitarian grounds, our human weakness would lead us to break them in other unjustified cases and that, to save us from temptation, God forbids the whole class of actions (Stout 1954, 13). Notice that God is now arguably playing a different role from that ascribed to him a few pages earlier. Here, his legislative perspective leads him to alter the *content* of the law based on the weaknesses of those who are to obey that law. Stout set the theological aspect aside and analyzed Austin's argument without it. He found Austin unable to defend the position given the example of a person who is certain his breach of the rule will never be detected. While one might object that it is unfair to break a rule that others are prohibited from violating, this is not a reason utilitarianism can accept (Stout 1954, 17). Why, he asked, is it not part of my special circumstances that I know my action will not be observed by others? The basic dilemma is this: if there is a causal link between my actions and those of others then act-utilitarianism can account for that link and change its prescriptions accordingly. If there is no causal link between actions and outcomes then there is no reason a utilitarian should be concerned. This is an argument for a narrow view of utilitarian orthodoxy, namely that it cannot include Kantian or other premises to help justify the shift to a legislative point of view. His argument was not so much that the position is wrong but that it is not utilitarian.

Stout was in some ways echoing the thought of others who had shown some sympathy toward rule-utilitarianism but suspected it needed support from something other than utility, perhaps an independent consideration related to fairness. The critique of J. J. C. Smart was even more scathing. He wrote as an unapologetic act-utilitarian who found rule-utilitarianism perverse and confused. His article "Extreme and Restricted Utilitarianism" identified the former with what we would call act-utilitarianism and the latter with rule-utilitarianism. Smart was pleased to be "extreme." Here we encounter the quotation in the epigraph at the beginning of this book. Why would someone obey a rule R in cases where one is convinced that breaking rule R will produce better consequences?

> But is it not monstrous to suppose that if we *have* worked out the consequences and if we have perfect faith in the impartiality of our calculations, and if we *know* that in this instance to break *R* will have better results than to keep it, we should nevertheless obey the rule? Is it not to erect *R* into a sort of idol if we keep it when breaking it will prevent, say, some avoidable misery? Is not this a form of superstitious rule-worship (easily explicable psychologically) and not the rational thought of a philosopher? (Smart 1956, 348–9)

These were perhaps the most rhetorically devastating sentences written against rule-utilitarianism in the twentieth century. David Lyons' book (mentioned below) was a more rigorous refutation, but Smart here captured succinctly what would become the running critique of rule-utilitarianism, that it was "superstitious rule-worship." The religious metaphor is telling. Bentham's act-utilitarianism was motivated by a rejection of morality based on divine law. Bentham sought to cleanse morality from religion's corrupting influence (Crimmins 1990). Smart may have seen rule-utilitarianism as a return to the superstitions that Bentham had tried to eliminate. Certainly Smart, like Bentham, was happy to reconsider the prevailing morality on the basis of utilitarianism rather than modify it to accommodate moral beliefs dependent upon superstitious belief in a divine legislator. The harsh language of Smart's critique seems to go beyond merely disagreeing, but to excommunicating from the profession of philosopher anyone who would indulge in such heterodoxy.

Smart argued that Sidgwick had gotten things right, in particular noting that we can apply the principle of utility to the question of what we should praise or condemn as well as to what we should do, and that these need not be the same (Smart 1956, 350; Sidgwick Methods, 428). Utilitarianism could, with logical consistency, include a command to praise people for following some other standard if encouraging others to follow suit would increase utility. He argued that while "restricted utilitarianism" is an appealing way to square utilitarianism with then current English moral sensibilities, the better path is to allow utilitarianism to critique those sensibilities.

Henry J. McCloskey (1957) attacked rule-utilitarianism from the opposite direction, as a critic of utilitarianism as such. He argued that there is no reason to bar exceptions if a practice won't be damaged by a particular action. He also noted that since rules conflict, rule-utilitarianism could collapse into act-utilitarianism as we use the latter to settle priorities between ever more specific rules. Against Rawls, he argued that punishing the innocent for the common good might actually be better on utilitarian grounds. In any case the empirical argument is uncertain, but our moral judgment is certain.

The most thorough critique of rule-utilitarianism was David Lyons' book *Forms and Limits of Utilitarianism* (1965). His book is important both for how he frames the debate historically and his practical critique of utilitarianism. He wrote "Admittedly, the classical utilitarian theories might not properly be characterized as purely simple utilitarian. None the less, partly through the influence of G. E. Moore (*Principia Ethica* and *Ethics*), in this century the traditional variety had come to be viewed as simple utilitarian, and Act-Utilitarianism as a coherent formulation of the predominant traditional theory" (Lyons 1965, 9). By "the classical utilitarians" he means people like Bentham and Mill. In any case, he notes that in the twentieth century act-utilitarianism is considered the default version of utilitarianism. Rule-utilitarianism arises in the twentieth century to avoid certain undesirable conclusions to which act-utilitarianism seems to lead.

Lyons focused on the question of how we determine the appropriate description for an act. This is important because if we are to ask what the consequences would be of everyone committing act A, we need a way of determining the appropriate description of A. Since utility is concerned with consequences, descriptions are relevant if they have some causal relationship to possible utilities. With this settled he then turns to the key issues that defenders of rule-utilitarianism had, in the past, employed in their justifications. They had noted that the utility of some acts depends on how many other people do them. These acts are nonlinear. If people start breaking promises, there comes a point where each broken promise does more damage than the earlier ones. There are also threshold effects. A few people walking on a given patch of grass has no negative effects but many doing so does. Since a full utilitarian description of an act needs to include everything related to its utility, it must account for how many other people are doing it or are likely to do it. This allows agents to weigh the effects of their act given what others do or may do, and once this is calculated there is no utilitarian reason to additionally consider counterfactual scenarios. In fact, once we give a full description of an act, rule-utilitarianism will collapse into act-utilitarianism. Act-utilitarianism need not be self-defeating since it can account for threshold effects with more precise descriptions of actions. In any case, act-utilitarianism could be coherently self-effacing. Lyons argued that the concerns raised by rule-utilitarians are better understood as an appeal to fairness that is not rooted in utilitarian concerns. Lyons thus seems to be aware of the hybrid nature of rule-utilitarianism.

John L. Mackie's (1985) "The Disutility of Act-Utilitarianism" attempted to show that act-utilitarians can avoid the counterutilitarian outcomes that people think follow from their position. Mackie was responding to those who say that if we imagine a world where people perfectly follow the dictates of act-utilitarianism we would find a morally disturbing absence of things like promises. Mackie argued that a world filled with perfect act-utilitarians could solve coordination problems simply by announcing an intention or command ("Go to your left!") and allowing all parties to make the corresponding utilitarian decision. With regard to promises, we actually do excuse people from upholding promises when doing so would have dreadful consequences, which is what act-utilitarianism would support. Additionally, even act-utilitarians can agree that the announcement of a promise creates new disutilities if it is then broken and that there would still be reason for act-utilitarians to utter the words and be partially guided by them. In a world where everyone was an act-utilitarian, no one would be bothered by this.

Notice where the debate has led us. First, the critiques are primarily about whether the rule-utilitarian position is consistent with utilitarian orthodoxy. Consideration of it as an explicitly hybrid approach that is trying to broaden the boundaries of utilitarianism by including other sorts of claims is mostly set aside (with Lyons as the most important exception). Put another way, much of the critique assumes that a utilitarian theory must be utilitarian all the way down, and that it is not enough that utilitarianism is used to select among moral rules or principles. Second, the refutations of rule-utilitarianism are quite powerful, and they have been framed by Lyons and Mackie in terms of what we might now call "ideal theory." Ideal theory imagines what system would be morally best in a world of perfect compliance (and possibly also unlimited cognitive ability). This is an interesting contrast to the "morality as legislation" model that implies that a legislator should account for the imperfections of those who are subject to the law. As rule-utilitarians attempted to salvage their position, this is the line of argument they adopted. The central issue is whether they can answer the question "why act as if you were legislating a code for others when, in fact, you are not?" The prevailing opinion among philosophers was that the above attacks succeeded in showing that rule-utilitarianism was unsustainable as a form of pure utilitarianism. They did not so much show that it was wrong as show that it could only be defended by having recourse to principles incompatible with utilitarianism strictly defined.

What was excluded from this analysis was sufficient attention to the fact that many of the people they criticized were not actually trying to stay within the narrow boundaries of utilitarianism, strictly defined. As we saw earlier in the chapter, many of the rule-utilitarians explicitly drew upon Kant or used "ideal-utilitarianism" as a way to incorporate claims about justice or unfairness more directly into their theories. We now turn to examples of philosophers from the late twentieth century who were prominent among rule-utilitarians to assess the role of Kantian arguments in their thought.

Hare, Harsanyi, and Brandt

Probably the most widely cited collection of essays on utilitarianism in the late twentieth century was *Utilitarianism and Beyond*, edited by Amartya Sen and Bernard Williams. In their preface they write that all of the papers in the volume are original except for two: "The exceptions are the papers of Hare and Harsanyi, which we have included because we thought it useful to offer, as a background to a collection that is largely, but not exclusively, critical of utilitarianism, two well-known and distinguished modern statements which offer arguments for the utilitarian outlook" (Sen and Williams 1982, vii). They go on to refer to Hare's account, in their introductory essay, as "an authoritative version of indirect utilitarianism" (15). Given this, it is surprising that both Hare and Harsanyi expressly embrace nonutilitarian aspects in their theories while still identifying as utilitarian. They are making the case for expanding the boundaries of utilitarian orthodoxy. Brandt did not follow the same approach in his version of rule-utilitarianism, but was nonetheless influential in promoting a view of morality as legislation.

Hare's article in the aforementioned volume (originally published in 1976) considers various cases where an action seems right (or not wrong) in a specific context but where everyone doing so would cause disutility. He rejects such acts because we would not want others to act on the same principle if they were in that situation. This seems like a deontological rather than consequentialist response. He then writes:

> Here is a point at which, perhaps, some will want to say that my Kantian or Christian variety of utilitarianism, based on giving equal weight to the prudent prescriptions or desires of all, diverges from the usual varieties so much that it does not deserve to be called a kind of utilitarianism at all. I am not much interested in that terminological question. (Hare 1982, 37)

He then notes that one could possibly arrive at the same conclusions without the aid of Kantian/Christian arguments, for example by stating that a deceased person is in fact harmed when what was promised to him is not done. He seems indifferent to the method by which his position is defended (38). Hare sees himself as an orthodox utilitarian, which is why he refers to his view as a "variety of utilitarianism," but acknowledges that others see this as a form of heterodoxy. He addresses this by saying he is uninterested in the terminology and more interested in whether his account is right, whether or not it is labeled as utilitarian.

Hare provided a more developed account of his position, which tried to combine act- and rule-utilitarianism, in his landmark book *Moral Thinking* (1981). Hare's ambitious goal in the book was to derive a theory of morality based on the logical meanings of basic moral terms like "ought." The quasi-Kantian aspect of his thought is his claim that to make a moral statement is to prescribe that things ought to be a certain way and to that extent to desire that thing be that way. A moral "ought" implies that if something is right or wrong, it is right or wrong in all similar situations and from all possible points of view. We can always conceive of situations where everything is the same but the positions of the people in question are reversed, and so we should only affirm principles if we would also affirm them when giving equal weight to the preferences of all affected parties. A universalization requirement is thus built in to the structure of the theory.

This universalization requirement is not yet an argument for rule-utilitarianism because an act-utilitarian could say that, by definition, the right act is in each case the one that produces the most good, counting everyone's preferences equally. The requirement to treat like cases alike is not enough to justify founding morality on general rules.

Rule-utilitarianism enters Hare's theory because he distinguishes between two levels of moral thinking, the critical and the intuitive. At the intuitive level we act on relatively simple moral principles that we have internalized such as "don't lie." Most of our moral decisions are made in this way. "Critical thinking aims to select the best set of prima facie principles for use in intuitive thinking. It can also be employed when principles from the set conflict *per accidens*" (Hare 1981, 49–50). If we were "archangels" with "superhuman powers of thought, superhuman knowledge, and no human weaknesses" (44), we could do all of our thinking at the critical level and would, in fact, be act-utilitarians. If we turned these extreme strengths into extreme weaknesses (the "*prole*") (45) we would be incapable of critical think-ing altogether and would want to be given simple intuitive principles to try to follow in order to act morally. Because human beings are in between these two extremes, we need a two-level theory of morality.

In this two-level theory, the critical level is where we decide which intuitive moral principles we want to try to inculcate in ourselves and others, for example our children. It is also the perspective that determines whether an action is, in fact, morally right.[5] We inculcate intuitive principles know-ing full well that what is truly right in a given situation is what the archangel would do in that situation and that the internalized intuitive principles will sometimes lead us to act contrary to those principles, for example telling the truth in cases where from the perspective of all parties it would have been better to lie. We inculcate these intuitive principles nonetheless because, knowing our limitations, we believe that in aggregate more people will have their preferences satisfied by proceeding in this two-level way. This is different from the esoteric "government house" utilitarianism of Sidgwick because, instead of dividing society into those who know morality at the critical level (and sometimes act from it directly) and those who simply act from the intuitive level, in principle all of us have access to both levels because we all have elements of both the archangel and the prole. Hare takes his approach to be a synthesis of Kant and utilitarianism (Hare 1981, 4).

Hare's approach raised important questions and a 1988 edited volume provided him with an opportunity to respond to a distinguished set of critics. For our purposes, two questions are of particular importance: 1) To what extent, in practice, can we appeal directly to the critical perspective

---

[5] Morally right here does not mean a true indicative statement in form of "X is wrong," since Hare thinks moral statements are prescriptions, not descriptions. A morally right prescription is one that is consistent with the underlying logic of morality and the relevant facts.

rather than just following the principles we have internalized? 2) Is this position stable, or is it liable to the familiar problems of other two-level utilitarian theories?

In answer to the first question, Hare is classified by some as an act-utilitarian and by others as a rule-utilitarian (Sen and Williams, as noted above). The confusion exists because, on the one hand, Hare would say that what is right is defined from the critical, act-utilitarian, perspective but that one of the acts requiring choice is which intuitive principles to inculcate in ourselves and others. It is a brute empirical fact that we do better with internalized principles like those of rule-utilitarianism. Yet Hare wants his intuitive principles to function as more than just rules of thumb, as a pure act-utilitarian would. Given that there are many prima facie intuitive moral principles, conflicts could be a rather common occurrence. If we have recourse to the critical position in such circumstances, we will effectively become rule-utilizing act-utilitarians. When pressed on this point by William Frankena, Hare insisted that he is both an act- and a rule-utilitarian because the dispositions selected at the critical level will practically function as rules that guide our moral decision-making, but the selection of dispositions/rules is an act that the archangel chooses on act-utilitarian grounds (Hare 1988, 226–7). Thus, faced with a situation where principles conflict, Hare seems to be saying that we ought not decide what to do by reverting to act-utilitarianism, since continuing to act according to the intuitive rules is a way of inculcating support for them and there are good act-utilitarian reasons for cultivating these dispositions. Harsanyi had claimed that reversion to the critical perspective in cases of conflicting principles would undermine the benefits of rules (Harsanyi 1988). Hare replied that in the standard cases where an act-utilitarian (but not rule-utilitarian) might break a promise "an omniscient and wholly impartial being might with confidence say that he ought to break [the promise]; but that a human being would be wise to keep it, in view of his inability to be sure that promise-breaking would be for the best in this case, and his liability to self-deception and special pleading" (Hare 1988, 244). Even in cases where our actions are secret, our decision to depart from the rule will weaken our resolve to follow the rule in the future and this is normally more than enough to justify, in this case, keeping the promise.[6]

---

[6] "[T]he expectation effects of the moral rule or code will be a factor in our choice of actions to the extent that actions have institution-weakening or institution-strengthening effects; and I hold, as a matter of empirical fact, that this is nearly always the case. At any rate, it is the case often enough for us to have stuck firmly to these rules, and to be glad that we have" (Hare 1988, 244–5).

This view has deep similarities to G. E. Moore's position with which we began the chapter, and also has some of the same empirical problems as Moore's. Just because exceptions to a rule are rare does not mean that there are not times when situation-specific information could make it clear that this is one of the exceptions. Similarly, if one acts rightly in breaking the rule it is not obvious that this will cause you to break the rule in other cases, provided that you have set a fairly high burden of proof to account for the special pleading and self-deception problems that Hare mentions. Bernard Williams pressed the objection that the

> thoughts are not stable under reflection; in particular, you cannot think in these terms if at the same time you apply to the process the kind of thorough reflection that this theory itself advocates. That is not a merely psychological claim. It is a philosophical claim about what is involved in effective and adequate reflection on these particular states of mind ... The more the theory represents the intuitive reactions as merely superficial, provisional, and instrumental, the fewer appearances [of conflicting with deeply held moral judgments] it saves. (Williams 1988, 190)

Hare replies by giving an analogy to a general who, for good reason, has internalized a principle of attacking the enemy when given the opportunity and who will therefore feel a strong conviction to do so in these situations, but who might still decide (with regret) not to attack because some other more important moral principle is in play or because doing so would lead to an unacceptable loss of life. This response seems to validate Williams' point – Hare makes the theory coherent, but in the process weakens the commitment to not break one's intuitive rules described above. It seems instead as if the general is in fact using act-utilitarian reasoning to determine whether to follow the rule.

What is most interesting for our purposes is that Hare's version, the most sophisticated attempt at wedding act- and rule-utilitarianism of the twentieth century, depends in a rather foundational way on Kantian universalization, which is not derived from consequentialist grounds. This makes his utilitarian theory, in my sense of the term, a hybrid one. I will say more about such theories in Part II. At the very least, Hare is a prominent case of the point made earlier, that many of the twentieth-century rule-utilitarians who were accused of inconsistency with their utilitarian foundations were explicit in including nonutilitarian commitments in those foundations.

John Harsanyi's rule-utilitarianism flowed from his interest in economics, rational choice theory, and their intersection with ethics. In an early article (Harsanyi 1976, originally published 1958) he specifically cites Harrod's article, discussed above, on the point that utilitarians can avoid the charge that there are no binding duties "if the utilitarian criterion is applied not to the consequences of each *single* act but rather to the cumulative consequences of the *general* practice of acting in a certain particular way (acting according to a similar rule) in all similar cases" (Harsanyi 1976, 32–3). He also notes a debt in this early work to Adam Smith's conception of the impartial spectator and to Kant's conception of universalizability (Harsanyi 1976, 28–30). His rationale is that moral rules are hypothetical imperatives:

> If the moral rules enjoin a particular act under certain conditions, this means that it is an objective fact, depending on certain logical truths and possibly also on certain empirical truths, that if anybody wants to follow the recommendation which a well-informed and intelligent impartially sympathetic observer would make [which for him is synonymous for wanting to act morally] he *must* perform this act under the specified conditions. (Harsanyi 1976, 34)

While one could imagine someone choosing to maximize utility in every particular act, Harsanyi maintains that this would not maximize utility because we would lose so much of our ability to rely on expectations, for example the ability to rely on promises.

Harsanyi continued this approach in his later work. The chapter in the Sen and Williams edited volume (1982a, originally published in 1977) again notes his debt to Adam Smith's impartial spectator and Kant's criterion of universality (which he takes to be similar to the Bible's golden rule) (Harsanyi 1982a, 39). He then mentioned, approvingly, Hare's universalizing approach to utilitarianism. This is hardly the introduction we would expect from someone who aspired to utilitarian orthodoxy, strictly defined. Later in the essay he claimed that antisocial preferences based on envy, sadism, or malice should simply be excluded from calculations, which again seems like a clear indication that his theory is not intended to stay within strict utilitarian orthodoxy. And yet, like Hare, he used utilitarian labels to describe his own approach repeatedly.[7] This should again be seen as a challenge to an excessively narrow definition of utilitarian orthodoxy, that only those who limit themselves exclusively to hedonistic

---

[7] Harsanyi consistently refers to his approach as utilitarian in other works as well (1977, 63–4; 1982b, 251). He also uses the legislative framework in these other works: "In other words, the question we have to ask is: If we were given the task of choosing a moral rule to regulate people's behavior in a certain type of situation, which would be the *moral rule whose adoption would best serve the social interest* (i.e., whose adoption would maximize our social-welfare function)?" (1977, 63).

consequences or something similar can be called utilitarians. Instead, he thought that since utilitarian reasoning does the work in regulating most of our ethical choices once we have adopted his system, this is more than enough to make it a member of the utilitarian family.

Brandt, in his later work, was more indirect in his reliance on non-utilitarian arguments. Even so, he did rely on the legislative model as a way of explaining both why rule-utilitarianism does not collapse into act-utilitarianism and why it provides a superior method for making moral decisions. Brandt in 1967 reminded his readers of the counterintuitive conclusions of act-utilitarianism. He called his revised view an "ideal moral code" theory.

> A moral code is "ideal" if its currency in a particular society would produce at least as much good per person (the total divided by the number of persons) as the currency of any other moral code. ... *An act is right if and only if it would not be prohibited by the moral code ideal for the society; and an agent is morally blameworthy (praiseworthy) for an act if, and to the degree that, the moral code ideal in that society would condemn (praise) him for it.* (Brandt 1992 [1967], 119–20)

By currency, Brandt meant a code that at least 90 percent of the population accepts, attempts to live by, and feels guilty if it breaks. This legislative approach allows for answers to key objections. Extraordinarily complex rules of the sort Lyons imagined (rules so complex that they yield the same conclusions as act-utilitarianism) would be too complex to inculcate in 90 percent of the population. Extraordinarily demanding duties would face a similar hurdle. One must look not only at the benefits of people acting in a certain way but also the costs of getting them to act that way (Brandt 1992 [1967], 126). The rules must also account for those who do not accept the principles or who apply them incorrectly.

This argument, however, leaves unanswered the question of why we should be deciding what is right in individual cases on the basis of a moral code rather than on an act-by-act basis. In 1967, Brandt's answer focused more on the unappealing conclusions of act-utilitarianism. In his important book published in 1979, *A Theory of the Good and the Right*, he claimed that appealing to intuitions is question-begging and that many of our intuitions reflect unsupportable prejudices (Brandt 1979, 16–23). His alternative was to base his theory on a concept of rational desires, where rational desires are those that would be retained following cognitive psychotherapy that would help the person with problems such as phobias, false beliefs, and desires that were artificially aroused in childhood, such as pressure to pursue a particular occupation (Brandt 1979, 11–12, 115–26). Given that we have desires, we should want rational ones, and given that societies do in fact have social moral codes we should ask ourselves what social moral code a rational person would want for the society to which they belong (Brandt 1979, 200–23). This provides a different route to viewing morality as a moral code with strong analogies to positive law.

In 1988, Brandt noted two different reasons for approaching morality from what I am terming a legislative point of view. The first is linguistic. Mill, according to Brandt, "seems to be relying on linguistic intuition; he says we *mean* or at least *imply* liability to 'punishment' (by guilt feelings and/or reprobation by others) when we say some act is morally wrong" (Brandt 1988, 344). As we have already seen, this linguistic argument relies on traditions of thinking about morality as a code that have theological roots and Mill (and Brandt) may have been relying on those assumptions about morality despite having secular theories. His second line of argument notes that Rawls, Harsanyi, and Scanlon all, in different ways, argue for determining what is right or wrong based on a code that is, in some sense of the word, benefit-maximizing (though Rawls and Scanlon include restrictions that diverge sharply from Harsanyi's rule-utilitarianism). Brandt then wrote:

> I do not assert that any of these proposals constitutes a knock-down argument that an action is morally wrong if and only if it would not be permitted by a benefit-maximizing moral system. But, in order to get on with the problems in formulating such systems, I shall assume that they show enough in this direction to make the concept of a benefit-maximizing moral system worth exploring. (Brandt 1988, 345)

While this is not enough to show that Brandt was a hybrid theorist, he was at least willing to appeal to philosophers who were not utilitarians to render his legislative approach more plausible.

Brandt attempted, in his approach, to avoid the paradoxical counterfactual shift by defining questions about morality as necessarily legislative. To be thinking about what is right or wrong is just to be thinking about what sort of social code you would want your group to have. This solution has its costs because it creates a separation between the questions "what should I do?" and "what moral code do I want my society to have?" The theory is not contradictory, but it also does not show that I can't have one moral code for myself and want another for my group to follow.

It is not the case that every defender of rule-utilitarianism was involved in stretching the boundaries of utilitarianism to include nonconsequentialist elements. Nor did all of the people mentioned in this chapter consistently align themselves with the hybrid position. Nonetheless, the above examples show that there were a significant number of thinkers who wrote in ways that acknowledged the value of hybrid approaches. They foreshadow the direction that I will pursue in Part II of this book, describing the type of hybrid theory that is needed to justify a shift to the legislative point of view. Before turning to Part II, I conclude Part I with a review of the historical argument.

Review of the Historical Argument

The Kantian philosopher Thomas Hill Jr., to whom we will return in the next chapter, provides a succinct summary of a commonly held view about the relationship between act- and rule-utilitarianism. "Rule-utilitarianism (RU) developed in response to objections to act-utilitarianism (AU) ... Among the many objections raised against AU in its various forms, the most persistent has been that it leads to counter-intuitive moral judgments" (Hill 2012, 207–8). The sorts of objections he has in mind are that

> If we use AU as a decision guide, it is argued, our ignorance and wishful thinking will often cause us to misestimate the expected utility of what we propose to do. More seriously, even if our estimates are correct, we will sometimes judge it permissible to do things that are dishonest, unjust, ungrateful, and disloyal because in many empirical circumstances, the honest, just, grateful, and loyal options are not utility-maximizing. (Hill 2012, 208)

Rule-utilitarians, by contrast, can argue that a general practice of allowing doctors to harvest the organs of healthy patients without their consent or allowing police officers to frame innocent persons would have terrible consequences. Since they define right and wrong in terms of an ideal code, they can show why these actions are wrong. If one includes the costs of getting most of the population to accept the moral code as part of the calculation, one can also explain why some particularly demanding forms of consequentialism would be rejected in favor of more moderate forms. It would be very difficult to convince 90 percent of the population that they must give to global charities until their level of well-being matches that of the worst-off person they could help.

The foregoing analysis presents a different way of understanding these debates historically. In the seventeenth and eighteenth centuries it was common to think of morality as legislation and to think of God as the legislator. These authors were not card-carrying utilitarians, but they were weakly consequentialist. They all thought that the content of the moral code was directly related to the likely consequences of the promulgation of that moral code. If there were two possible codes and an omniscient lawgiver could foresee that one would better bring about, in practice, the lawgiver's desired consequences, that would give the lawgiver a reason to legislate and promulgate the rule with better consequences. In making these judgments, the lawgiver would account for the natural drives, biases, and fallibility of those who would be under the law in the same way that a rational human legislator considers the limitations of those who will be bound by human laws.

To be sure, we have seen that the criteria used for membership in the club of "consequentialists" or "utilitarians" reveals much about the underlying assumptions of the one doing the classification. There was, in fact, a secular shift with Bentham, and some people make secularism essential to utilitarianism. They often focus on the claim that God plays no significant role in the theory, particularly with respect to the existence of moral obligations. A theory that must invoke "because God commanded it" as the explanation for why there are moral obligations seems rather opposed to the spirit of Bentham's project. While this is true enough, we have seen that God's presence in the earlier theories did more than explain the existence of moral obligations and motivate moral behavior, it also defined the perspective from which assessments are made about what is right or wrong. Thus, even if the theorists we have studied are not pure utilitarians or even pure consequentialists, they are part of the history of consequentialism in this respect. They formulated a way of thinking about ethics that both assumed that morality has a legislative shape and that consequentialist reasoning from a legislative perspective is, at least in part, necessary for thinking rightly about morality.

John Locke rejected religious persecution from a legislative perspective, arguing that the alternative, understood as a publicly known general rule, would require fallible human rulers to enforce the religion they thought to be true, a dubious prospect. George Berkeley used Locke's same form of argument to rebut one of Locke's other major claims, the legitimacy of revolution. Berkeley argued that a publicly known rule authorizing active resistance to the government would be abused too often by fallible subjects. Francis Hutcheson heroically attempted to synthesize the legislative perspective with an account of morality that emphasized God as the architect who designs our moral sense such that it accords with God's will as well as with the metaphor of the "spectator." Hutcheson's version of the legislative point of view was even more emphatic in making the production of happiness the object of the moral code, while acknowledging the way human limitations alter the content of the moral code.

Hutcheson's attempted synthesis did not hold together. Joseph Butler deemphasized the legislative perspective and put the architect metaphor at the center of his theory. He also articulated the basic objection that morality based on act-by-act benevolence leads to unacceptable violation of valuable moral rules. David Hume, by contrast, relied on the spectator metaphor. Hume repeatedly noted a natural tendency of humans to rule-based thinking without claiming that this must be traced to divine design (as in the architect metaphor). In doing so, the tendency to rule-based thinking became, in an important sense, descriptive rather than normative. Given the rule-based tendencies of human beings, there are good pragmatic reasons to think of justice *as if it were* a legislative code although, metaphysically, it is not.

Hume's approach created a fork in the road: would theism continue to ground the legislative perspective or was it possible to use it in a purely secular consequentialist theory? William Paley opted for the former approach, but Jeremy Bentham was far more influential in opting for the latter. Bentham's agenda was consciously and aggressively secular. He was also much more willing than most to revise his specific moral judgments to align with the theory of utilitarianism. In other words, he was not particularly troubled by counterintuitive conclusions. He confronted the problem that, on purely consequentialist grounds, it is unclear why one should be constrained by imaginary rules of justice. Given that I as an individual, by my actions, do not actually create a law that others must obey, why should I base my ethical decisions on what I would legislate if, counterfactually, I did have such a power? Bentham's strategy was twofold. First, he focused his energies on situations where human beings actually do legislate. There is no counterfactual perspectival shift when you tell actual legislators to think legislatively. Second, he reframed our public moral judgments as a kind of participation in a legislative practice. If the law of opinion shapes human behavior by offering reputational rewards and sanctions and if people often decide who to praise and blame on the basis of conformity with publicly known rules, then when I decide whether to support or criticize the commonly held moral rules of the day I am engaging in something like a legislative enterprise, an enterprise that can be guided by utilitarian principles. This strategy portends institutional utilitarianism, discussed below, which attempts to rescue utilitarianism from many of its counterintuitive conclusions by restricting its scope to laws, policies, and institutions.

Bentham's great nineteenth-century successors, John Stuart Mill and Henry Sidgwick, grappled with the consequences of this trajectory. Both Mill and Sidgwick emphasized the compatibility of the principle of utility with the use of subordinate rules in practical decision-making. The practical benefits of a known rule about keeping promises, for example, could give utilitarians a reason to affirm such a rule. Publicly affirming a moral position, as with Bentham, continued to be analogous to legislation and therefore subject to a legislative calculus. Moral norms in a society have a meaningful influence over actions and often facilitate reputational rewards and punishments in the same way that traditional legislation does. For Mill, this created a tension regarding public moral expression. On the one hand, Mill championed the right (and perhaps even duty) of people to publicly declare what they really think about what is right and what is wrong. On the other hand, one must censor one's own public moral statements because of strategic legislative considerations, as Mill sometimes did. Sidgwick faced this dilemma and fully embraced its radical conclusion – that morality must be esoteric. What we say is right and wrong may need to diverge from what we know actually is right or wrong in a particular case. What to publicly affirm is just one more action subject to its own utilitarian analysis and it may deviate from a distinct utilitarian analysis of what one should do. Sidgwick, and perhaps Mill, previewed an approach to the legislative perspective, which views it as a decision-making procedure rather than the criterion for right and wrong.

In the twentieth century, utilitarians were attempting to answer the charge that utilitarianism should be rejected because it failed to square with widely held moral intuitions. In particular, Ross' pluralist critique of utilitarianism claimed that its oversimplified framework neglected other, independent, moral principles like justice and honesty. Rule-utilitarianism was revived in part to show how a utilitarian framework could arrive at the "right answers" regarding questions where these values were implicated. It faced the powerful objection that following an ideal rule when breaking it would produce better outcomes was, for a consequentialist, superstitious rule-worship. Several strategies emerged to defend it. One strategy was to consciously embrace a hybrid theory with non-consequentialist (often Kantian) elements. These approaches foreshadow contemporary accounts that use a consequence-sensitive legislative perspective infused with Kantian elements.

The hybrid approach is not, of course, the only available way for thinking about morality as if it is, to some extent, akin to legislation. In Part II I will first survey the four leading contemporary options when utilizing the legislative point of view before describing the benefits of an explicitly hybrid approach and the sort of justification such an approach needs in the last chapter.

PART II

*Contemporary Approaches
to the Rule-Consequentialist Paradox*

CHAPTER 6

Four Contemporary Options for Resolving the Paradox

This chapter examines four contemporary strategies to rehabilitate the legislative perspective in the face of the criticisms that strict consequentialism seems incompatible with the counterfactual reasoning that the legislative point of view often requires. The three main consequentialist options are 1) to restrict legislative consequentialism's scope to the design of rules, policies, and institutions (Goodin, Johnson, and Schauer); 2) to follow Sidgwick and accept a disjunction between moral rules and moral right (Lazari-Radek and Singer); or 3) to justify a consequentialist legislative perspective based on its fit with our moral judgments using something resembling a reflective equilibrium approach rather than having consequentialism itself be the foundation (Hooker). These approaches are not mutually exclusive but rather represent distinctive strategies to resolve the paradox. A fourth option is a Kantian, nonconsequentialist one (Hill and Parfit). While our historical focus has been on the consequentialist stream of thought on rules, there is an alternate nonconsequentialist stream of thought that also frames right and wrong in a legislative manner. This chapter explores these four options and argues that none of them alone is able to justify the decision to adopt a counterfactual legislative perspective of the sort specified in the introduction, paving the way for the discussion of an alternative, hybrid approach in the next chapter.

Institutional Consequentialism

One contemporary strategy for defending the legislative point of view is to restrict its scope to genuinely legislative contexts. The biggest justificatory problem for the legislative perspective is explaining why you should act as if you were drawing up rules for others to follow when, in fact, you are not. Institutional consequentialism tries to solve this problem by confining utilitarianism such that one avoids counterfactual cases. This strategy is able to capture some of the benefits of the legislative point of view in that one is deliberating about what actual laws and policies should be and trying to decide what law would be best, accounting for all the practical difficulties that are likely to follow when the law is adopted. It is only a limited version of the legislative point of view because while it embraces legislative thinking in legislative contexts, it rejects the extension of the legislative point of view to nonlegislative contexts and also rejects counterfactual use of the legislative perspective in legislative contexts. Before proceeding, it will be helpful to review three distinctions that were described in the Introduction, as these will coincide with the three philosophers I discuss in this section.

The first distinction is the simplest of the three. We have seen that, historically, the legislative point of view was often used to determine standards of right and wrong that apply to decisions made in nonlegislative contexts. The legislative point of view was often used to determine the standard of conduct for individuals as such, not merely for those making laws. What I am calling the institutional strategy adopts the legislative perspective but does not claim that it provides consistently sound ethical guidance for individuals who are not deliberating about what our laws, policies, or institutions should be.

The second distinction is more complex: the difference between legislative and nonlegislative contexts is separate from the distinction between factual and counterfactual deliberation. Legislative context is about whether I am in a situation where my actions contribute to shaping a rule that others will follow whereas in nonlegislative contexts my action is not oriented toward the adoption of an action-guiding rule. Factual deliberation is where I choose to consider only the consequences that are likely to flow from my action's contribution toward bringing about the adoption of a rule. In counterfactual deliberation, I consider consequences that are not causally affected in any significant way by the decision I will make. A state legislator thinking only about what law will produce good consequences for their state is using factual reasoning in a legislative context, but a state legislator discerning whether it is right to vote for a law by considering what laws other states should also adopt is thinking counterfactually in a legislative context (assuming a weak causal connection between the decision of that state regarding the law and the decisions of other states regarding their laws).

The two are easily conflated because the use of the legislative perspective in a nonlegislative context is always counterfactual, but contexts and deliberative approaches should be distinguished because in legislative contexts there is still a choice to be made about whether one will use the legislative perspective counterfactually or not. Suppose, as in Locke's argument, a monarch is deciding whether or not to tolerate those who dissent from the national religion and has full power to enact the rule of his choice regarding dissenters. His context is as legislative as possible. He is deciding what rule will be adopted for his country. He still faces a choice about whether to give weight to the dictates of a counterfactual legislative perspective. He could, as Locke and Paley advised, consider whether a more general rule, that applies to himself and to other kings and instructs them to use their power to bring people to the true religion, would be beneficial or not. If he does so, he is using the legislative perspective counterfactually since the monarch is not actually in a position to legislate for other countries even though the monarch is still in a legislative context with respect to his own country. Alternatively, he could reject the counterfactual frame and simply decide what rule about religious toleration is best for his own country. Limiting the legislative perspective to legislative contexts thus removes the most obvious set of counterfactual cases, but it does not provide a reason for counterfactual use of the legislative perspective more generally.

The third distinction has to do with how much weight we assign the dictates of the legislative perspective. All versions of the legislative point of view must give it at least some weight, but some do so in an absolute sense. The rules derived from that perspective are to be followed in all cases. Rule-consequentialists can, in this sense, be as absolutist about rules as Kantians, although the content of the rules will be different. This distinction can interact with the others since the weight we attach to the dictates of the legislative perspective may be stronger in cases where there is an actual rule promulgated by authoritative institutions or widely accepted as a moral norm. Informal norms can still constitute "institutions," in the sense I am using it here, as they can be promulgated and incentivize compliance with rules as do formal institutions.

Robert Goodin, Conrad Johnson, and Frederick Schauer all utilize a consequentialist version of the legislative perspective and try to avoid the paradoxes by restricting the scope to institutional contexts. Goodin's approach illustrates the first distinction in that he explicitly circumscribes the use of consequentialist reasoning to specifically legislative contexts and denies that it provides the standard of right in private contexts. Johnson's approach highlights the second distinction in that he thinks that only existing practices that are justified on consequentialist grounds are right-defining. He rejects the idea that counterfactual optimific rules can be right-defining. Schauer underscores the third distinction, which is that we can assign varying weights to the dictates of the legislative perspective. I will take up each of the three in turn.

Robert Goodin, in his book *Utilitarianism as a Public Philosophy*, argues that utilitarianism "can be a good normative guide to public affairs without its necessarily being the best practical guide to personal conduct" (Goodin 1995, 4). When writing constitutions, drafting laws, or promulgating policies we really are acting in a legislative capacity. One need not be a member of a traditional legislative body, what matters is that one is in a position to enact rules that have authority. Whether the particular actor is a judge setting precedent, a bureaucrat formulating regulations, or a member of parliament voting for a law, the object of one's decision is a publicly known rule. In such settings, there is nothing counterfactual about the legislative point of view. One is actually shaping legislation.

Goodin makes a credible case that restricting utilitarianism in this way actually moves it closer to the primary interests of its classical proponents. Bentham and Mill were primarily interested in large public questions like constitutional reform, penal reform, and the rights of women. Goodin approvingly quotes J. S. Mill's own assessment of Bentham:

> It is fortunate for the world that Bentham's taste lay rather in the direction of jurisprudential than of properly ethical inquiry. Nothing expressly of the latter kind has been published under his name except the "Deontology" – a book scarcely ever ... alluded to by any admirer of Bentham without deep regret that it ever saw the light. (Goodin 1995, 12)

We saw in Chapter 3 that Goodin (and Mill) has a valid point. Bentham really did focus his energies on questions of a legislative nature and said little about the ethics of individual decisions apart from legislative frameworks.

Goodin claims that his approach is orthogonal to the traditional act versus rule debate because it is about who (public officials v. private persons) is guided by utility rather than what (acts v. rules) the doctrine applies to (Goodin 1995, 60–1). I am unpersuaded by Goodin on this point. If it was about "who," it would apply to public officials in their secret, nonpublic choices. Public officials can sometimes wield public power in ways that do not generate publicly known policy. Yet when explaining why his approach upholds rights Goodin states, "My point is instead that public officials cannot systematically violate people's rights, as a matter of *policy*, and expect that policy to continue yielding the same utility payoffs time and again" (Goodin 1995, 70). Goodin explicitly states that he is talking about policies and that his logic would not hold in cases of discretionary decisions that do not set precedents for other decisions. Goodin's approach really is about *what* utilitarianism applies to (public rules) rather than *who* applies it. Given the counterintuitive implications of act utilitarianism at the individual level, this is a sensible way to try to salvage what is most plausible about the theory, but it requires setting aside the legislative point of view in large swaths of life where it may actually be helpful. We have seen that the legislative perspective has informed our understanding of what is right in contexts other than public policy, and I will argue in the next chapter that there are good reasons for this. Goodin's approach does not try to resolve any paradoxes, but rather to sidestep them by limiting his scope to only those cases where the main paradox does not arise.

A problem with Goodin's approach is that since consequentialism does appear to make universalistic claims, it seems ad hoc to stipulate that it only applies to public contexts. This is parallel to the traditional objection against rule-consequentialism. Goodin anticipates this objection and notes various ways in which some aspects of utilitarianism traditionally thought to be vices are not. They may actually be virtues in public contexts. His article, "Government House Utilitarianism" (in Goodin 1995, 60–77) makes essentially the same point. He clarifies that he is using the term not to defend Sidgwick's esoteric morality, but rather to make the claim we have been discussing, that public officials have obligations to make decisions on a utilitarian basis that private citizens do not. He again emphasizes the ways in which many of the problems arising from utilitarianism when embraced as a personal moral code are actually strengths in public policy. These reasons are intended to make the distinction justified rather than ad hoc. Interpersonal utility comparisons, for example, are actually easier in a policy context where there is no alternative to relying on general estimates. Impartiality is easier to justify in public contexts than in family life. A legal framework of rights is of great utility. In making these arguments and in forgoing the "outsmart" option of simply affirming the counterintuitive conclusions ("yes, frame the innocent person"), Goodin opens the door to assuming that there are some values other than utilitarian ones at work. These nonutilitarian values provide the explanation for why it is that there should be limits to consequentialism's reach. If this is so, more explanation is needed for why those other values apply only to private situations. If pressed, Goodin might defend his position by using the strategies in sections two or three. He might claim that, in the end, we adopt different decision rules in public and in private because using nonutilitarian decision rules in private life produces more utility. The fact that he is unwilling to reject esoteric morality in principle but rather treats it as an empirical question points in this direction. If so, the comments in the next section on disjunctive consequentialism would apply to him as well. Alternatively, Goodin could be using a strategy similar to Hooker's (see below), arguing for a version of consequentialism based on its acceptability to nonutilitarian moral intuitions. The tone of the two chapters mentioned in his book fits with that theme, and if that is his strategy the comments made in the section discussing Hooker would apply here as well.

For present purposes, Goodin is important because his rhetorical strategy is simply to disregard defending utilitarianism outside of legislative contexts and instead defend it from within them, thus eliminating the problematic need for a counterfactual perspectival shift. I will argue in the next chapter that Goodin is right – that the reasons for assuming the legislative perspective are stronger in political than in apolitical contexts, but that the argument for why this is the case is stronger if we acknowledge nonconsequentialist reasons when explaining the greater weight of the legislative point of view in public contexts. Moreover, once we acknowledge these reasons, we cannot simply assume that, while they can be invoked to justify the shift to the legislative perspective, they should then be set aside while we employ purely consequentialist considerations to work out the content of the rules or principles that inform what is right or wrong.

Conrad Johnson, in his book *Moral Legislation: A Legal-Political Model for Indirect Consequentialist Reasoning*, argues that we have good reasons to think that rules that are justified on consequentialist grounds define what is right and wrong. His approach is also restrictive, focusing on actual institutions. Unlike Goodin, he focuses on the perspective of the private person, not the policy maker. His argument is about the claims that widely accepted rules make on us, and he explicitly rejects the idea that counterfactual rules, rules that would be beneficial if they were adopted, are important for determining what is right. He thus shows how one can use a restricted strategy not to restrict the contexts of application (since his examples include the moral rules of individuals in everyday decision-making) but instead to reject deliberative strategies that are counterfactual versions of the legislative point of view.

According to Johnson, individuals who always claim permission to depart from the rules when doing so could create still greater benefits undermine the benefits of having the rule. Rules allow for mutual trust and reliance, but they require "that everyone abdicates title to engage in unlimited individual maximization" (Johnson 1991, 7) to achieve this. In

Johnson's formulation, the legislative perspective can determine what is right and wrong and restrict our individual actions, but it never does so counterfactually. Rather, his argument is that if a rule or practice already exists and is accepted, we can have reason, as consequentialists, to allow that rule to define what is right rather than understanding right to be defined from the situated perspective. He is suspicious of disjunction strategies, which will be discussed in the next section. He thinks that, practically speaking, to acknowledge something as right is to commend doing it. Moral rules for him are not mere decision rules that help us get to the right answer more often, but actually define what is right if there is an existing practice that is justified on consequentialist grounds. His position differs from more typical rule-consequentialism, which defines what is right in accord with the rule that would be best if it were adopted, and instead looks only at rules that have already been adopted. What he calls the "Moral Legislation model" is an approach that "represents *existing* rules as right-defining under certain conditions" (Johnson 1991, 118, my emphasis).

Johnson is right that there are some benefits of the legislative perspective that are only attained when there is an existing rule or practice. Like Hume, Johnson sees the value of known rules and practices and of adhering to rules even in cases where the underlying rationale for the rule does not hold, not because of deontological reasons but because of certain brute facts about human psychology (Johnson 1991, 59–64). These brute facts (such as our desire for assurance as to what others will do and our tendency to depart from rules too often and in self-serving ways), when combined with a consequentialist commitment to produce the best outcome, give us reasons to act according to the rule in question. Some of these brute facts, however, apply just as much to decision-making when there is not an already established rule as to cases where there is. If we can use these considerations to determine whether or not a rule is, on the whole, good in its consequences and thus worthy of our support, we can use the same considerations to evaluate and propose rules.

Johnson's main hesitation about this is a worry that it will be used to justify individualistic deviation from rules, and we would lose the benefits of having a shared rule that is recognized as binding. It is right and proper to revise our moral and legal codes, but there needs to be a real separation of the legislative and executive modes, so to speak. If we can convince enough of our fellow citizens to adopt the new rule, it will no longer be hypothetical, and we can take it as our new basis. Until then, while we may legislatively engage in advocacy we must, in the meantime, submit to the rules that are already existent. This reveals that Johnson's main concern is with how binding moral rules are. He does not actually provide an argument against using the legislative point of view to determine what rules to advocate for, including moral rules along the lines of the "moral expression as legislation" position that was popular with nineteenth-century utilitarians. He provides an argument for why consequentialist rules that are already widely accepted are binding even in exceptional cases, and in this he sidesteps one part of the counterfactual problem: he never has to imagine obeying a rule that exists only counterfactually. He does not, however, propose an argument either for or against a more expansive use of the legislative perspective in cases where no rule exists or where we are in trying to decide which rule to advocate for.

Johnson's position assumes an all or nothing weight to the dictates of rules. If we are free to make individualized judgments about whether to depart from the rules, the whole system unravels. Our final example of the institutional approach, that of Frederick Schauer, challenges this assumption. In his book *Playing by the Rules: A Philosophical Examination of Rule-Based Decision-Making in Law and in Life*, Schauer differentiates four ways of thinking about rules (Schauer 1991, 93–100). Pure particularism (1) ignores rules whenever the background considerations that justified the original adoption of the rule no longer apply. Rules can still be used as rough guides or time-saving devices, but it is rule-worship to obey a rule in exceptional cases where following the rule undermines the objective of adopting the rule in the first place. Rule-sensitive particularism (2) gives more weight than particularism to rules because it acknowledges that our actions impact rules and moral norms and that this must be taken into account. If my failure to follow a rule will affect the future behavior of others, as a consequentialist I must consider this before deviating from a widely accepted rule, particularly if doing so is likely to encourage behavior that has negative consequences or undermines trust in a valuable norm. Schauer wants to go one step further to what he calls "presumptive positivism" (3). This allocates more weight to rules than rule-sensitive particularism but less than the option that gives rules absolute weight (4). Under presumptive positivism (3), you depart from the rule not just when you think it is harmful (including harms to future decision-making by yourself or others), but on more compelling grounds. This amounts to something like a "compelling interest test" in the law where one must be quite confident that breaking the rule is justified before doing so. One might require a high likelihood that breaking the rule will produce significantly less harm than following it. Schauer thinks this greater adherence to rules is a good thing but wants to stop short of rule absolut-ism, which he finds difficult to justify in a theory that has a substantial consequentialist aspect. It is difficult to explain why you must abide by a rule in an exceptional case if following it, for example, leads to the extinction of human life.

Schauer's reason for wanting to give rules this degree of weight is that there are both advantages and disadvantages to rule-based decision-making. Rules force us to consider only some of the morally relevant features of a situation rather than all of them. Doing so has a cost, as illustrated in the standard rule-worship examples, because in those cases morally relevant information is ignored when we follow the rule anyway. But rule-following can also have benefits. Sometimes we are more likely to arrive at the right action by following a rule than by engaging in "all things considered" particularistic decision-making. Rules speed up decision-making and thus reduce costs. Rules increase reliance, predictability, and certainty and thus help us coordinate our actions with others. These reasons are sufficient to justify the shift from particularism to rule-sensitive particularism, but not to presumptive positivism. A rule-sensitive particularist can give weight to rules for all of the above reasons. To justify a stronger shift, we need to note that there are other reasons for preferring rule-based decision-making than the aforementioned. Schauer argues that we use rules, not only to make decisions, but also to allocate power both institutionally and chronologically. Rules grant to some people, rather than others, the right to make certain decisions. Thus, there are special reasons to emphasize rules that apply to a person who is a "designer of a decision-making environment" (Schauer 1991, 98). Such a person is not merely creating rules but setting the parameters for who is authorized to make rules for others. We can give greater weight to rules because we want the ability to allocate power and jurisdiction.

By restricting his argument to those who are constructing decision-making environments, Schauer is acknowledging that the stronger forms of the legislative point of view are restricted to people who are actually in a legislative context, designing rules and institutions. That is why I classify his approach as one that focuses on institutionalized expressions rather than counterfactual ones. Thus, there can be asymmetries when we com-pare the perspective of the legislator with the perspective of the ordinary citizen. Since Schauer's position provides only a strong presumption for following the rules rather than an absolute obligation, citizens and officials may, at times, rightly break the rules. It does not follow, however, that the law must grant exemptions from punishments in those cases. Actual legislators may think that a rule giving such exemptions would encourage so much deviation from the rule that the exemption would lead to more harm than benefit. Schauer comes close to advocating for the sort of esoteric morality that we will examine in the next section but stops short. He does not claim that those with high levels of wisdom or insight should promulgate moral doctrines they know to be incorrect. He assumes the same knowledge about what is right and wrong is available to all. Instead, he reasons that since it is difficult psychologically to punish people when they have broken a rule rightly and produced good consequences, the better option is to have severe punishments for breaking the rule that apply only in cases where bad consequences follow from breaking the rule. Such a rule would reinforce presumptive positivism by giving us an extra incentive to be extremely sure we are right before breaking the rules (Schauer 1991, 133).

In the end, Schauer, like the others in this section, sees value in rules but does not provide an argument for the extension of the legislative point of view to nonlegislative contexts or for using counterfactual versions of the legislative perspective to guide action.

Since I have already talked about the benefits of rule-based decision-making in legislative contexts, let me close this section by noting a fundamental cost of rejecting the legislative point of view in nonlegislative contexts. Public officials can find themselves in situations where they have discretionary power and where their use of that power will not create a precedent. A counterfactual use of the legislative perspective could still be helpful in such circumstances. Consider a state contemplating a preemptive strike against another country. The actions of one country in one instance will not by itself change the international norm. The best estimates might indicate that the benefits to be gained by a preemptive strike, in this instance, outweigh the costs (including the cost of a weakened norm). A rule-sensitive particularist should consider how one's action will affect the prevailing norm, but in this case the impact of one violation of the principle seems negligible. If the state was in a position to think of itself as credibly designing a system of rules, that would provide a reason to think in these terms, but the state is not in such a legislative context. Perhaps the rule-sensitive particularist could argue that cases of preemptive strike are classic instances where particularistic decision-making by the actor in question is less likely to arrive at the right decision than rule-based decision-making given that reasons of self-interest can often cloud a state's judgment about whether the strike is truly necessary. This seems like a valid argument for abiding by an internationally recognized rule even if violating the rule will not significantly discredit the rule. But it seems like there is value in pushing further and arguing that even in the absence of an existing international rule a state should consider what rule, counterfactually, would be best to regulate the decisions not only of itself but of other countries considering preemptive strikes. In the next chapter I will present more of the positive case for such counterfactual deliberation. The arguments become even stronger in cases where we consider actions that are easier to keep secret than preemptive military strikes. If the action is truly secret, there is no harm to the underlying norm. In the original theological version of the legislative perspective, this problem was avoided because the authors assumed the existence of a God who sees what is done in secret and judges conduct according to known rules.

The general theme of these strategies is that they try to realize as many of the benefits of rules and the legislative perspective as possible without actually saying that counterfactual uses of the legislative perspective are relevant for determining actual standards of right and wrong. In some cases, they simply specify that consequentialism is defensible in legislative contexts as a public philosophy rather than in private contexts and in doing so simply set aside the interesting cases where it might be helpful to use the legislative point of view in nonlegislative contexts. In other cases, they focus on why consequentially beneficial rules are binding even in cases where deviation from the rules could be even more beneficial. While Johnson and Schauer disagree about how much weight the rules should be given, both of them construct arguments that hinge on the actual existence of rules rather than counterfactual reasoning about what the rules should be. The institutionalist consequentialism strategy does not, therefore, provide a defense of the paradoxical shift to the counterfactual legislative point of view. It is, rather, a retreat from it.

Disjunctive Consequentialism: Separating Moral Rules and Moral Right

A second contemporary approach acknowledges the value of the legislative perspective in nonpublic situations and tries to avoid the rule-consequentialist paradox by denying that the useful moral rules we publicly affirm (and perhaps act upon) are actually the standard of right and wrong. This approach typically embraces what Schauer termed "rule-sensitive particularism." Individuals cannot possibly calculate the probable consequences of the various options open to them each time they face a decision.

Moral rules greatly simplify decision-making, lowering costs. The rules can also be constructed to account for the likely biases of those making the decisions, reducing the number of wrong decisions in the aggregate, even if not in every instance. Rules are also very helpful for coordinating behavior. Many actions that are relatively harmless if done by one person can be very harmful if done by many. People have greater security if they can reliably predict that others will respect shared moral norms. Given these advantages for rule-based decision-making, a consequentialist could argue that, on consequentialist grounds, one's choices should normally be guided by rules justified from a legislative point of view even though the ultimate standard of right and wrong is actual consequences and may diverge from the publicly affirmed rules.

There are actually three disjunctions to discuss in this section. One is a disjunction between a decision procedure and the standard of right. I may adopt a rule to guide my decision-making even though I know it tracks imperfectly with the standard of right and that I could try to follow the standard of right directly. If my goal is simply to produce the best consequences possible, I can evaluate the two decision procedures on consequentialist grounds and choose the procedure that will yield the best outcomes and this need not be the decision procedure of always acting directly on the principle "maximize happiness" or "produce the best consequences." Once we have affirmed this distinction on consequentialist grounds, it is difficult to avoid affirming a second disjunction between what we know about what is actually right and the decision-rule we recommend that others follow. This second disjunction simply moves from a first-person application to a second-person application. If decision-rules and standards of right can be separated and consequentialism is the standard for making decisions, then if commending an indirect decision-rule to others produces better consequences than if they act on the principle "produce the best consequences" then we should do so.

These two disjunctions then lead to the third and most problematic one. It is psychologically difficult to condemn actions we know are actually right and to praise actions that are actually wrong. It can also be difficult to adhere to a decision procedure when one strongly suspects that it is diverging from the true standard of what is right. One way of addressing this is for most people to think that the decision-rule actually is the standard of right while only a few people are aware the above disjunctions actually exist. Additionally, since people differ in their intelligence, moral knowledge, moral judgment, and character, it does not automatically follow that everyone must use the same decision procedure. Those who have greater knowledge may be able to maximize consequences more effectively by allowing themselves more permission to depart from the publicly affirmed norms than they would grant others. Whereas in the second disjunction I encourage others to follow the same decision procedure that I follow, in the third there are two (or more) sets of decision procedures for different people. Some will likely think that the decision-rule they have been taught is the standard of right for everyone, even if it is not. Believing this would make it psychologically easier to follow the rule.

We outlined the impressive historical roots for the disjunctive approach and the reasons why the logic of pure consequentialism leads to embracing all three disjunctions in previous chapters. Mill thought that the direct pursuit of happiness was self-defeating and that alternative decision procedures could be justified on consequentialist grounds if the latter, on average, led to better consequences. We have seen that Sidgwick openly advocated for an esoteric morality and would have affirmed the validity of all three disjunctions. Making moral statements is an act, and if acts are judged by their consequences then the right thing to do, in principle, is to mislead people about morality if doing so gets them to internalize moral beliefs that in practice produce better consequences than simply teaching them consequentialism.

Katarzyna de Lazari-Radek and Peter Singer (2014) provide a contemporary defense of Sidgwick's approach. They acknowledge that this means that this entails a publicity requirement (that we act on moral rules that we would want to be publicly known). For example, Lazari-Radek and Singer believe that consequentialism requires people to make far larger contributions to the global poor than they are likely to make. If most people in rich countries were told they must sell almost everything and give it to the poor, most would ignore the instruction completely. If setting a more moderate standard leads to more money going to the global poor, that is reason enough to advocate for the more moderate standard (Lazari-Radek and Singer 2014, 295). If permission to use torture will be frequently misused, it may be right to teach people that torture is always wrong even though, on consequentialist grounds, this is not true (296).

This approach has long had its critics. Bernard Williams criticized this view for the sort of divided self that it leads to, as I must separate my public moral proclamation from my private views of right and wrong. (This is in addition to his criticisms of the way utilitarianism overrides our projects and commitments in a particularly objectionable way.) If consequentialism supports inculcating beliefs that truth-telling is right for reasons that go beyond consequentialism, can we really maintain both views in the same person? And if the alternative is dividing society into two groups, only one of which is privy to the truth about right and wrong, this is disturbing as well (Williams 1985, 107–10). As a public philosophy it risks self-serving behavior by those who inculcate as true in others what they themselves believe to be useful but false. At a private level it may be psychologically impossible to relate to the moral code in the necessary way if one knows that it is not actually the standard of right. While one can logically separate decision procedures and theories of right, it may be very hard to do this psychologically, and consequentialist theories cannot just dismiss the way psychology impacts actual practice.

An important factor here is whether the publicity condition defended by Rawls (1971) and Gert (2005) is important for reasons that are not fully captured by consequentialism. Unless one is willing to claim that it is, the disjunction strategy we are describing culminates in Lazari-Radek and Singer's conclusion, unappealing though it will be to most. Perhaps thinking of ourselves as under a moral law that is publicly shared with others expresses values of a Kantian nature that are important apart from the practical benefits of publicity. There are certainly reasons that are available for blocking all three of the disjunctions and especially the last. These reasons, some of which will be discussed in the next chapter, are nonconsequentialist reasons.

The disjunction strategy is needed precisely because there is no moral authority that governs by rules and sees what is done in secret, as was assumed in the earlier historical theories. The disjunction strategy can salvage some of the benefits of the legislative point of view but only at the cost of rendering the strategy either elitist or psychologically implausible. In a sense, the problem is the same as with institutional consequentialism. Both positions resist invoking the legislative point of view counterfactually. Both strategies can apply the legislative point of view to the question of which norms we should persuade others to internalize and accept. The difference is that the former strategy works by simple restriction of scope while the latter position works by separating decision procedures about what to do and what to commend from the actual standard of right.

One part of the psychological difficulty comes from a sort of infinite regress problem. Suppose I advocate for a moral rule because I know people, in the absence of the rule, will make poor choices because they are biased in their own favor. Suppose I then confront a situation where the rule seems to restrict me from doing what I think will be best overall. I then ask whether my assessment that I can produce better consequences by breaking the rule might be biased. That, after all, was the original reason for using the rule rather than direct consequentialism as the decision procedure. I then ask whether all people are equally biased and equally in need of the restriction. I then ask whether I may be biased in my assessment of whether I am less biased than most people, and so on. This whole line of thought is necessary because there is not actually a legislator who legislates for cases like the one I am deliberating about. A decision procedure that I select because I think it will lead to good consequences does not have the same authority as an actual rule promulgated by a moral authority. The further I get from contexts where my decision actually creates a new rule (perhaps because my opinion about moral rules is only one opinion among millions, perhaps because my action will be secret), the less fitting the legislative point of view seems.

A different way of exploring the problem is to recall, as noted in the Introduction, that we can think about conceptions of rationality as including an account of the perspective from which rational deliberation begins. A consequentialist theory understands rational deliberation to rank alternatives based on the expected value of their consequences. If I am an individual facing a specific decision, and the decision is not about a legislative matter, rationality seems to dictate that I make the decision that leads to the best consequences. This approach leads to something analogous to a collective action problem. In a collective action problem, rational decision makers can end up with suboptimal outcomes even though they are aware of what is happening and why. Each fisherman can see that it would be better if everyone complied with a rule to not overfish, but, in the absence of such a rule, the rational thing for each fisherman to do is to overfish. The fisherman knows that his overfishing contributes to a problem that will ultimately harm him, but in the absence of a coordinating norm the decision he faces is individual and situated, not legislative. Abiding by the norm while others do not would, from a situated perspective, be irrational. The fish supply will be depleted either way, but he will be poorer in the short term if he restricts his fishing.

Pure consequentialism leads to an altruistic version of the same problem. A group of altruists could agree that we would have better overall consequences if everyone abided by a given rule, but awareness of this is not enough to render it rational for those altruists individually to act on that rule if no one has actually legislated it. In some cases where our actions are sufficiently public and our interactions with others recur frequently this problem might be overcome. But in cases where we can keep our actions secret, it will not be obvious why one should shift from the situated perspective to the legislative perspective. This is also true in cases where the benefits of breaking the rule are high because our single action will not make a significant difference to whether the rule is upheld or is breached by others. Even if a consequentialist can see that everyone adopting a nonconsequentialist decision procedure would lead to better consequences, that does not mean that consequentialist individuals will act rationally if they use the nonconsequentialist decision procedure. If I embrace a consequentialist theory of rationality and the choice I face is individual and situated, the rational course of action may lead to a suboptimal outcome.

The disjunction strategy can account for much of the value of rules, as can the rule-sensitive particularism of Schauer that we discussed in the previous section, but it cannot account for the truly counterfactual use of the legislative point of view. If it could, the esoteric morality would not take hold since, as we will see in the next chapter, the legislative point of view can be defended and specified such that publicity is one of its requirements. Absent nonconsequentialist reasoning, the disjunctive strategy leads to the conclusion of esoteric morality. It naturally leads to viewing moral pronouncements as a kind of legislative activity subject to its own distinct calculation, which can differ from the calculation about what one should do in a particular case, particularly in cases where one's actions will remain secret. To continue to abide by the rule in cases where it seems clear that breaking it would produce better consequences in order to avoid esoteric morality is to partake of the rule-worship for which rule-utilitarians were criticized. Since you are not forming a rule that others would follow, indirect decision rules will have their limits. This is not a logically contradictory position, but it is psychologically difficult and morally troubling. A decision-rule that I know does not track with the actual standard of right may not hold the same authority as one does that is understood to coincide with right and wrong. Rules designed to counteract systematic overestimates of our own abilities cause strain if the theory allows us to give more leeway to ourselves than we do to others.

Rawlsian Rule-Consequentialism: Brad Hooker

As noted in Chapter 5, some of the late twentieth-century rule-consequentialists tried to overcome the paradox by appealing to moral considerations independent of consequentialism. The most prominent contemporary version of this approach is Brad Hooker's rule-consequentialism (Hooker 2000). His thought combines elements from

R. M. Hare and Richard Brandt. Both Hare and Brandt, as noted in the previous chapter, acknowledge debts to nonutilitarian sources. What moral code would be chosen by persons who have successfully overcome various forms of irrationality? Brandt argues that they would choose a code based on some version of utilitarianism. Brad Hooker takes a similar view of what a "moral code" is, as we will see, while also borrowing from Rawls. In Hooker's case he defends rule-consequentialism as the theory that would be chosen using Rawls' method of reflective equilibrium. In this section I focus on Hooker as the best example of an approach that tries to justify the shift to a consequentialist legislative perspective by appealing to nonconsequentialist considerations.

Hooker argues that we should define what is right based on what accords with the moral code that would produce the best consequences, accounting for the costs of getting high levels of societal commitment to the principle. He thinks the strength of such a code is that it can account for many of our existing moral beliefs while also credibly helping us solve moral dilemmas. In other words, a crucial part of the case for his rule-consequentialism is that it yields more attractive ethical outcomes than other competing approaches.

In order for him to arrive at attractive results, he specifies his theory, as Brandt had done, in a way that draws very heavily on the legislative metaphor. To know what is right I must enter the legislative chamber, so to speak. I imagine myself proposing a moral code that is akin to a law. I must ask myself all the same questions that an actual legislator would need to ask: how hard will it be to gain sufficient support from others to get this change to the accepted code adopted? How hard will it be to get people to comply with the code once adopted? How will different people interpret the code differently? How much will increased complexity in a code make it harder to follow? How might the code be misapplied in practice? These are precisely the questions that legislators ask, and Hooker's approach to morality requires people to ask these same questions in situations where they are not, in fact, legislators.

What is of present interest in this approach is that its main attraction is that it can better match most people's moral judgments while still providing a theoretical explanation for those judgments and giving guidance on difficult moral questions. It achieves this by insisting that we act according to a code that an ideal legislator would propose for human beings as they are, given their various limitations (selfishness, bias, laziness, etc.). Hooker thus needs to answer the recurring objection: why should one act on such principles given the certain knowledge that often one is not legislating for others when one acts on a principle? What justifies the perspectival shift from that of a situated agent looking at actual circumstances and probable consequences of a particular decision to that of a legislator with the power to impose a code on other people when one does not have that power? Hooker answers this objection using Rawls' influential method of "reflective equilibrium" in which we select principles based, in part, on how they are able to account for our considered moral judgements about particular cases. In some cases we adjust our judgments about particular cases and in other instances we adjust our principles depending on the relative strength of our considered moral judgments about each case (Hooker 2000, 9–23). Hooker argues that rule-consequentialism is superior to both act-utilitarianism and Kantianism because it better accounts for our considered moral judgments. Most people give much more weight in their moral judgments to consequences than Kantians do, and rule-consequentialism can account for this. Compared with act-consequentialism, rule-based versions can provide a more straightforward explanation for why we should respect the rights of others even in instances where those rights could be secretly violated and produce better consequences.

Hooker's specific formulation is carefully crafted to avoid the most common objections against rule-consequentialism.

> RULE-CONSEQUENTIALISM: An act is wrong if and only if it is forbidden by the code of rules whose internalization by the overwhelming majority of everyone everywhere in each new generation has maximum expected value in terms of well-being (with some priority for the worst off). The calculation of a code's expected value includes all costs of getting the code internalized. If in terms of expected value two or more codes are better than the rest but equal to one another, the one closest to conventional morality determines what acts are wrong. (Hooker 2000, 32)

It avoids the paradox, as noted above, by relying on reflective equilibrium rather than consequentialism to justify the approach as a whole. Thus, if we say "but couldn't you produce even better consequences if you broke the rules sometimes?" he can respond that the decision procedure was not selected on consequentialist grounds. Hooker avoids several other objections by specifying that right actions track with an "ideal code" that includes the costs of getting that code "internalized" by around 90 percent of the population. This avoids the objection that rule-consequentialism will collapse into act-consequentialism because we will generate incredibly complex rules that functionally mimic the act position. Very complex codes are ruled out because it would be either impossible or prohibitively costly to bring 90 percent of the population to internalize such a code. The problem of overdemandingness is also dealt with through this device. Given the strength of natural drives and moral judgments in favor of some forms of partiality toward friends and family, it is better to have rules that accommodate these rather than go through the very costly (and perhaps impossible) steps needed to bring 90 percent of the population to the place where they accept moral rules that tell them their drowning spouses are entitled to no more concern than drowning strangers (Hooker 2000, 75–85). Hooker calls his approach consequentialist rather than utilitarian because he thinks the rules better square with our moral convictions if equality is one of the considerations used to rank possible outcomes independent of average or total utility (55–65).

Although it is beside the main point of the current book (because it relates to the already extensively discussed question of moral obligation rather than the less discussed question of what justifies the perspectival shift), I will briefly note an interesting problem with this approach that we might call endogeneity. Reflective equilibrium approaches depend on our considered moral judgments about both principles and specific cases, but if those moral judgments depend on brute facts about human psychology or western history this raises interesting questions. Hume, we have seen, thought it was simply a fact about human psychology that rule-based thinking seems to better square with our moral judgments. Today one might try to provide an evolutionary explanation for why this is so. But if we think that the reason rule-based thinking fits our moral judgments better is explained by the fact that it gave our ancient ancestors an advantage in the race to produce viable offspring, we might question whether to view such moral judgments as generating obligations. Alternatively, if rule-based moral reasoning fits our considered moral judgments better than act-by-act reasoning due to historical inertia (contemporary sensibilities, though more secular, are nonetheless shaped by a history of thinking about morality in terms of divine law) it raises similar questions for those who think the theology of those earlier thinkers misguided. These are questions that the earlier theological theories did not face because they assumed that our faculties were designed by God in such a way that we could use them to correctly track with morality, although, of course, those theories faced the alternate challenge of justifying those beliefs about God and about divinely anchored moral obligations.

For present purposes, the more important objection to Hooker concerns whether nonconsequentialist commitments should play a larger role in his theory than they do. When we use the method of reflective equilibrium, there is no a priori restriction on our moral judgments and so there is nothing to prevent our intuitive sense of fairness, for example, from explaining why we prefer one moral theory's conclusions to another. In Hooker's articles that preceded *Ideal Code*, he advocated for a version of consequentialism where fairness itself was one of the goals by which a code of rules should be assessed. In *Ideal Code*, he backtracked from that claim, as will be discussed below. Nonetheless it is significant in terms of what it tells us about his approach – he was consciously trying to stretch the boundaries of what counts as consequentialism.

In his book, Hooker retreats from his initial claim by saying that competing moral codes should be measured in terms of aggregate well-being with a preference for equality. Yet nonconsequentialist considerations are arguably in play in two different ways. First, he admits that aggregate well-being should be weighted to coincide with a priority for the least well off. He presents this as an alternative to directly invoking fairness, and, while inequality is less contested in what it means than is fairness, it is hard to avoid suspecting that substantive (nonconsequentialist) beliefs about fairness are what motivate including the stipulation in the first place. Utilitarians normally justify redistribution to the poor based on the increased marginal benefit that a poor person receives from a sum of money relative to the marginal loss to a rich person who loses that same sum of money. The introduction of an additional equality consideration when selecting moral rules signals that something other than utilitarian considerations are needed to correspond with our considered moral judgments. The most plausible explanation is that we not only think that inequalities make the poor a more efficient utility investment than the rich, but that we also think inequality creates unfair differences in opportunities or outcomes. Rawls, of course, utilized considerations of fairness in his use of reflective equilibrium and it seems likely that Hooker does too, although he arrives at different conclusions about how much inequality is permissible.

A second instance of nonconsequentialist thinking is Hooker's discussion of discrepancies between the ideal code of morality and the currently accepted code of morality. Hooker thinks we should act on the ideal code but believes this needs to be qualified: we should not act on the ideal code in cases where it would lead to a disaster or to significant unfairness (Hooker 2000, 121–4). Although one might be able to define a disaster in purely consequentialist terms as an event that involves massive decreases in human welfare, "significant unfairness" cannot be explicated in a similar way. The need to add this phrase, in addition to the disaster exception, again seems to be a clear signal that nonconsequentialist considerations are at work. Here again, in order to more closely fit with our moral judgments, nonconsequentialist considerations seem to work their way into the actual content of the theory.

At this point I should acknowledge a terminological problem in the above argument. I am assuming above that if we invoke a notion of fairness such as "giving each person what they deserve" that a nonconsequentialist norm of desert has been introduced into the theory. On the other hand, some consequentialists could reply that there is no problem in including such elements in a consequentialist theory (Pettit 1989). We could have a consequentialism of desert, for example, where outcomes are ranked based on the extent to which people get what they deserve, and we select rules that maximize that outcome of people getting what they deserve. Or, alternatively, we could decide that torture should be rejected so strongly that we select rules that are chosen because they minimize instance of torture or even minimize cases where people are morally obliged to commit acts of torture. If my torturing one person would prevent ten people from torturing or being tortured, a minimize-torture consequentialist would affirm my act of torture. In other words, all of these things can be redescribed as a type of outcome and therefore the object of consequentialist maximization. The argument I am making does not hold against those who define consequentialism so capaciously and who also embrace the legislative point of view. In a sense, the next chapter is providing a framework precisely to enable more capacious understandings of what a legislator might consider a morally good outcome. Hooker, however, is not defending that position and represents a significant school of thought where consequentialism involves some, but less extensive, departure from utilitarianism.

Hooker is aware that there is another approach that can also claim a high degree of fit with our considered moral judgments – Ross-style pluralism. If there is a plurality of prima facie moral duties and we use something like moral intuition to assess their relative strength, we can arrive at a system that will fit our considered moral judgments closely. Hooker thinks that his approach is superior to pluralism in that it can give a more systematic account of our moral judgments and provide more guidance in cases involving unresolved moral issues (Hooker 2000, 104–7). Instead of simply saying we must use judgment in choosing among prima facie duties when they conflict, he thinks we have a theory to tell us how much weight each duty should be ascribed: as much as is compatible with a code that maximizes aggregate well-being.

Pluralists can argue that, given the way nonconsequentialist commitments are used to justify the theory and modify it so that it arrives at more intuitively acceptable outcomes, it would be strange to think that those same nonconsequentialist considerations should not operate more directly in making actual decisions. Hooker allows nonconsequentialist considerations of fairness into the set of reflective equilibrium considerations that justify the decision to think in terms of rules rather than on an act-by-act basis. He then allows these considerations in again by incorporating equality (and likely fairness) into the definition of what counts as a good outcome and still again when listing circumstances where we could justify an exception to the rules. Given all of these exceptions, it is not clear that there are strong reasons against more thoroughly including nonconsequentialist elements into the theory. This pushes us back toward pluralist theories that rely more directly on nonconsequentialist premises rather than incorporating them indirectly through the use of reflective equilibrium and commonly held moral judgments (Dale Miller 2013; Montague 2000). The approach I will describe in Chapter 7 has affinities with Hooker's position in its use of appeals to reflective-equilibrium-style arguments, but it opens the door to a more extensive incorporation of nonconsequentialist elements (or, if you prefer, very capacious understandings of consequentialism) that shape the rules that are selected from the legislative point of view and the extent to which those rules are decisive for determining what is right.

Kantians and the Legislative Point of View: Hill and Parfit

While the historical survey in this book focused on approaches that were at least partly consequentialist, it is well known that Kant also used legislative metaphors for thinking about morality. He thought we should consider whether our maxims can be thought of as a universal law and told us to think of ourselves as legislating members of a kingdom of ends (Kant G, 16). What is interesting about Kantian approaches is that they explain the shift to the legislative perspective more directly. If we have independent reasons for thinking that morality is expressed in universal laws, that we should think of ourselves and others as having equal and reciprocal standing to act as moral agents thinking about these questions, and that acting on moral principles that can be justified from this perspective is a way of respecting the dignity of others, we have the building blocks for explaining why the shift to a legislative point of view is reasonable, even though the decisions reached within the legislative point of view may be quite different than in a more consequentialist theory.

There are different Kantian versions of the legislative perspective that include some consequentialist elements.[1] I will focus first on Thomas Hill's version and then on Derek Parfit's Kantian turn in *On What Matters*. Hill writes:

> In several previous essays, I have sketched an alternative way of thinking about moral rules drawn from Kant's idea of ideal moral legislation in a "kingdom of ends." The main idea is that everyday decision-making should be guided and constrained by rules (mid-level principles) that would be endorsed by rational moral "legislators" who deliberate under specified conditions, including autonomy and respect for humanity as an end in itself. As in RU [rule-utilitarianism], deliberation about moral rules must take into account reasons for and against having rules with respect to various areas of life, but in the Kantian alternative these reasons are not fixed by an over-arching concern to maximize utility. Consequences matter, but only in ways prescribed and limited by the Kantian values stipulated in the legislative framework. (Hill 2012, 217–18)

Notice first that in his theory the scope is not limited to public affairs, it applies to "everyday decision-making" and that moral rules arrived at through a legislative approach guide us in those decisions. Notice second that the goal of the legislator need not be the maximization of utility. In both of these respects, Hill's approach is parallel to many of the seventeenth- and eighteenth-century thinkers we have studied.

Our interest in Hill's approach is not primarily to decide whether it is the right interpretation of Kant or whether it is, in the end, persuasive. Rather, it is to show how the introduction of nonconsequentialist commitments can provide an alternative way to ground the legislative point of view. Kantians can derive a commitment to publicity from their interpretation of the duty to show respect for humanity. Seeing both myself and others as mutual participants in a shared framework of moral rules is one way of expressing respect. The commitment to respecting autonomy can be used to argue that moral agents must know the moral rules that they and others must follow. Thus, a Kantian approach can arguably provide

---

[1] David Cummiskey, for example, argues that Kant's own argument actually points to a consequentialist interpretation of his theory because a commitment to human dignity as priceless does not mean we can't say that preserving the dignity of two is not better than preserving the dignity of one (Cummiskey 1996). In his theory, Kantian values structure deliberation in terms of universal laws, but he allows room for consequentialist reasoning in the selection of those laws.

grounds for three of the key assumptions of the counterfactual legislative perspective that are difficult to sustain on purely consequentialist grounds: 1) a scope of application that includes everyday decision-making, 2) a generality requirement that gives shared moral rules a prominent place in moral deliberation, and 3) a publicity requirement that the principles adopted be publicly known.

Another element of the legislative point of view has to do with altering the content of the rules in view of possible noncompliance and misapplication of the rule. My argument in this book assumes that a theory need not be wholly consequentialist, but it should be consequentialist in at least this sense. Despite the reputation for recalcitrance that Kantians have on this point, in his version of Kantianism, Hill is willing to go some distance in this direction as well. In a discussion of terrorism where he considers a general permission that might be given to authorities to risk killing one innocent person in order to save more than one, he gives as one reason for rejecting such a rule from the legislative point of view the fact that it would invite abuse (Hill 1992, 216).

Interestingly, the previous chapter noted variations on this approach in the work of a number of thinkers. They were more utilitarian and less Kantian than Hill, but all of them acknowledged the need for nonconsequentialist commitments to ground the shift to what we have called the legislative point of view. All of these hybrid positions have historically struggled to gain adherents because they are thought to share the same weakness as Ross' pluralist intuitionism. We may lack the necessary theory for knowing how to combine the consequentialist and nonconsequentialist elements of the theory.

Hill's work shows how Kantian thinking can be used to justify the shift from the question "which act?" to the question "which rule?" utilizing nonconsequentialist reasons. This style of argument will be very important in the next chapter. Nonetheless, there are reasons not to fully endorse Hill's position. Although Hill makes some accommodations to render a Kantian legislative point of view more "realistic" in the sense I specified in the Introduction, many will find that consequentialist reasoning still plays too small a role in selecting principles. He does, for example, allow us to consider abuse of a rule when deciding whether to accept that rule, which not all Kantians do. Despite this, there are reasons to think that Kantian criteria are being given too much weight in selecting the rules from the legislative point of view. The arguments made against Hooker apply in an inverse way against Hill. If Hooker's theory gains plausibility by more directly including considerations for fairness into the theory, so might Hill's gain plausibility if more traditional consequentialist concern for improving human well-being could be incorporated into his Kantian approach. It is beyond the scope of this book to try to offer a defense of this claim (namely, that approaches that mix Kantian and consequentialist considerations more fully are more attractive than approaches that skew heavily one way or the other), but I think that it is a sufficiently plausible claim that it will motivate the reader to explore, in the next chapter, a framework that allows for such theories. The main point is to note that one could accept Kantian reasons for assuming the legislative point of view while believing that those reasons are not always decisive in determining the content of the rules selected from the legislative point of view.

Derek Parfit's *On What Matters* (2011–2017) is a recent and very prominent attempt to defend a legislative approach to ethics that combines Kantianism with consequentialism (and contractualism). Parfit defends rule-consequentialism as the best moral theory, but arrives at that conclusion by way of a unique interpretation of Kant and changes to Kant's theory that he believes make the theory more tenable while still being in the spirit of Kant's project (a claim that many Kantians will reject). We saw in the previous chapter that it was actually fairly common in the mid-twentieth century for some rule-utilitarians to present their theories as hybrid theories that combined Kantian and utilitarian elements, with Kant providing a justification for framing moral questions in terms of rules that was different from what utilitarianism alone could provide. Parfit provides a much more in-depth version of this same approach, and he explicitly identifies his theory as a hybrid one. Toward the end of Volume 1 (2011), he writes:

> If Kantian Contractualism implies Rule Consequentialism, as I have claimed, that does not make the resulting view wholly Consequentialist. Though this view is Consequentialist in its claims about which principles we ought to follow, it is not Consequentialist either in its claims about *why* we ought to follow these principles, or in its claims about which *acts* are wrong. This view, we might say, is only *one-third* Consequentialist. (Parfit, 1:417–18)

If one looks only at the criteria for selecting moral rules, Parfit's theory seems fully consequentialist, but it is only one third consequentialist because he uses a combination of Kantian and Contractualist arguments to explain why we are thinking about right and wrong in terms of moral principles and why it is appropriate to apply consequentialist criteria.[2]

---

[2] Parfit stops short of claiming that there is a perfect identity between Kantian contractualism and rule-consequentialism: "There may be other cases in which these kinds of Contractualism conflict. And Kantian Contractualism may sometimes conflict with Rule Consequentialism. I believe that, in all or

Parfit spends considerable time working through different variations on Kant's approach including the formula of universal law and the prohibition on treating people as moral ends before deciding that the position that best captures Kant's underlying goals, and the one that is most defensible, is this: "Everyone ought to follow the principles whose universal acceptance everyone could rationally will, or choose" (1:378). Parfit then argues that, from an impartial perspective, we have more reason to choose these principles than any other principles. He also claims that all of us have a sufficient reason to do what is impartially best (as consequentialism recommends) and thus all of us could potentially will optimific principles to guide our conduct. We might have other reasons to not choose these principles, such as reasons of self-interest, but these reasons are not decisive.

> But in the thought-experiments to which the Kantian Formula appeals, we would *not* be choosing principles from an impartial point of view. Our choices would affect our own lives, and the lives of those other people to whom we have close ties, such as our close relatives and those we love. So we might have strong personal and partial reasons *not* to choose the optimific principles. (Parfit, 1:379)

A person could, for example, rationally choose to follow the optimific principle at great personal cost. These personal costs would provide reason to reject the principle, but not a decisive reason. Lastly, there are no nonoptimific principles "that everyone would have sufficient reason to choose" (378). Rule-consequentialism emerges as the one approach that everyone could choose, although not the one everyone would choose. This is enough for rule-consequentialism to be the moral theory selected by Kantian contractualism.

Parfit is not arguing that in deciding what principles everyone could accept that we use our existing moral intuitions or common-sense morality, because Kantian contractualism is meant to supply principles of right and wrong and not be dependent on preexisting principles. Parfit calls this prohibition on using our existing moral intuitions to decide what views can or cannot be universally accepted the "Deontic Beliefs Restriction" (1:287). Parfit does not, however, think we have to totally reject our moral intuitions.

---

nearly all important cases, everyone could rationally choose that everyone accepts some optimific principle. But there may be cases in which everyone could also rationally choose some significantly non-optimific principle" (Parfit, 2:159). He claims possible compatibility between them, not that it is impossible for a rational person who adheres to Kantian contractualism to occasionally deviate from rule-consequentialism.

If Contractualists make such claims, they can defend the Deontic Beliefs Restriction without rejecting our moral intuitions as worthless. On these versions of Contractualism, it is only while we are asking what Contractualist formulas imply that we should not appeal to our beliefs about the wrongness of the acts that we are considering. We can appeal to these beliefs at a later stage, when we are deciding whether we ought to accept these formulas. (1:370)

An important example of how this would work is Parfit's treatment of pain and suffering. He thinks that we all have nondeontic reasons to view pain as bad, as something we have reason to avoid. This is not a moral claim that we ought to avoid pain or a claim that pain is morally bad, which would violate the Deontic Beliefs Restriction, simply a claim that pain provides a reason to make the pain cease. He also believes that pain is impersonally bad, that we have a reason to choose that others not suffer that is not based on a moral obligation to minimize pain or a claim about pain's moral badness. Just as our own pain provides a reason, so does the pain of others (371–2). He thus defines "best" in the "impartial-reason-implying sense" (Parfit, 1:372). If pleasure and pain were the only things that could provide these sorts of impartial reasons, Kantian contractualism would seem to imply some form of utilitarianism. Parfit, however, seems more interested in versions of contractualism that hold to a broader set of considerations that generate nondeontic impersonal reasons. He thinks consequentialists could hold that "how well things go depends in part on how benefits and burdens are distributed between different people" (1:373). He also thinks that "The goodness of some outcomes might depend in part on facts about the past. It might be better, for example, if benefits went to people who had earlier been worse off, or if we kept our promises to those who are dead, or if people are punished only if they earlier committed some crime" (1:373–4). In these examples, distributions or relations to the past would need to give us reasons apart from the belief that inequality is wrong or that punishing the innocent is wrong.[3]

Parfit makes it clear that this Kantian approach relies upon a counterfactual thought experiment: "But in the thought-experiment to which the Kantian Formula appeals, I would have the power to choose

---

[3] "The goodness of outcomes may in part depend on other facts, such as facts about how benefits and burdens are distributed between different people, or facts that are not even about people's well-being. If everyone could rationally choose that everyone accepts some autonomy-protecting principle, this might be one of the principles whose acceptance would make things go best, even if this principle's acceptance would not on the whole best promote everyone's well-being. Rule Consequentialism need not take this Utilitarian form, or any other wholly *welfarist* form" (Parfit, 2:150–1).

which principles everyone would accept, both now and in all future centuries" (1:382). The fact that one's choice is being framed in this way is what enables Parfit to say that one has sufficient reason to choose principles that might be detrimental to one's interests or of those one cares about since one would be weighing these things against the altered course of human history where there is widespread acceptance of the principle we propose.

Parfit thinks we would not choose act-consequentialism, even though it directs us to do what is impartially best, because we would have to internalize a set of beliefs and motives in order to live as act-consequentialists that would be detrimental:

> But the good effects of everyone's acts would again be outweighed, I believe, by the ways in which it would be worse if we all had the motives that would lead us to follow AC [act-consequentialism]. As before, in losing many of our strong loves, loyalties, and personal aims, many of us would lose too much of what makes our lives worth living. So this version of the Kantian Formula does not require us to be Act Consequentialists. (Parfit, 1:406)

Parfit notes that we will need different versions of rule-consequentialism depending on whether we can expect full compliance and success in acting upon the principles that are selected. He also notes that we will need different principles in the more common case where we can expect non-compliance and mistakes:

> For example, it is one question *what we ought all ideally to do* if we suppose that we would all succeed. Our answers to this question will be our *ideal act theory*, or what some call our *full compliance theory*. It is another question what we ought to do when we know that some other people will act wrongly. Some call this our *partial compliance theory*. We can also ask what we ought to try to do when we take into account various other facts, such as facts about the mistakes that people would be likely to make, and facts about people's motives, desires, and dispositions. (Parfit, 1:407)

Here we see outright endorsement of the legislative point of view in that error and noncompliance are taken into account in selecting the principles that will bring about the best consequences.

In defending rule-consequentialism, Parfit is aware that following optimific rules will sometimes cause us to act in ways that are not optimific, creating the following dilemma.

> If we are not Act Consequentialists, we may think:
>   We could often reasonably want and hope that things will go in the ways that would be best.
>   It would often be best if some people acted wrongly.

Therefore

We could often reasonably want and hope that some people will act wrongly.

I call this the *Argument for Moral Ambivalence*. (3:349)

This dilemma arises because, for everyone except act-consequentialists, success in following our moral theory may not produce the best outcomes, for example because we are following an optimific rule in a case where things would go better if we broke the rule. In Volume 3, Parfit engages with the act-consequentialist position since he wants to avoid accepting this argument.

While he could have simply invoked the earlier Kantian argument and argued that it gives us adequate reason to abide by optimific principles even in these cases, Parfit tries instead to build an argument that would be more easily accepted by the act-consequentialist critic. He writes:

What matters most is how well things go.

Things would on the whole go best if we have optimific motives and we accept and try to follow optimific rules.

Therefore

We ought to have such motives and we ought to try to follow such rules. (3:432)

Here Parfit opts for something akin to the disjunction strategy discussed earlier in the chapter, arguing that what matters most is how well things go; things will go better if we become motive-/rule-consequentialists rather than act-consequentialists. Rule-consequentialism can better handle cases where a very large number of acts have a cumulatively large effect but an almost undetectable effect when disaggregated (Parfit, 3:421–32). He also thinks that the second premise is supported by the claim that "On some views, we ought to follow certain rules, not because we have too little time or too little evidence to make good predictions, but because we would make such predictions under some distorting influence" (3:419). This is a way of answering the charge that rule-consequentialism is, in Smart's terminology, "superstitious rule-worship." Even if we agree that what matters most is how well things go, and even if we know that acting on an optimific rule will sometimes not make things go as well as they could, we may have enough reason to think that the bias of personal benefit, for example, will make us poor judges of when it is safe to disobey the optimific rule. One ambiguity in this argument is whether accepting and following optimific rules includes believing that those rules define rightness or whether they are decision procedures we have reason to follow even though they do not define right. Hooker's Kantian argument for rule-consequentialism takes the former position, while an act-utilitarian might only affirm the argument based on the latter interpretation, leaving a gap.

His other strategy for shrinking the gap between rule- and act-consequentialism is to argue that act-consequentialists can answer some of the typical challenges to their position by including a robust account of nondeontic badness. For example, he writes of utilitarians that "Their mistake is not their belief that the numbers count, but their belief that it makes no moral difference how benefits and burdens are distributed between different people" (Parfit, 2:196). If the inequality of burdens contributes to an outcome's nondeontic badness, a consequentialist would be able to conclude that we have moral reason to prefer outcomes where this does not happen, all else being equal. Someone might believe that a person being intentionally killed is worse than being accidentally killed, or that someone being used as a means is worse than someone not being used as a means and that the explanation for this badness is the wrongness of intentional killing or using someone as a means. Parfit appreciates that this framing can explain why we would not harvest the organs of one patient to save five others while we might make a different decision if killing one patient would lead to a vaccine that could save five million. There might be enough nondeontic badness in killing the patient to outweigh the deaths of five, but not the deaths of five million.

Critics will argue that this is circular because the wrongness of the act is explaining the badness of the act and badness is also the explanation for wrongness in a consequentialist theory. Parfit denies this. An act-consequentialist could conceive of deceiving people as something that is nondeontically bad (Parfit, 3:400). For example: "It might be intrinsically bad to deceive or coerce people even when such acts would be on balance justified, or be what we ought to do, because these acts would save other people from great harm. Since these acts would be in these ways intrinsically bad though they would not be wrong, their intrinsic badness would be nondeontic" (Parfit, 3:400). These strategies could decrease the gap between act-consequentialism and other theories, including Parfit's preferred rule-consequentialism, that track more closely with common-sense morality.

The approaches of Hill and Parfit provide two contrasting examples of hybrid justifications for the legislative point of view, though they differ greatly in their content. Hill's position makes fairly small deviations from standard Kantian conclusions. He is willing to consider hypothetical generalizations about the mistakes that might be made if a principle were universally adopted but rejects consequentialist weighing of outcomes for deciding which principle should be legislated. Parfit, by contrast, uses Kantian arguments to justify a rule-consequentialist theory. I have already noted that many people will find Hill's position insufficiently consequentialist and that that gives us reason, in the following chapter, to consider ways that Kantian considerations could be used in a more consequentialist way. That critique is inapplicable to Parfit, whose theory is more likely to be rejected for being too consequentialist (as some critics in Volume 2 of *On What Matters* say) (Parfit, 2:35, 83). I conclude this chapter by differentiating my proposal outlined in the following chapter from Parfit's position.

In what follows, I adopt an approach that allows more direct appeals to our moral judgments than Parfit's Kantian contractualism allows. This is in part because I am unpersuaded that nondeontic badness can do the necessary work to justify a theory that will match closely enough with our overall moral judgments to be acceptable. Parfit is willing to allow us, in the end, to reflect on the theory that we have developed and reject it if it is too out of step with our considered moral judgments. I think we should acknowledge that many of our reasons for wanting principles that all could accept, for caring about the distribution of burdens, for preferring that innocent people not be punished, and so on, are misdescribed as nondeontic. Or, put differently, the nondeontic versions of these are likely too weak to justify an acceptable moral theory. The approach I will use in the next chapter is like Parfit's in that it combines Kantian justifications with consequentialist principles, but it does so by asking about the plausibility of the necessary premises, given our considered moral judgments. It is also a weaker version of consequentialism than Parfit's since it does not insist that only consequentialist considerations count in selecting the rules that count toward what is right or that those rules are the only things that determine what is right. It will be a weaker and more ecumenical theory that makes the case for a counterfactual legislative perspectival shift and for thinking that the resulting rules count in favor of an action's being right or wrong.

CHAPTER 7

A Hybrid Defense of the Legislative Perspective

My goal in this chapter is not to defend a particular solution to the question "What is right?" It is rather to explore the moral reasons for posing the question "What is right?" in a particular way and to show why those reasons are stronger in political than nonpolitical contexts. We have seen in the historical survey of Part I that the shift from the style of argument prominent in Locke, Cumberland, Berkeley, Shaftesbury, Hutcheson, Butler, and Paley to the style of argument in the works of Hume, Bentham, Mill, and Sidgwick was a consciously secular shift. We saw in the previous chapter that there are three main contemporary consequentialist alternatives for utilizing the legislative point of view but none of them are adequate to justify the particular form of the legislative point of view that is of interest here. The type of legislative position I am interested in justifying is moderate in its strength: it is one that factors into our beliefs about what is right rather than merely being a decision procedure, but it is not always decisive in its weight. It is realistic in that one considers the limitations and biases of actual agents rather than idealized ones in selecting the principle or rule. It is consequentialist in the weak sense that the content of the rules or principles is rightly adjusted to better achieve the morally legitimate goals of the legislator. It is counterfactual in that it asks the person to include considerations about what principle would be appropriate for some larger group than the group for which the person is actually making the decision.

The above version of the legislative perspective can be employed as a thought experiment by an individual trying to discern which action is the right action to perform because historically this is how the idea was utilized. In practice, actual legislators are more likely members of a collective legislative body than absolute monarchs who can simply enact the law of their choice. Although the legislative perspective can be monological, it will often be better employed dialogically, where we make legislative proposals to others and listen to their counter proposals, as would members of a legislative body. Since one of the strengths of the legislative point of view is its ability to account for disagreement, dialogue that utilizes the legislative point of view will normally improve legislative deliberation where possible.

My goal is not to definitively prove that we must adopt this version of the legislative point of view but instead to argue that this is a plausible moral position and that, if it is to be upheld, the defense is most likely successful if it follows the hybrid approach I describe below. I will draw upon the historical study of Part I by noting the moral commitments that informed the earlier theological versions of the legislative point of view. These commitments were a mixture of consequentialist and nonconsequentialist claims, and so the proposed theory will need to include both sorts of claims. I will specify what these claims are and then argue that in each case a secular translation of the claim is at least morally plausible and certainly worthy of consideration.

The legislative point of view is a perspective one may take when weighing questions where the general moral rule or principle that would be best has weight in determining what specific action is right. I have noted that our particular interest is in cases where this is counterfactual, and that we are concerned with the use of counterfactual deliberation both in legislative and nonlegislative contexts (see the Introduction and Chapter 6). Legislative context is a matter of degree both in terms of whether the decision context aims at rule change or maintenance and the level of efficacy an agent has to change the rules. Absolute monarchs have full power to set down the law of their choice, while a member of a legislative body may have one vote out of hundreds. The legislator is still in a more legislative context than the private citizen whose public moral statements will have a much smaller impact on the prevailing moral norms in society. The point is that this context sometimes makes the question "what rule should be adopted?" the obvious one because it is clear from the context that what you are doing is, in fact, adopting some rule. The legislators who, for campaign reasons, vote against a good bill that they know will not pass anyway are, to an extent, opting out of the legislative point of view because "what rule should be adopted?" is not really the question driving their voting. They are instead asking a different question, "Which way of voting will help me stay in office?" If they view their vote as part of a complex strategy for securing the passage of other rules that they think should be adopted on their merits, their actions are legislative in a qualified sense. There are two main implications of the above distinction. The first is that the stronger the legislative context of the decision maker, the less paradoxical it is to ask, "what rule should be adopted?" because in strongly legislative contexts there is nothing counterfactual about asking that question. Since our interest is in the more paradoxical counterfactual cases, it is to those cases that the justifications below are addressed. The second is that, as noted in the Introduction, the counterfactual use of the legislative perspective as a method of deliberation is possible in any of these contexts, even the most strongly legislative context imaginable. Whether one finds oneself in a legislative context is something of a brute fact, but the decision to adopt a counterfactual legislative perspective is always an option and it is a shift that stands in need of justification. In this chapter, I explore what that justification might look like.

The Benefits of a Hybrid Version of the Legislative Point of View

Before proceeding to explain the specific commitment needed to adopt the above version of the legislative point of view, a view I will argue likely requires a hybrid framework, it will be helpful to state more positively the reasons why such a view is attractive. Since I have argued that there are multiple versions of the legislative point of view, a fair case for the hybrid view I will present must acknowledge what is attainable by versions of the legislative point of view that are not hybrid, helping us compare the hybrid and purist approaches (whether consequentialist or nonconsequentialist).

From the foregoing analysis, we can identify some beneficial elements of the legislative point of view that are available on purely consequentialist grounds, shared with the hybrid view. We can begin with the value of rules. Sometimes the legislative point of view is not counterfactual because the question before us really is "which rules should we adopt?" This is most obviously true for actual legislators, people drafting binding regulations, or setting in place policies that will govern the workings of an institution. It is also true, however, that sometimes the question before us is what moral rules we would like our society to embrace. The view of people like J. S. Mill and Henry Sidgwick that I called "moral expression as legislation" is correct in that there will, in fact, be some kind of moral code that is taught in a society (or perhaps competing codes in societies with deep moral conflict). Given that there will be, a consequentialist can answer the question "which code?" by answering "the one that will produce the best consequences." The differences between rule-consequentialism and motive-consequentialism (or conscience-consequentialism) are not important here insofar as the latter tries to produce people who have the right sorts of moral reactions by means, in large part, of inculcating rules.

Both versions arrive at the question "what moral code do we want our society to have?" in a way that is not counterfactual.

A factual version of the legislative point of view follows naturally in this situation, and if we assume that at least part of what makes a moral code a good one is that people's lives go better because they are bound by it (as opposed to a bad code or no code), there is room for legislative framing to significantly influence how we think about that moral code. We can think about how difficult it would be to bring about widespread acceptance of a moral code, the fallibility of those who will try to live according to the code, and the characteristic biases that might impede their judgment. The moral code cannot be overly complex or it will be too costly to try to bring about its widespread acceptance. Given that limitation, there will inevitably be instances where the rules conflict, or seem to be a poor fit when applied to a very unusual situation. Here act-consequentialists (who, as we have seen, can think legislatively when the question before them is "what rule?") may note that the rules were always just rules of thumb that we use to simplify moral teaching and moral decision-making. We can resolve conflicts and ambiguities, when they occur, by direct reference to consequences. Rule-consequentialists normally include among their rules an escape clause that instructs a person to break other rules in cases where following the rule will produce great harm. Rule-consequentialists reason that our legal codes do this effectively and that our moral codes can as well (Brandt 1992, 151). Legal codes include justifications and exceptions (you may exceed the speed limit driving to the hospital in an emergency) and, in practice, moral codes do too. If I break my promise to have lunch with you because I stop to save the life of someone in a traffic accident, it is extremely unlikely that I will receive any moral censure.

Nonconsequentialists can of course object at several points. Some might deny that consequentialist criteria have any relevance in determining what moral code should be taught, but I take this to be a minority position and one that leads to rather counterintuitive conclusions (and hence a reason for rejecting the purist nonconsequentialist alternative). More common would be those who think that consequentialist reasoning needs to be restrained or modified in certain ways. For this latter group, as long as consequentialist reasoning has some role to play in the selection of the moral code, the legislative point of view will have some relevance, even if not always decisive relevance. Since my goal is to defend some weight, not necessarily decisive weight, for the legislative point of view, this latter sort of nonconsequentialist challenge can be set aside for the moment. Indeed, I will argue later in this chapter that I agree with this nonconsequentialist critique and prefer the introduction of nonconsequentialist considerations and thus favor weak consequentialism. My point here is simply to note which attractive aspects of the legislative point of view are available to a purely consequentialist approach.

If we replace the question "what codes would be best?" with the question "for which code should I advocate?" the legislative point of view will remain pertinent for strategic reasons. Moral principles are easier to inculcate in people when they have some degree of reciprocity, at least among those viewed as equals within the moral system. Publicly saying "this is the code I recommend for everyone else, but I intend to act on a different code because of my superior wisdom" is unlikely to draw significant support. Likewise, if I interpret "best" as "best for me" and advocate accordingly, I am unlikely to be an effective advocate. (There is of course the possibility of insincere advocacy, where one advocates for moral principles in part because they benefit oneself but where one looks for justifications that obscure this motivation. This is a valid concern and will factor in the discussions below.)

Thus far we have talked about the role of the legislative point of view when approaching the question "what is the moral code that my society should adopt?" What resources from the legislative point of view are available when the rather different question "what should I do?" is under consideration? We have seen that purely consequentialist positions struggle to explain why what is right is defined by the counterfactual question "what would the ideal code recommend in this case?" Nonetheless, indirect consequentialists can maintain that there are times when acting on the rules arrived at through the legislative point of view are more likely to yield better consequences than trying to act directly on the principle "maximize happiness." This might be because particularistic judgments are more likely to be self-interested or otherwise fallible. Asking the question "what rule would I want other fallible people to act on?" may be a more reliable way of accounting for one's own fallibility if we, psychologically, tend to underestimate our own bias or other cognitive limitations. Acting on the rule increases the ability of others to predict and rely upon my behavior and can help support the general acceptance of the rule. Insofar as I think using the legislative point of view helps me arrive at the action that produces the best consequences in this particular case, there is no paradox for a consequentialist to ascribe some weight to the legislative point of view when making decisions.

While these uses of the legislative point of view are available to a pure consequentialist, I think a stronger position would incorporate nonconsequentialist commitments, and so in the remainder of this section I want to lay out the general reasons why I think a hybrid position is superior. The premises I will outline in the next section are for a version of the legislative point of view that gives greater weight to counterfactual considerations than a strong consequentialist position validly can.

The first consideration is that while it is true that when asking the question "what should the moral code be?" the legislative view follows naturally, we are rarely in a situation where this is the specific question (or the only question) before us practically. The influence of any one person on the moral code of society as a whole is normally so small as to be negligible. If my influence is negligible, my moral reason for taking on the legislative point of view when making moral pronouncements diminishes. Even within my smaller sphere of influence, I often have less influence on what norms are accepted as right than the factual version of the legislative position demands. The main problem we have seen, throughout the book, is that while the legislative point of view has power if we start with certain questions, it is more difficult to explain why those are the right questions to ask. We could invoke principles such as that it is wrong to publicly advocate for a moral code while intending to break that same code, but why is this wrong on purely consequentialist grounds? If one exempts oneself in order to harm others, a consequentialist could object to the exemption, but why would departures from the legislative point of view motivated by beneficence be wrong?

Brandt's version (Chapter 5) simply asks what moral code we would want our society to have. He assumes that some sort of universalization requirement applies which prevents us from asserting that society should have the moral code that gives our group more of what we, particularly, want. But his reasoning here falters. It is true that we will not prove very persuasive if we advocate a "moral code to benefit me" position to others, but if there are no nonconsequentialist constraints and the only consideration is what I want, it is not clear what is instrumentally irrational about proposing a code and secretly acting contrary to that code. If I am not actually in a position to enact a code by my statements, why give serious weight to the code's dictates in my actions? I can have considerably stronger influence on the moral codes adopted by smaller groups of which I am a part. Parents have significant influence over the sort of moral code their children will adopt. A religious leader may have influence over the moral codes of those in a particular church. Nonetheless, the question "what moral code should my subgroup adopt" is still quite different than "what should the moral code be for my whole society."

There is no shortage of examples of both parents and pastors who have taught one thing and done another. Why not inculcate in your children a different moral code than the one you proclaim for the outside world if it could give your children a competitive advantage?

Second, positions like Mill's seem to assume a foundational commitment to pursuing human happiness for all, not just myself, as the starting point of moral thinking. People may harm others as a result of selfish actions, but such actions are wrong. This sort of position can restrict deviations from the legislative point of view to altruistic ones, but it still has its own concerns. If it is human happiness that justifies the rule, and greater human happiness can be obtained by secretly breaking the rule, this form of consequentialism gives strong reasons to break the rule. Realistically, only some people will have the education to understand the underlying consequentialist theory on which the moral code rests and thus be in a position to think of utilitarianism in this way. What to do and what to commend really are separate acts, and it is hard to see why Sidgwick was wrong to conclude that the consequentialist assessments should be done separately and may diverge.

Attempts to avoid this esoteric morality, without resorting to nonconsequentialist considerations, are unpersuasive. Consider Alan Gibbard's (1984) consequentialist argument. He argues that an esoteric morality would deprive us of the benefits of sincere discussion about ethical theories and that it would produce strains that would weaken our commitment to the basic moral principles. Let us take these points in turn. Proponents of esoteric morality have often conceived of it as a knowledge that could be shared among a select group of people who understand morality's true basis. These people would not be bereft of opportunities for sincere discussion among each other. Second, while this consideration might give us reason not to endorse esoteric morality publicly (since if we did, people might question our commitment to our subsequent statements, particularly on certain topics) there is still a difference between what I should endorse and what I should do. If consequentialism alone is right, then the proposition that what produces the best consequences is right is something of an incorrigible fact. If that fact, made widely known, produces negative consequences it is not at all clear that the losses that come from individual self-censorship in ethical discussions will outweigh those.

This leads to his second reason, which is that esoteric morality would undermine our commitment to basic moral principles. Here, I agree with Gibbard that it would. Knowledge that the rule is not really the standard of right (or part of it), but rather an imperfect means to an end, will change my perception of the rule. Given that cognitive limitations are one of the factors that determine the content of the moral code, and given that the sorts of people who will know that morality is esoteric will tend to be much more educated than the general population, the thought that a different code will be beneficial for people like me, with my greater knowledge (or intelligence?), is difficult to resist. Of course, the more people who think this way, the more we lose the benefits of coordinated behavior and the more we risk undermining commitment to the basic moral principles themselves. Some consequentialists seem to reason that because the outcome, in the aggregate, of a series of individual choices, would produce bad consequences then obviously consequentialism could not choose that outcome. This is a mistake. The whole point of rational choice exercises like the prisoner's (or prisoners') dilemma is to note that individually rational choices can lead to suboptimal outcomes, and, as Parfit (1984) has pointed out (see the Introduction), altruistic consequentialists can have collective action problems just as much as selfish individualists. I may know that if everyone were to think of the rules the way I am thinking of them, the moral code would be undermined, but it is still true that my own actions have a limited effect on what others will do, particularly when my actions can be performed secretly. At the end of the day, when the decision is which action to perform (as opposed to which moral code to advocate for) for the pure consequentialist, one cannot change the question to "which rule would be best?" The nature of situated consequentialist reasoning can thus create a moral collective action problem.

A third reason for moving beyond the purely consequentialist understanding of the legislative point of view is that pure deontology and pure consequentialism both lead to moral conclusions that most people find troubling. The Kantian insistence that the rules that govern us be formulated with little or no concern for the consequences of their content leads to conclusions such as not telling a lie though millions of people die. Pure consequentialism has trouble, as we have seen, handling cases where we can secretly exempt ourselves from a generally applicable rule and, for example, increase utility by bringing about the conviction of an innocent person. A hybrid theory can include deontological considerations so that the moral conclusions we reach are a much better fit with our considered moral judgments. To take the most obvious example, it can include a publicity requirement that rules out esoteric morality as a matter of principle, rather than making it an empirical question. Thus far, the hybrid position I am advocating is similar to Hooker's in that it makes use of a reflective

equilibrium argument for the theory and incorporates a publicity requirement as a premise rather than a questionable empirical conclusion.

The sort of hybrid theory I sketch below, however, goes beyond Hooker
in that it provides a more transparent account of the ways that nonconsequentialist and consequentialist considerations interact. One alleged short-
coming of hybrid theories is that they are more vague than pure theories.
Pure consequentialism or pure Kantianism may yield more definite conclusions than approaches that ask us to attempt to combine elements of
very different approaches in a single theory. This problem cannot be
completely eliminated, and it must be said, in fairness, that in the end
the theory I describe will not be able to give a formula for how conflicting
rules will be prioritized or the exact amount of weight that the conclusions
drawn from the legislative point of view should have in our overall moral
judgment in any particular situation. My own view is that, in the end, a less
precise theory is better than a wrong theory, and the vagueness of theories
that are a better fit with our moral judgments may simply be a reflection of
the limitations of our theories, limits that are better acknowledged than
hubristically defied.

With that caveat in mind, the hybrid legislative point of view that I will
describe provides a structure within which deontological and weak consequentialist considerations interact with each other and can thus reduce some
of the ambiguity. Deontological commitments to think of morality as having
the characteristics of a shared moral law, publicly available to all, are
particularly important in framing which question we are answering. They
make it clear why the question "what is the best moral code?" is directly
relevant to the question "what should I do?" Once these parameters are in
place, weak consequentialist thinking has a greater role to play as we work
out the content of those rules. The content of the rules should be adjusted to
better promote the moral goals of the legislator, accounting for the difficulty
of bringing about acceptance and compliance with the rule, the fallibility
and bias of those who will interpret and apply it, and so on.

Within those parameters, there is a lot left open-ended. This framework
is not intended to determine the answer to all ethical questions so much as
to provide a framework for thinking about those questions. Much will
depend on how we define the set of moral goals at which the legislator aims.
These could be some version of a utilitarian account of well-being, in
which case the resulting theory would be similar to the rule-
consequentialism of Hooker. But one could also allow nonconsequentialist
considerations to play a much stronger role in defining what the moral
goals are. One could imagine a rights-consequentialist account that

prioritizes ensuring that certain rights are maximally protected and chooses the content of the rules with that end in view. Although I have emphasized Kantianism in my nonconsequentialist account, there is nothing to prevent an account of human virtue from figuring prominently in the goals of the legislator. Moreover, much of the attraction of virtue ethics comes from the sense that both pure consequentialism and pure Kantianism are too rigid and exclude too much morally important information. They are both reductionist. A hybrid theory that allows a place for contextual judgments about the relative priority of rules when they conflict can partially capture what makes a virtue ethics approach attractive.

In what follows I describe the set of premises one would need to endorse to use the morality as legislation framework in a sufficiently strong form that the counterfactual questions about what rule would be best if I were formulating a law are relevant to what is right and wrong here and now, even though I am not, factually speaking, in a position to legislate for all those I imagine following the rule. Hopefully the foregoing gives a sufficient sketch of why a hybrid theory might be attractive, and the next section makes the case that a successful translation is possible from the theological version of this theory to a contemporary secular version.

The Moral Commitments Necessary to Endorse Morality as Legislation and Their Plausibility

Our goal is to identify the moral commitments that make the counterfactual shift to the legislative perspective helpful, not merely as a decision rule for how to act, but as actually having weight in determining what is morally right. Historically, these positions were held on the basis of a theistic natural law theory where an actual legislator, God, expresses his will through general rules that can be known through human reason. God's will was taken to create obligations, and the communication of the moral law through reason to all human beings ensured a kind of publicity. In this situation there was not a counterfactual perspectival shift. These theories are hybrid in that they included both weak consequentialist and nonconsequentialist elements. While God was thought to use at least some weakly consequentialist reasoning in determining the content of the moral law, the fact that God's will determined what was right, or that we were obligated to obey that will, often was not defended on consequentialist grounds. In what follows I systematically identify the moral commitments that were present in the religious versions of the theory and translate those into more general moral claims that a secular theory would need to endorse in order to justify a shift to the legislative perspective. By calling these alternate positions secular I do not mean that only people who reject religion can endorse them, but rather that they do not require affirmation of the theistic content of the original theories.

I attempt to establish the plausibility of the secular claims by appealing to what I think are widely shared, though not universally shared, moral judgments. As with reflective equilibrium approaches, a closer match with our considered moral judgments counts as evidence in favor of a moral claim being valid. Although I will provide some brief remarks to make the case for the plausibility of these claims, attempting a full defense of them that might persuade people who, for example, reject even the weakest version of consequentialism or publicity requirements, is beyond the scope of this book. As noted in my remarks on Hooker in the previous chapter, our considered moral judgments today are influenced by the history described in Part I. The past tendency of western philosophers and theologians to think of morality as rule-like, for example, may make the claims below seem more plausible now. Granting this, I do not think a better approach is available. One that foregrounds the historical influences so that we can make considered moral judgments about them as well mitigates the danger somewhat.

1A) Theistic claim: *God's declarations of what is right should inform moral decision-making.*

1B) Secular claim: *What is right should inform moral decision-making.*

The secular version will drop the claim about God, but it would still need to hold that what is morally right carries authority and should shape our decisions. Christine Korsgaard, stating what she takes to be a widely held assumption, writes "when you think an action is right, you think you ought to do it – and this consideration at least frequently provides you with a motive for doing it" (Korsgaard 1996a, 11). The reason for mentioning this comparatively uncontroversial claim is that what I have called the consequentialist disjunction position does not endorse it. With the disjunction position, it does not follow from the fact that something is right that I have reason to do it since the best decision procedure may diverge from the standard of right. I will not say much in defense of this position since I take the disjunction position to be the minority position, and I am only trying to show the plausibility of the legislative point of view, not to prove it. In any case, much of what could have been said here will be addressed when defending the publicity claim in 3B. I have stated the position weakly as "rightly informs" rather than strongly as "always deter-mines" so as not to enter into a debate about the limitations of morality's claims on us.

2A) Theistic claim: *God declares what is right, at least in part, via general rules.*

2B) Secular claim: *Morality itself, and not just our decision procedure, is at least partly rule- or principle-based.*

For the secular theory I change the terminology from "general rules" to moral rules and principles since I take both rules and principles to be derivable from the legislative point of view and there is no need to adjudicate here between the relative importance of rules and principles. Moral rules are often thought of as specifying what is or is not to be done, while principles tell us what sorts of factors count in favor of something being right or wrong (Zamzow 2015, 123). Ross' prima facie duties are normally thought of as principles rather than rules. In saying that both rules and principles can derive from the legislative point of view, I mean that in either case we can evaluate a proposed rule or principle by consid-ering that rule or principle as one that is not merely for us, but one that would apply to people more generally and that those people should know that it does apply to them.

In contrast to strong versions of the disjunction strategy, rules and principles help us discern what is actually right, not just what decision we should make. We need not think that all moral thinking is principle-based or that the rules are exhaustive, but we should agree that there are significant moral decisions that will be made with reference to principles or rules. Pure consequentialists can affirm this since any given consequential-ist theory can be stated as a principle or set of principles ("right actions maximize utility," for example). Although extreme particularists will deny the claim that morality is even partially rule-based, most people accept that it is. Virtue ethicists can argue that virtuous agents are, in part, people who are adept at discerning which moral principles are applicable in a particular circumstance and what weight those principles should have.

3A) Theistic claim: *God legislates moral rules that are both general and public.*

3B) Secular claim: *Moral rules and principles are general and public.*

In natural law theories, there was assumed to be one code for all humanity, although the rules could justifiably be broad enough to allow different applications or modifications in different contexts. "Generality" refers to the fact that the rule or principle applies to a class of cases that are similar in morally relevant ways rather than referring only to a particular case. "Publicity" refers to the idea that these moral rules should be available to all those to whom they apply and that the success of the principles should not depend on their secrecy.

In affirming the publicity of principles, we need not endorse a version of the argument for the transparency of reasons that would undermine the idea that some reasons are agent-specific or agent-relative (Korsgaard 1996b; Portmore 2001 and 2003; Wallace 2009). That I have a reason to visit my sick friend need not imply that you have the same reason, but it would imply that there is a general principle about the goodness of visiting sick friends that applies to those who have friends who are sick. If someone challenged this principle by pointing to instances where visits would be unwelcome, one could respond by restating the principle in a more general way, for example that the relationship of friendship provides a moral reason to show care for one's friend and leaves it open whether visits are always the right way to show care. One could also note that the principle in question is sometimes outweighed by other competing principles. All of these fairly standard moves are permissible within the constraints of 3B.

I take this principle to be sufficiently broad that it could be endorsed from a variety of different standpoints. John Rawls is perhaps the most famous twentieth-century proponent of these requirements. Rawls insisted that two of the conditions a theory of right must meet are that its principles be both general and public (Rawls 1971, 131–3).[1] "First of all, principles should be general. That is, it must be possible to formulate them without the use of what would be intuitively recognized as proper names, or rigged definite descriptions. Thus the predicates used in their statements should express general properties and relations" (131). Rawls, at least in his early work, also imposes a constraint of universality: "A principle is ruled out if it would be self-contradictory or self-defeating, for everyone to act upon it" (132). This is then linked to the publicity condition where the fact of the principle being publicly known and affirmed does not undermine it: "the general awareness of their universal acceptance should have desirable effects and support the stability of social cooperation" (133). Rawls in his later work (1993) continued to affirm publicity and generality but clarified that generality need not mean that the principles of justice we adopt would hold in all times and all places. In recognition of the controversial nature of claims about universality, I have not included it in my list of criteria since I think the

---

[1] See also his discussion of publicity in Rawls 1993, 66–71.

combination of generality and publicity is sufficient to justify a shift to the legislative point of view provided the other principles are affirmed. I need not claim that my principles are universal, but the generality requirement would apply to both myself and those with whom I am in dispute. When engaging in moral reasoning with others I need to search for common moral principles that apply to them as well as me and that could be publicly known and endorsed by them and by me.

In Rawls' original formulation these are constraints on principles of justice that will determine the basic structure of society, not principles for individual decision-making, at least in the first instance. Is this framework applicable for expansion to decision-making more broadly? In Rawls' framework, he uses a legislative frame to determine the principles of justice: the parties in the original position see themselves as establishing binding principles. As one works through the four stages (1971, 195–201), the constraints on knowledge imposed by the veil of ignorance are gradually relaxed as the earlier stages guide deliberation at the later stages. By stage four people are making judgments that are particular and not legislative but doing so using a framework that is thoroughly legislative. It is meant to provide some guidance even when the actual laws do not conform to the best principles of justice: the counterfactual thought experiment about what principles would be legislatively selected carries weight in specific judgments. In this sense, Rawls' principles track with what is affirmed in 3B. His main point is to show that we are not required to use the full veil of ignorance for other types of decision-making, not to deny that the principles of publicity and generality can have a wider scope than the original position.

Endorsement of 3B does not depend on a specific endorsement of Rawls. Rawls is influenced by Kant, and so it is unsurprising that the principles of generality and publicity receive strong support in that tradition (Davis 1991). As noted in Chapter 6, Hill's contemporary Kantian account assumes the importance of a legislative perspective in part because that frame forces us to think in terms of general and public principles. Nor is endorsement restricted to Kantians. Hooker's rule-consequentialism affirms it (Hooker 2000, 32, 79, 85–6). Commenting on Sidgwick's esoteric morality, he writes, "Such paternalistic duplicity would be morally wrong, even if it would maximize the aggregate good" (85). It is also affirmed by Bernard Williams in his famous critique of utilitarianism: self-effacing theories that violate transparency impose unacceptable costs on the moral agents who would adopt that perspective (Williams 1985, 109–10).

A secular theory would need to hold that the moral principles in question are not specifically tailored to each person but rather are part of a shared moral code that is known to the people under that code. If I deny the principle of generality and claim that the moral code that applies to me or my allies is different from the moral code that applies to everyone else, I no longer affirm the moral equality of persons in the same way and no longer respect them in the same way. Legislation, in its paradigm form, is both general and public. In order to adopt the legislative point of view, one needs to affirm a view of morality that is compatible with giving moral weight to both generality and publicity. This claim is not uncontroversial as strong versions of moral particularism would deny it (Hooker and Little 2000). Nonetheless it is a plausible secular principle and one crucial to affirming the legislative point of view.

4A) Theistic claim: *Those addressed by God's law are expected to act in their capacity as moral agents to interpret and apply those rules.*

4B) Secular claim: *Moral rules and principles address people as moral agents who must interpret and apply those rules and principles.*

Plausible moral rules will need to include terms that require the moral judgment of those who act on them as they interpret and apply the rule. Since rules and principles will be open to contestable interpretations and applications, I should not claim a right to greater latitude in interpreting and applying than I recognize for others who are also moral agents, just as I am. To claim for myself the right to assume my preferred interpretations and applications of the rule in assessing the viability of the rule is to usurp the equal right of other moral agents to interpret and apply the moral principles that apply to them. If I deny others the ability to act as moral agents either by keeping secret from them the principles that apply to them or by insisting that they must interpret the rules exactly as I do, I also show a lack of respect for them.

Again, and unsurprisingly, this is fairly easy for Kantians to affirm. Hill writes:

> The ideal of moral agents as jointly legislating moral laws, I suggested, urges us to curb our moral self-complacency by consulting others, listening to divergent views, and submitting our own convictions to criticism. But, unfortunately, we see ample evidence that, even among reasonable, con-scientious people, real moral discussion often fails to produce the conver-gence of judgment that Kant expected among ideally rational legislators with autonomy. This is one reason, among others, that the principle that we should regard each person as a rational, autonomous legislator of moral laws

cannot serve by itself as a determinate decision guide. The idea behind the principle, however, can still help to frame morally appropriate attitudes. (Hill 2000, 45)

In this formulation, the ideal would be for all of us to see ourselves as legislators and converge on the same publicly known principle. The reality is that unanimity will not happen, but the desire to respect the equal right of others to act as moral agents on the same terms as ourselves reflects, as Hill states, a morally appropriate attitude.

The legislative perspective as I define it is broad enough to express the same underlying idea in different ways. If we think literally of a nation full of individuals all legislating different laws, we are confronted with a picture of chaos. We could instead think of people as proposing laws to each other while recognizing the requisite moral interpretations and decisions needed to apply the proposed principles and that others retain their moral agency in doing so. For example, a proposal to restrict hate speech should account for the differences that may arise as to what constitutes hate speech and not be premised on the assumption that one's preferred interpretation will prevail, any more than, in Locke's original example, one could claim the right to engage in religious persecution based on the assumption that everyone would affirm your judgment about which religion is true.

5A) Theistic claim: *God foresees, and considers as morally relevant, likely noncompliance with rules and misapplication of rules as well as the cognitive limitations of those bound by the rule.*

5B) Secular claim: *Foreseen noncompliance with (and misapplication of) moral rules and principles is relevant to the considerations of the merits of those moral rules and principles, as are the cognitive limitations of those bound by the rule or principle.*

While some versions of ideal theory consider idealized agents whose rational capacities, moral judgment, and so on greatly exceed those of real people, the shift to the legislative point of view as defended here requires this more realistic picture of legislative deliberation. The principles that guide us are principles for people like us, people with these same limitations. There is, of course, controversy about how much the realities of nonideal theory impact what is right in particular circumstances. Gerald Allan Cohen thought Rawls granted too much to nonideal theory in that he was willing to justify inequalities under the difference principle by accepting the limited altruism of workers and their resulting need for economic incentives to be productive and to develop their abilities (Cohen 2008). Consequentialist theories tend to embrace this position, as do those that are Humean. The rules we have were selected because they work for people with the typical faults and limitations of human beings. Were we to imagine a different rational species with different needs, abilities, and characters, different principles might be better, at least once we work down toward more practical principles (David Miller 2013). There are some strong Kantian positions that might deny this, holding that morality must be the same for all rational beings, whether human or divine. In our historical study, we saw that the theistic theories often assumed that the differences between humans and God helped explain differences in what was morally permissible for humans and God.

It is also worth making a few reflections on how this distinction relates to the longstanding debates about ideal and nonideal theory. Simmons (2010) defends the Rawlsian perspective that we begin with ideal theory where we make realistic (nonutopian) assumptions about human nature, but where we also assume conditions in which the ideal can be achieved and where people affirm that ideal. Nonideal theory focuses on problems of noncompliance with principles of justice, duties, and priorities under conditions that make achieving our principles of justice difficult or impossible. The position I have sketched has affinities with nonideal theory in that problems of noncompliance and contextual factors that make justice or right hard to achieve are accounted for in the legislative point of view, but this leaves open a role for ideal theories of justice to play. Ideal theories may help us determine the goals of the legislature even if the specific principles we adopt from the legislative point of view must be adjusted given nonideal circumstances. One important difference is that, in the traditional way of thinking about problems of noncompliance in nonideal theory, people know what is demanded of them but choose to act unjustly. In the legislative perspective, our disagreement about what is right and just is built into the model itself. Our theories need to account for this (Waldron 1999). We can think of two distinct rationales for doing so. One, which could be accepted without the need for a counterfactual perspectival shift, is simply that a heuristic that forces me to account for the errant opinions of others will improve the odds of me selecting the right principles if people in general (and myself by implication) tend to underestimate their own fallibility. If I think this decision procedure helps me identify the principles that determine what is right, there is no counterfactual shift to justify since I am simply selecting the method most likely to identify what is right in this circumstance. A second possible reason is different; namely, that through the decision to think of principles as shared and recognizing the different interpretations of contestable moral terms of others, we express a respect for the moral agency of others.

6A) Theistic claim: *God can adjust the code so that God's purposes are better promoted when promulgated under realistic conditions.*

6B) Secular claim: *Moral codes can be adjusted in order to better further the underlying moral values of that code.*

In the theistic theories, God sometimes adjusted the content of the moral law so that God's purposes would be fulfilled, and God was, at least in this limited sense, consequentialist. Even if the use of force to bring people to the true religion was in itself a good thing, the general principle would be rejected because application of a general rule to use force in religious matters by fallible rulers would result in fewer people adopting the true religion, not more.

In the secular theory, having specified the morally defensible goals of the legislator, it is appropriate to adjust the content of the rules to better further those legislative goals. Most theories would endorse this, but deontological purists would insist that what is right is defined independently of good consequences and cannot be adjusted to produce better consequences. Consider the classic example of whether or not one may torture a suspected terrorist to reveal the location of a bomb. One might hold that there is something particularly wrong about torture such that one should not use it, even if it would likely save many lives. Suppose we grant this and then consider a situation where, by torturing one person, we can stop one hundred other people from being tortured ("torture only to minimize instances of torture"). If we allow torture in this case, it would be an example of modifying the content of the moral code in order to better achieve the underlying value of that code. It does involve a shift to looking at things from the perspective of a legislator who cares about the aggregate instances rather than just the perspective of a situated agent who might be more concerned that he or she not torture.

The Legislative Point of View and Hybrid Justification

While I think all six of these claims are individually plausible, the problem is found in affirming all of them in the same theory. As noted above, the theistic theories combined nonconsequentialist divine command theories with weakly consequentialist reasoning about the content of those theories. Often, unstated assumptions about the nature of morality itself (that it is based on general, publicly accessible rules) were never subjected to tests for whether or not these assumptions were justifiable on consequentialist grounds. These nonconsequentialist commitments helped justify a counterfactual perspectival shift that cannot be justified on consequentialist grounds alone. The challenges of twentieth-century rule-utilitarianism can largely be understood as trying to maintain this hybrid theory on a purely consequentialist basis or trying to stretch the boundaries of utilitarian orthodoxy to include nonconsequentialist components. Lyons (1965, 182–97) was right in his suggestion that rule-utilitarianism seems to require a commitment to something other than utility in order to work.

The legislative point of view models an attractive way of thinking about morality. Rules help finite creatures of limited knowledge who are prone to bias make better decisions. Thinking of ourselves as moral agents who share a common moral framework with other moral agents and, in our limitations and fallibility, have an equal right and should have an equal opportunity to interpret and apply the rules of that common framework, shows respect for others and expresses one aspect of moral equality. It also acknowledges a rightful place for consequentialist thinking: we should sometimes modify rules to account for the likely consequences if such a principle were widely adopted. The historic interest in rule-consequentialism testifies to the attractiveness of this picture. What we have seen from our historical study is that the problem is not so much with the attractiveness of the picture but with the attempt to justify it within a purely secular, consequentialist framework. In its original formulation, a more complex set of considerations, some of them theistic, grounded the approach. Attempts to utilize the approach without recourse to nonconsequentialist commitments will continue to leave questions unanswered about what will motivate the counterfactual perspectival shift of thinking of ourselves as legislators when we know we are not.

Once the legislative point of view is liberated from the dominion of purely consequentialist approaches it not only helps justify the starting point but also broadens the set of considerations that one can consider when deliberating from that point of view. Nonconsequentialist commitments can affect the goals of, and not merely serve as constraints on, the legislator. In real life, people who serve in legislatures and deliberate about laws are motivated by a variety of purposes, some consequentialist and some not. The same breadth is available to those who wish to use the legislative point of view as a device for thinking ethically in nonlegislative situations. If we are to utilize the legislative point of view as specified above, it will require a hybrid theory that includes both consequentialist and nonconsequentialist commitments.

The Legislative Point of View and Political Ethics

We have seen that the legislative point of view can be used in a variety of contexts, political and apolitical, legislative and nonlegislative. In all of these cases what is of most interest is what motivates the counterfactual perspectival shift to ask what rule we would propose if legislating for some larger group even when, factually speaking, we are not. The case for making the counterfactual perspectival shift is stronger when facing ethical dilemmas in political contexts than in apolitical contexts, as is the degree of weight that should be assigned to the dictates of that perspective. In the Introduction, I opted for a focal case approach to defining what is deemed a political context rather than trying to define the necessary and sufficient conditions. I opted for this approach because it seems that there are a variety of factors that can count in favor of something being political, not just one, and that something being political is a matter of degree rather than dichotomous. "Political" may be a Wittgensteinian family resemblance term (Wittgenstein, 67) where there are common features but none of them are either necessary or sufficient. My main claim here is that, in general, the more political a context is the stronger the claims of the legislative perspective. To the extent that is true, we also have more reason to stop and take the time to think about our decisions from the perspective of the legislative point of view, all else being equal. The greater weight a consideration has in determining what is right, the riskier it is to ignore it. Even in the most political context imaginable, the legislative point of view might provide only some of the relevant information for discerning which action is right. It is nonetheless significant that in political contexts the weight we should attach to the legislative perspective increases. In this section I try to explain why that is.

We can begin by noting several contextual descriptions that count in favor of a decision being political: 1) the subject matter at stake is how the coercive power of the state will or may be employed, 2) the subject matter at stake is what set of moral norms will prevail that regulate public life or set boundaries between the public and the private, or 3) the decision maker has assumed a public office such that the official acts (in some sense) in the name of the people. Remember that the political context dimension is distinct from the legislative context dimension which has to do with whether or not we aim to bring about the adoption of an authoritative rule (whether a law or a norm) and how much efficacy our actions have in doing so. While these often overlap, they do not always coincide since there can be apolitical rule-making and political actions that do not aim at the establishment of a rule. Throughout the book we have noted that it is easier to justify the shift to the legislative perspective when one is in a legislative context because in these contexts the legislative perspective (which asks us which rule should be adopted) is not counterfactual as we really aim at a rule. Here the point is different, namely that political contexts increase our reasons to take on the legislative point of view, setting aside whether or not the context is legislative. By definition, the use of the legislative perspective aims at the adoption of a general rule and is, in that sense, legislative, but the person in question may use that only to guide their own actions rather than engaging in action to actually bring about the adoption of a new rule (although the person would likely think it good that that rule in question be observed by others). The legislative perspective can be used in political contexts to adopt a rule only for oneself. Another way of seeing whether there is greater weight for the legislative point of view in political contexts, irrespective of legislative context, is by comparing instances where one seeks to change a political norm and noting that the outcome of legislative deliberation holds more weight than it would if the context were not political. If we keep the legislative context constant but vary how political the context is, we can see if political context changes the appropriate weight. Lastly, we can examine cases where someone aims at norm change or legal change but knows that their actions are unlikely to affect the prevailing norms or laws. The context is here political, but the legislative context is weak.

One factor that counts toward describing a context as political is whether what is at stake is how the coercive power of the state will or may be used. Some stark examples of political but not legislative contexts are the use of violence by state actors such as law enforcement and the military. While their violent actions may be expressions of rule-following, in many cases they are not, as there is a significant amount of discretion available to government agents about how to use force and they may use force with no intention of setting a public precedent for how force will be used in similar instances. Even if some would want to classify their actions as less political than those of the politicians who pass the laws and issue orders, their actions are nonetheless part of a political context as they deploy the state's coercive power. If someone would prefer to describe them as "public" contexts rather than "political" contexts I would be more interested in arguing that the legislative perspective makes stronger claims on us in such public contexts than in arguing about the distinction between the public and the political. For simplicity I will simply call these instances political. In the example in the Introduction, a legislator faces a decision about whether to use their political influence to help a campaign contributor get a government contract. Here too, the coercive power of the state is in play since the money that will be spent to pay the contract is collected through mandatory taxes backed by legal punishments.

The claim that the legislative point of view is stronger in political cases than apolitical ones depends upon the claim that the nonconsequentialist commitments embodied in claims 3B and 4B are stronger, all else being equal, in political contexts than in apolitical ones. We have more reason to think of our actions as right because they align with rules that are public, general, and addressed to others who have an equal right to interpret and apply those principles according to their own judgment. As noted earlier in the chapter, there is a Kantian aspect to the plausibility of 3B and 4B, as Kantians often ask that we think of ourselves as legislating alongside other persons who have an equal right to legislate. The laws and principles that guide the use of coercive force impinge on the autonomy of others in a way our private lives do not (Korsgaard 1996b). The Kantian concern (shared by many non-Kantians as well) that coercive actions are a particularly important threat to individual autonomy provides the basic justification for the claim that, in contexts where what is at stake is how coercive power will be employed, the claims of the legislative perspective are correspondingly stronger. Coercive acts restrict the freedom of others, and limiting these acts to those that can be justified on the basis of a shared framework that recognizes the moral agency of others has advantages over claiming the right to unilaterally use the state's coercive power in ways that you would reject if others acted on the basis of the same principle but with different specific judgments.

This claim holds even in cases where the context is political but not legislative. Consider a police officer trying to decide what principles to use when deciding whether or not to use lethal force. These norms will significantly shape how the police officer makes split-second decisions in the line of duty since our particular judgments are partially determined by the principles we hold. A police officer could simply ask what principles will produce the best outcomes if they follow them, or could ask what principles would be best for police officers in some larger group (the city in question, for example). In practice, the police officer does not actually think that adopting a set of principles will cause others to adopt those same principles, and the police officer might also reasonably believe that they could adopt a set of principles for making decisions without making public to others what those principles are. If one's decision is questioned, one could always look for the best available principle that justifies one's action in a given case. One could thus, as a police officer, adopt the disjunction strategy of separating what one should do in specific instances from what norms one publicly supports or affirms. Nonetheless, I think the police officer should attach greater weight to the dictates of the legislative point of view than a private citizen. Some of the reasons do not depend on counterfactual reasoning. Accounting for the bias of police officers generally (for example, biases related to race or social class that influence perceptions of threat) might be a more reliable way of accounting for one's own bias if we tend to systematically underestimate our own bias even as we recognize it in others. Other justifications do depend on counterfactual reasoning. There is a kind of respect shown for fellow citizens by acting only on a rule that one would want other fallible people to act upon as well. Recognizing that the use of lethal force by the state poses particularly grave risks to the autonomy of others, constraining oneself by acting on universalizable principles expresses respect for others as free and equal fellow citizens.

It counts in favor of a context being political that what is at stake is how the power of the state will or may be used. The phrase "may be" is included because part of politics is determining what is legally permissible as well as what is actually done. Political action might protest the killing of an unarmed person by the police with the goal of changing the norms that guide police officers who are deciding whether to use potentially lethal force or the process by which police officers are held accountable. Again, contexts where what is at stake is what may be done coercively by the state have stronger claims than rules or norms in nonpolitical contexts for similar reasons to those given above. What the state may do to us is important for our freedom and standing within society apart from what is actually done in particular cases. Republican theorists, such as Philip Pettit (1997), have made much of this point, but one need not adopt the republican point of view in total to grasp that something of particular importance is at stake in establishing what the state may do to people, and that different answers to this question show varying degrees of respect for other persons. Notice that in this case it can be private citizens who are in a political context because of their decision to engage in protest. Thus far we have noted that a context becomes more political because of its subject matter rather than because of any official position the person holds, namely the subject of how the state's coercive power will be used.

I also include as one factor that counts toward a political context that it seeks to impact the moral norms that regulate our public life or that define the boundaries between the public and the private. These are both important arenas of political contestation. In the example of political protests against police violence, the protestors might aim at legal changes or changes in the prevailing nonlegal norms that govern police conduct. Social movements to stop sexual harassment normally aim both to change the legal system and transform the prevailing attitudes toward what counts as acceptable behavior. There are basic rights that people have and opportunities that they need in order to flourish as citizens. The more directly our actions and decisions affect these things, the more political the context is. For example, if public shaming makes it impossible for a subset of the population to exercise its political rights, the shaming is political even if done spontaneously by private citizens on social media. While every norm may not be political, some norms clearly impact a person's ability to live in public spaces and to exercise basic rights. In these contexts we have reason to take the legislative point of view as having greater weight for reasons similar to the ones discussed above concerning coercion.

As we have seen, Mill thought that social norms could be coercive and a much bigger threat to freedom, in some cases, than traditional laws. The reputational sanctions that people experience when they are known to have broken a widely accepted norm can be much more significant than many legal penalties and thus raise concerns about autonomy. They are also, like traditional laws, part of a shared framework of rules that can bind together members of a community. Part of the justification for taking the legislative point of view is that it shows respect for your fellow citizens as free and equal members of a common political community, and the informal norms that shape our ability to participate in that political community are deserving of protection.

For example, when private citizens consider joining in or initiating public shaming, they have more reason to subject their judgments to the legislative point of view than in more private actions. A private citizen who did so might consider what principles to regulate public shaming would be chosen without assuming that it will always be done by wise and discerning people or by those who share one's views about politics, economics, race, gender, or religion. Some acts of shaming that seem fully justified looking only at this situated instance seem less so when considered as part of a broad framework that one would want fellow citizens to also apply, knowing that many of them would direct their shaming at very different targets. This would not require the abolition of public shaming. Nor would it ensure that everyone who adopted the legislative point of view converged on the same position about what should be shamed and to what extent, but the heuristic in such cases would provide a restraint by providing a nonconsequentialist reason for not assuming that you are entitled to shaming prerogatives your fellow citizens should not have. Public shaming acts occupy a kind of middle ground, contextually, between more public moral utterances that are less political in nature and explicitly political enactments.

A third factor that counts toward describing a context as political and that influences the weight accorded to the legislative point of view is whether a person holds public office. Those who hold public office have a special responsibility to show respect for others in the way the legislative point of view requires. We might think that the main difference between private citizens and public officials is that private utterances have, in most cases, a small impact on the moral norms of our society. In other words, public officials are more likely to be in a genuinely legislative position than private citizens. While this may be true, it is not the relevant point here since in all cases it is the counterfactual nature of the perspectival shift that needs justification and that is as true for one group as the other. The issue is rather that those who are discharging the duties of a public office show a greater degree of disrespect for others when they fail to think of the moral principles on which they act as part of a shared framework with others. Those who hold public office act in the name of the public and are thus rightly subjected to a higher burden of public justification. Public office carries with it a greater degree of responsibility to be impartial in making decisions than in cases where people do not hold such offices.

Consider the following argument. If one thinks of Bernard Williams' famous example about the man who, when faced with saving his wife or a stranger, stops to think about whether it is ethically permissible to show favoritism toward his wife and has had, therefore, "one thought too many," the illustration draws its strength not just from the intensity of marital affection but partly from the private nature of the decision (Williams 1981, 18). Were the man in question a legislator contemplating a law about nepotism and deciding whether its adoption would harm his family members who have benefitted from nepotism, we would be less likely to regard taking on the legislative point of view as one thought too many, even if furthering the interests of his family is particularly central to his life projects. Likewise, a public official deciding whether to award a contract to his wife's company could have recourse to the legislative point of view without having one thought too many. We are more likely to say that failure to think about whether the principle is one that should guide other political officials is one thought too few.

I conclude this section by noting that Williams is right that certain forms of moral reasoning are burdensome. The legislative perspective forces us to abstract to a larger number of cases, to consider our own fallibility more acutely, and to aspire to a more impartial level of justification. As we noted in the discussion of Mill in Chapter 4, we can think of our public moral expressions as a type of legislation since they shape powerful norms that can then inflict significant reputational sanctions. Unless we accept that the degree of weight accorded to the legislative perspective is greater in political circumstances, we are forced into the position that we have an equal duty to pay heed to the dictates of the legislative point of view in all circumstances. A person who had to run every public moral statement, every parenting decision, every church activity, every hobby or pastime through the legislative grid might reasonably claim that all of life is not a legislative chamber and that we need some space and protection from its encroachments. This does not mean that the legislative perspective cannot potentially apply in these areas, only that its claims are weaker and more easily overridden and, in some cases, sufficiently weak that a person could disregard it blamelessly. In practice, people will need to develop a sense of when to engage in legislative deliberation since in many cases people will, rightly, make decisions without thinking of it at all. To the extent that people can almost immediately grasp whether the context in which they act is political, they will be better able to discern whether to reason in a legislative manner and whether to afford more or less weight to the outcome of that deliberation.

Conclusion

Many people find it intuitively attractive to use the thought experiment "what if everyone acted that way" and apply it in at least a partially consequentialist manner, considering the likely consequences of real people attempting to act on the proposed principle. When they do so, they think of this as a factor that counts in favor of whether the action is right or not. In some cases, they may engage in a more fully developed version of the legislative point of view where the difficulty of gaining widespread compliance with a proposed norm counts as a reason against thinking the norm is actually correct. The appeal of this way of thinking is that it seems to match more closely with most people's considered moral judgments than simple act-consequentialism or strict Kantianism. It has also proved hard to justify the counterfactual perspectival shift that is needed in cases where your decision will not significantly impact the norms or rules that will guide others. Strict act-consequentialists will reject it because it seems irrational to perform the action that will not produce the best consequences in this particular case just because of a counterfactual hypothesis. Strict Kantians will object to the consequentialist considerations that go into deciding which principles to affirm. What I have called the legislative point of view thus sits uneasily in either of these frameworks.

In this book I have tried to explain why this is so by exploring the history of this question. There is a long history of thinking about morality that combines some elements of consequentialist reasoning with nonconsequentialist commitments to thinking of morality as having an intrinsically law-like character. These theistic theories were neither strictly consequentialist nor strictly nonconsequentialist, but many of our moral sensibilities are still shaped by this tradition. Apart from historical inertia, this combination of commitments yields a framework that seems to help us think through moral questions in a sensible way. If we understand the historical tradition out of which this way of thinking arose it will be clearer why a purely consequentialist defense of it fails, opening the door for us to be more explicit about the sorts of secular commitments one would need to justify the use of this framework. I have argued that the commitments are all plausible ones for a contemporary thinker who does not accept the original theological framework, but that the commitments combine both consequentialist and nonconsequentialist considerations. A secular defense of this approach will, I think, need to synthesize these elements. We must both care about the consequences of principles we hold when those are adopted by real people and desire to show respect for others by acting on public, shared moral principles in a way that is more than just consequentialist.

I have not tried to make the stronger claim that the dictates of the legislative point of view are always the last word on morality, only that it can justifiably influence whether actions are right or wrong. It will not do so equally in all cases. The nonconsequentialist grounds for making the counterfactual perspectival shift seem to me to be stronger in the political realm than in the private realm. The use of this framework in political ethics shows respect for our fellow citizens and acknowledges the greater argumentative burden that is needed when our actions are coercive or impact the basic political rights of others.

Works Cited

For older works, the original publication date is given in parenthesis. For editions of works that reproduce multiple works, the parenthetical date is the date for the latest work included in the collection, using the editor's dating where possible. Reproductions of collected works give in parenthesis the date of the original collected works' publication.

Albee, Ernest. (1901) 1962. *A History of English Utilitarianism*. New York: Collier Books.

Anscombe, Gertrude Elizabeth Margaret. 1958. "Modern Moral Philosophy." *Philosophy* 33: 1–19.

Austin, John. (1832) 1995. *The Province of Jurisprudence Determined*. Edited by Wilfrid E. Rumble. Cambridge: Cambridge University Press.

Baier, Annette. 2010. *The Cautious Jealous Virtue: Hume on Justice*. Cambridge, MA: Harvard University Press.

Bentham, Jeremy. (1789) 1988. *The Principles of Morals and Legislation*. New York: Prometheus Books.

Bentham, Jeremy. (1822) 2003. *The Influence of Natural Religion on the Temporal Happiness of Mankind*. New York: Prometheus Books.

Bentham, Jeremy. (1834) 1983. *Deontology Together with a Table of the Springs of Action and Article on Utilitarianism*. Edited by Amnon Goldworth. Oxford: Clarendon Press.

Berger, Fred R. 1984. *Happiness, Justice, and Freedom: The Moral and Political Philosophy of John Stuart Mill*. Berkeley: University of California Press.

Berkeley, George. (1712) 1901. "Passive Obedience, or the Christian Doctrine of Not Resisting the Supreme Power, Proved and Vindicated upon the Principles of the Law of Nature." In *The Works of George Berkeley, Volume Four*. Oxford: Clarendon Press.

Berman, David. 1994. *Idealism and the Man*. Oxford: Clarendon Press.

Birks, Thomas Rawson. 1874. *Modern Utilitarianism: Or the Systems of Paley, Bentham, and Mill Compared*. London: MacMillan.

Brandt, Richard. 1959. *Ethical Theory: The Problem of Normative and Critical Ethics*. Englewood Cliffs, NJ: Prentice-Hall.

Brandt, Richard. 1979. *A Theory of the Good and the Right*. Oxford: Clarendon Press.

Brandt, Richard. 1988. "Fairness to Indirect Optimific Theories in Ethics." *Ethics* 98: 341–60.

Brandt, Richard. (1967) 1992. "Some Merits of One Form of Rule-Utilitarianism." In Richard Brandt, *Morality, Utilitarianism, and Rights*. Cambridge: Cambridge University Press.

Brink, David O. 2013. *Mill's Progressive Principles*. Oxford: Clarendon Press.

Broad, Charlie Dunbar. 1916. "On the Function of False Hypotheses in Ethics." *International Journal of Ethics* 26(3): 377–97.

Bull, Hedley, Benedict Kingsbury, and Adam Roberts. 1990. *Hugo Grotius and International Relations*. Oxford: Clarendon Press.

Butler, Joseph. (1867) 2006. *The Works of Joseph Butler: Containing the Analogy of Religion and Sixteen Celebrated Sermons*. London: William Tegg [reprinted by Elibron Classics].

Campbell, Charles Arthur. 1948. "Moral Intuition and the Principle of Self-Realization." *Annual Philosophical Lecture, Henriette Hertz Trust, Proceedings of the British Academy*, Vol. 34. London: G. Cumberlege.

Cohen, Gerald Allan 2008. *Rescuing Justice and Equality*. Cambridge, MA: Harvard University Press.

Cohon, Rachel. 2008. *Hume's Morality: Feeling and Fabrication*. Oxford: Oxford University Press.

Crimmins, James E. 1990. *Secular Utilitarianism: Social Science and the Critique of Religion in the Thought of Jeremy Bentham*. Oxford: Clarendon Press.

Crisp, Roger. 1997. *Routledge Philosophy Guidebook to Mill on Utilitarianism*. Abingdon, UK: Routledge.

Crisp, Roger. 2015. *The Cosmos of Duty: Henry Sidgwick's Methods of Ethics*. Oxford: Clarendon Press.

Cumberland, Richard. (1672) 2005. *A Treatise of the Laws of Nature*. Translated by John Maxell and edited by John Parkin. Indianapolis, IN: Liberty Fund.

Cummiskey, David. 1996. *Kantian Consequentialism*. New York: Oxford University Press.

Dancy, Jonathan. 2004. *Ethics without Principles*. Oxford: Clarendon Press.

Darwall, Stephen. 1995a. *The British Moralists and the Internal "Ought" 1640–1740*. Cambridge: Cambridge University Press.

Darwall, Stephen. 1995b. "Hume and the Invention of Utilitarianism." In *Hume and Hume's Connexions*, edited by Michael Alexander Stewart and John P. Wright, 58–82. Philadelphia, PA: Pennsylvania State University Press.

Davis, Kevin R. 1991. "Kantian 'Publicity' and Political Justice." *History of Philosophy Quarterly* 8(4): 409–21.

Dennett, Daniel and Asbjørn Steglich-Petersen. 2008. *The Philosophical Lexicon*. www.philosophicallexicon.com.

Donner, Wendy. 1998. "Mill's Utilitarianism." In *The Cambridge Companion to Mill*, edited by John Skorupski, 255–92. Cambridge: Cambridge University Press.

Donner, Wendy. 2009. "Mill's Moral and Political Philosophy." In *Mill*, edited by Wendy Donner and Richard Fumerton, 13–143. Malden, MA: Wiley-Blackwell.

Donner, Wendy. 2011. "Morality, Virtue, and Aesthetics." In *John Stuart Mill and the Art of Life*, edited by Ben Eggleston, Dale E. Miller, and David Weinstein, 146–68. Oxford: Oxford University Press.

Eggleston, Ben. 2011. "Rules and Their Reasons: Mill on Morality and Instrumental Rationality." In *John Stuart Mill and the Art of Life*, edited by Ben Eggleston, Dale E. Miller, and David Weinstein, 71–93. Oxford: Oxford University Press.

Ewing, Alfred Cyril. 1953a. "What Would Happen If Everybody Acted Like Me?" *Philosophy* 28: 16–29.

Ewing, Alfred Cyril. 1953b. *Ethics*. London: English Universities Press.

Ewing, Alfred Cyril. 1959. *Second Thoughts in Moral Philosophy*. London: Routledge & Kegan Paul Ltd.

Forbes, Duncan. 1975. *Hume's Philosophical Politics*. Cambridge: Cambridge University Press.

Forde, Steven. 1998. "Hugo Grotius on the Ethics of War." *The American Political Science Review* 92(3): 639–48.

Forsyth, Murray. 1982. "The Place of Richard Cumberland in the History of Natural Law." *Journal of the History of Philosophy* 20(1): 23–42.

Fuchs, Alan E. 2006. "Mill's Theory of Morally Correct Action." In *The Blackwell Guide to Mill's Utilitarianism*, edited by Henry R. West, 139–58. Malden, MA: Blackwell.

Gert, Bernard. 2005. *Morality: Its Nature and Justification*, Revised Edition. Oxford: Oxford University Press.

Gibbard, Allan. 1984. "Utilitarianism and Human Rights." *Social Philosophy and Policy* 1(2): 92–102.

Gill, Michael B. 2006. *The British Moralists on Human Nature and the Birth of Secular Ethics*. Cambridge: Cambridge University Press.

Goodin, Robert E. 1995. *Utilitarianism as a Public Philosophy*. Cambridge: Cambridge University Press.

Gray, John. 1996. *Mill on Liberty: A Defense*, Second Edition. Abingdon, UK: Routledge.

Grotius, Hugo. (1625) 1925. *The Law of War and Peace*. Translated by Francis W. Kelsey. Indianapolis, IN: Bobbs-Merrill.

Haakonssen, Knud. 2000. "The Character and Obligation of Natural Law According to Richard Cumberland." In *English Philosophy in the Age of Locke*, edited by Matthew A. Stewart, 29–47. Oxford: Clarendon Press.

Hardin, Russell. 2007. *David Hume: Moral and Political Theorist*. Oxford: Oxford University Press.

Hare, Richard Mervyn. 1981. *Moral Thinking: Its Levels, Method, and Point*. Oxford: Clarendon Press.

Hare, Richard Mervyn. 1982. "Ethical Theory and Utilitarianism." In *Utilitarianism and Beyond*, edited by Amartya Sen and Bernard Williams, 23–38. Cambridge: Cambridge University Press.

Hare, Richard Mervyn. 1988. "Comment." In *Hare and Critics*, edited by Douglas Seanor and Nicholas Fotion, 199–203. Oxford: Clarendon Press.

Harman, Gilbert. 1977. *The Nature of Morality: An Introduction to Ethics*. New York: Oxford University Press.

Harris, John. 1975. "The Survival Lottery." *Philosophy* 50(191): 81–7.

Harrison, Jonathan. 1952–1953. "Utilitarianism, Universalization, and Our Duty to Be Just." *Proceedings of the Aristotelian Society* 53: 105–34.

Harrison, Jonathan. 1981. *Hume's Theory of Justice*. Oxford: Clarendon Press.

Harrison, Ross. 1983. *Bentham*. Abingdon, UK: Routledge.

Harrod, Roy Forbes. 1936. "Utilitarianism Revised." *Mind* 45(178): 137–56.

Harsanyi, John. 1976. "Ethics in Terms of Hypothetical Imperatives." In John Harsanyi, *Essays on Ethics, Social Behavior, and Scientific Explanation*. Dordrecht: D. Reidel Publishing.

Harsanyi, John. 1982a. "Morality and the Theory of Rational Behavior." In *Utilitarianism and Beyond*, edited by Amartya Sen and Bernard Williams, 39–62. Cambridge: Cambridge University Press.

Harsanyi, John, 1982b. "Rule Utilitarianism, Rights, Obligation, and the Theory of Rational Behavior." In John Harsanyi, *Papers in Game Theory*. Dordrecht: D. Reidel Publishing.

Harsanyi, John. 1988. "Problems with Act-Utilitarianism and with Malevolent Preferences." In *Hare and Critics*, edited by Douglas Seanor and Nicholas Fotion, 89–99. Oxford: Clarendon Press.

Hebblethwaite, Brian. 1992. "Butler on Conscience and Virtue." In *Joseph Butler's Moral and Religious Thought: Tercentenary Essays*, edited by Christopher Cunliffe, 197–207. Oxford: Clarendon Press.

Hill, Jr. Thomas E. 1992. *Dignity and Practical Reason in Kant's Moral Theory*. Ithaca, NY: Cornell University Press.

Hill, Jr. Thomas E. 2000. *Respect, Pluralism, and Justice*. Oxford: Oxford University Press.

Hill, Jr. Thomas E. 2012. *Virtue, Rules, and Justice: Kantian Aspirations*. Oxford: Oxford University Press.

Hooker, Brad. 2000. *Ideal Code, Real World: A Rule-Consequentialist Theory of Morality*. Oxford: Clarendon Press.

Hooker, Brad and Margaret Olivia Little, eds. 2000. *Moral Particularism*. Oxford: Clarendon Press.

Hume, David. (1739) 1978. *A Treatise of Human Nature*. Edited by Lewis A. Selby-Bigge and Peter H. Nidditch. Oxford: Clarendon Press.

Hume, David. (1748) 1998. *An Enquiry Concerning the Principles of Morals*. Edited by Tom L. Beauchamp. Oxford: Oxford University Press.

Hume, David. (1777a) 1994. *Political Writings*. Edited by Stuart D. Warner and Donald W. Livingston. Indianapolis, IN: Hackett.

Hume, David. (1777b) 1985. *Essays: Moral, Political, and Literary*, Revised Edition. Edited by Eugene F. Miller. Indianapolis, IN: Liberty Fund.

Hutcheson, Francis. (1725) 2008. *An Inquiry into the Original of Our Ideas of Beauty and Virtue in Two Treatises*, Revised Edition. Edited by Wolfgang Leidhold. Indianapolis, IN: Liberty Fund.

Hutcheson, Francis. (1728) 2002. *An Essay on the Nature and Conduct of the Passions and Affections, with Illustrations from on the Moral Sense.* Edited by Aaron Garrett. Indianapolis, IN: Liberty Fund.

Hutcheson, Francis. (1745) 2007. *Philosophiae Moralis Institutio Compendiaria, with a Short Introduction to Moral Philosophy.* Edited by Luigi Turco. Indianapolis, IN: Liberty Fund.

Hutcheson, Francis. 1755. *A System of Moral Philosophy, in Three Books.* Glasgow: R. and A. Foulis.

Irwin, Terrance. 2008. *The Development of Ethics: A Historical and Critical Study. Volume II: From Suarez to Rousseau.* Oxford: Oxford University Press.

Johnson, Conrad. 1991. *Moral Legislation: A Legal-Political Model for Indirect Consequentialist Reasoning.* Cambridge: Cambridge University Press.

Kant, Immanuel. (1785) 1997. *Groundwork of the Metaphysics of Morals.* Edited by Mary Gregor. Cambridge: Cambridge University Press.

Kant, Immanuel. (1797) 1996. *The Metaphysics of Morals.* Edited by Mary Gregor. Cambridge: Cambridge University Press.

Kaye, Frederick Benjamin, ed. 1988. *Introduction to* The Fable of the Bees or Private Vices, Publick Benefits *by Bernard Mandeville.* Indianapolis, IN: Liberty Fund.

Kirk, Linda. 1987. *Richard Cumberland and Natural Law: Secularization of Thought in Seventeenth-Century England.* Cambridge: James Clarke & Co.

Korsgaard, Christine. 1996a. *The Sources of Normativity.* Cambridge: Cambridge University Press.

Korsgaard, Christine. 1996b. "The Reasons We Can Share: An Attack on the Distinction between Agent-Relative and Agent-Neutral Values." In Christine Korsgaard, *Creating the Kingdom of Ends*, 275–310. Cambridge: Cambridge University Press.

Lazari-Radek, Katarzyna de and Peter Singer. 2014. *The Point of View of the Universe: Sidgwick and Contemporary Ethics.* Oxford: Oxford University Press.

Leidhold, Wolfgang, ed. 2008. *Introduction to* An Inquiry into the Original of our Ideas of Beauty and Virtue *by Francis Hutcheson*, Revised Edition. Indianapolis, IN: Liberty Fund.

Locke, John. (1689a) 1983. *A Letter Concerning Toleration.* Edited by James Tully. Indianapolis, IN: Hackett Publishing Company.

Locke, John. (1689b) 1988. *Two Treatises of Government.* Edited by Peter Laslett. Cambridge: Cambridge University Press.

Locke, John. (1690) *An Essay Concerning Human Understanding.* Edited by Peter Nidditch. Oxford: Clarendon Press, 1975.

Locke, John. (1703) 1997. *Political Essays.* Edited by Mark Goldie. Cambridge: Cambridge University Press.

Locke, John. (1706) 1996. *Some Thoughts Concerning Education* and *of the Conduct of the Understanding.* Edited by Ruth W. Grant and Nathan Tarcov. Indianapolis, IN: Hackett Publishing Company, Inc.

Locke, John. (1823) 1963. *Works of John Locke*, 10 vols. London: Thomas Tegg [reprinted by Scientia Verlag Aalen].

Lyons, David. 1965. *Forms and Limits of Utilitarianism*. Oxford: Clarendon Press.

Lyons, David. 1976. "Mill's Theory of Morality." *Nous* 10: 101–20.

Mabbott, John David. 1939. "Punishment." *Mind* 48(190): 152–67.

Mabbott, John David. 1953. "Moral Rules." *Proceedings of the British Academy* 39, 97–117.

Macbeath, Alexander. 1952. *Experiments in Living*. London: Macmillan and Co.

Mack, Eric. 1999. "The Alienability of Lockean Natural Rights." In *Persons and Their Bodies: Rights, Responsibilities, Relationships*, edited by Mark J. Cherry, 143–176. Dordrecht: Kluwer Academic Publishers.

Mackie, John L. 1982. *The Miracle of Theism: Arguments for and against the Existence of God*. Oxford: Clarendon Press.

Mackie, John L. 1985. "The Disutility of Act-Utilitarianism." In *Persons and Values* edited by John L. Mackie and Penelope Mackie, Vol. 2, 91–104. Oxford: Clarendon Press.

Mandeville, Bernard. (1732) 1988. *The Fable of the Bees or Private Vices, Public Benefits* (2 vols), edited by Frederick Benjamin Kaye. Indianapolis, IN: Liberty Fund.

McCloskey, Henry John. 1957. "An Examination of Restricted Utilitarianism." *The Philosophical Review* 66: 466–85.

McKown, Delos B. 2004. *Behold the Antichrist: Bentham on Religion*. Amherst, NY: Prometheus Books.

Mill, John Stuart. (1969) 1985. *Collected Works*. Edited by John M. Robson. London: Routledge & Kegan Paul and Toronto: University of Toronto Press.

Millar, Alan. 1992. "Butler on God and Human Nature." In *Joseph Butler's Moral and Religious Thought: Tercentenary Essays*, edited by Christopher Cunliffe, 294–315. Oxford: Clarendon Press.

Miller, Dale E. 2010. *J.S. Mill*. Cambridge: Polity Press.

Miller, Dale E. 2011. "Mill, Rule Utilitarianism, and the Incoherence Objection." In *John Stuart Mill and the Art of Life*, edited by Ben Eggleston, Dale E. Miller, and David Weinstein, 94–119. Oxford: Oxford University Press.

Miller, Dale E. 2013. "Hooker on Rule-Consequentialism and Virtue." *Utilitas* 25 (3): 421–32.

Miller, David. 2013. *Justice for Earthlings: Essays in Political Philosophy*. Cambridge: Cambridge University Press.

Montague, Phillip. 2000. "Why Rule Consequentialism Is Not Superior to Ross-Style Pluralism." In *Morality, Rules, and Consequences: A Critical Reader*, edited by Brad Hooker, Elinor Mason, and Dale E. Miller. Lanham, MD: Rowman and Littlefield.

Moore, George Edward. (1903) 1954. *Principia Ethica*. Cambridge: Cambridge University Press.

Moore, George Edward. (1912) 1961. *Ethics*. Oxford: Oxford University Press.

Morison, William Loutit. 1982. *John Austin*. London: Edward Arnold.

Nowell-Smith, Patrick Horace. 1954. *Ethics*. Harmondsworth, UK: Penguin.

O'Flaherty, Niall. 2019. *Utilitarianism in the Age of Enlightenment: The Moral and Political Thought of William Paley*. Cambridge: Cambridge University Press.

Paley, William. (1785) 2002. *The Principles of Moral and Political Philosophy*. Indianapolis, IN: Liberty Fund.

Paley, William. (1802) 2008. *Natural Theology*, edited by Matthew D. Eddy and David Knight. Oxford: Oxford University Press.

Parfit, Derek. 1984. *Reasons and Persons*. Oxford: Clarendon Press.

Parfit, Derek. 2011–2017. *On What Matters* (3 volumes). Oxford: Oxford University Press.

Parkin, Jon. 1999. *Science, Religion and Politics in Restoration England: Richard Cumberland's* De Legibus Naturae. Woodbridge, UK: The Boydell Press.

Parrish, John M. 2007. *Paradoxes of Political Ethics: From Dirty Hands to the Invisible Hand*. Cambridge: Cambridge University Press.

Pettit, Philip. 1989. "Consequentialism and Respect for Persons." *Ethics* 100(1): 116–26.

Pettit, Philip. 1997. *Republicanism: A Theory of Government and Freedom*. Oxford: Clarendon Press.

Portmore, Douglas W. 2001. "Can an Act-Consequentialist Theory Be Agent Relative?" *American Philosophical Quarterly* 38(4): 363–77.

Portmore, Douglas W. 2003. "Position-Relative Consequentialism. Agent-Centered Options, and Supererogation." *Ethics* 113: 303–32.

Proast, Jonas. 1691. *A Third Letter Concerning Toleration*. Oxford: Early English Books Online Text Creation Partnership, http://name.umdl.umich.edu/A559 26.0001.001.

Rawls, John. 1955. "Two Concepts of Rules." *The Philosophical Review* 64(1): 3–32.

Rawls, John. 1971. *A Theory of Justice*. Cambridge, MA: Harvard University Press.

Rawls, John. 1993. *Political Liberalism*. New York: Columbia University Press.

Rosen, Frederick. 2003. *Classical Utilitarianism from Hume to Mill*. Abingdon, UK: Routledge.

Ross, William David. (1930) 2002. *The Right and the Good*. Oxford: Clarendon Press.

Ryan, Alan. 1974. *J. S. Mill*. London: Routledge and Kegan Paul.

Scarre, Geoffrey. 1996. *Utilitarianism*. Abingdon, UK: Routledge.

Schauer, Frederick F. 1991. *Playing by the Rules: A Philosophical Examination of Rule-Based Decision-Making in Law and in Life*. Oxford: Clarendon Press.

Schneewind, Jerome B. 1977. *Sidgwick's Ethics and Victorian Moral Philosophy*. Oxford: Clarendon Press.

Schneewind, Jerome B. 1998. *The Invention of Autonomy: A History of Modern Moral Philosophy*. Cambridge: Cambridge University Press.

Schofield, Thomas Philip. 1987. "A Comparison of the Moral Theories of William Paley and Jeremy Bentham." *The Bentham Newsletter* 11: 4–22.

Schultz, Bart. 2004. *Henry Sidgwick – Eye of the Universe: An Intellectual Biography*. Cambridge: Cambridge University Press.

Schultz, Bart. 2017. *The Happiness Philosophers*. Princeton, NJ: Princeton University Press.

Scott, William Robert. 1900. *Francis Hutcheson: His Life, Teaching, and Position in the History of Philosophy*. Cambridge: Cambridge University Press.

Sen, Amartya and Bernard Williams. 1982. *Utilitarianism and Beyond*. Cambridge: Cambridge University Press.

Shaftesbury, Third Earl of (Anthony Ashley Cooper). (1711) 1999. *Characteristics of Men, Manners, Opinions, Times*, edited by Lawrence E. Klein. Cambridge: Cambridge University Press.

Sidgwick, Henry. (1902) 1988. *Outlines of the History of Ethics*. Indianapolis, IN: Hackett Publishing Company.

Sidgwick, Henry. (1907) 1981. *The Methods of Ethics*, Seventh Edition. Foreword by John Rawls. Indianapolis, IN: Hackett Publishing Company.

Simmons, A. John. 1992. *The Lockean Theory of Rights*. Princeton, NJ: Princeton University Press.

Simmons, A. John. 2010. "Ideal and Nonideal Theory." *Philosophy and Public Affairs* 38(1): 5–36.

Singer, Marcus George. 1958. "Moral Rules and Principles." In *Essays in Moral Philosophy*, edited by Abraham Irving Melden. Seattle: University of Washington Press.

Skorupski, John. 1989. *John Stuart Mill*. Abingdon, UK: Routledge.

Smart, John Jamieson Carswell. 1956. "Extreme and Restricted Utilitarianism." *Philosophical Quarterly* 6: 344–54.

Sobel, Jordan H. 2009. *Walls and Vaults: A Natural Science of Morals (Virtue Ethics According to David Hume)*. Hoboken, NJ: John Wiley & Sons.

Stephen, Leslie. 1900. *The English Utilitarians* (in three volumes). London: Duckworth.

Stewart, John B. 1992. *Opinion and Reform in Hume's Political Philosophy*. Princeton, NJ: Princeton University Press.

Stout, Alan Ker. 1954. "But Suppose Everyone Did the Same." *Australasian Journal of Philosophy* 32: 1–29.

Temkin, Larry S. 2019. "Being Good in a World of Need: Some Empirical Worries and an Uncomfortable Philosophical Possibility." *Journal of Practical Ethics* 7 (1): 1–23.

Ten, Chin Liew. 1980. *Mill on Liberty*. Oxford: Clarendon Press.

Toulmin, Stephen. 1950. *The Place of Reason in Ethics*. Cambridge: Cambridge University Press.

Tuck, Richard. 1979. *Natural Rights Theories: Their Origin and Development*. Cambridge: Cambridge University Press.

Tuck, Richard. 1999. *The Rights of War and Peace: Political Thought and the International Order from Grotius to Kant*. Oxford: Oxford University Press.

Tuckness, Alex. 1999. "The Coherence of a Mind: John Locke and the Law of Nature." *Journal of the History of Philosophy* 37(1): 73–90.

Tuckness, Alex. 2002. *Locke and the Legislative Point of View*. Princeton, NJ: Princeton University Press.

Tuckness, Alex. 2008. "Locke's Main Argument for Toleration." *Nomos (Yearbook of the American Society for Political and Legal Philosophy)* 48: 114–38.

Tuckness, Alex. 2010. "Retribution and Restitution in Locke's Theory of Punishment." *Journal of Politics* 72(3): 720–32.

Urmson, James Opie. 1953. "The Interpretation of the Philosophy of J. S. Mill." *The Philosophical Quarterly* 3: 33–9.

Voitle, Robert B. 1984. *The Third Earl of Shaftesbury, 1671–1713*. Baton Rouge: Louisiana State University Press.

Waldron, Jeremy. 1999. *Law and Disagreement*. Oxford: Oxford University Press.

Wallace, R. Jay. 2009. "The Publicity of Reasons." *Philosophical Perspectives* 23: 471–97.

Whelan, Frederick G. 1985. *Order and Artifice in Hume's Political Philosophy*. Princeton, NJ: Princeton University Press.

Whewell, William. 1852. *Lectures on the History of Moral Philosophy in England*. London: John W. Parker and Cambridge: John Deighton.

White, Morton. 1978. *The Philosophy of the American Revolution*. New York: Oxford University Press.

Willard, Dallas. 2018. *The Disappearance of Moral Knowledge*. New York: Routledge.

Williams, Bernard. 1981. "Persons, Character, and Morality." In Bernard Williams, *Moral Luck*, 1–19. Cambridge: Cambridge University Press.

Williams, Bernard. 1985. *Ethics and the Limits of Philosophy*. Cambridge, MA: Harvard University Press.

Williams, Bernard. 1988. "The Structure of Hare's Theory." In *Hare and Critics*, edited by Douglas Seanor and Nicholas Fotion. Oxford: Clarendon Press.

Wittgenstein, Ludwig. (1953) 1958. *Philosophical Investigations*, Third Edition. Translated by Gertrude Elizabeth Margaret Anscombe. Englewood Cliffs, NJ: Prentice Hall.

Zamzow, J. L. 2015. "Rules and Principles in Moral Decision Making: An Empirical Objection to Moral Particularism." *Ethical Theory and Moral Practice* 18: 123–34.

Index

Mill, John Stuart, 100, 101, 137, 154, 192, 213
  act-utilitarianism and, 108
  defense of freedom of expression of,
    112–13
  example of counterfactual legislative
    perspective in, 110
  historical background of, 101–2
  legislative perspective and, 107–12, 114–18
  moral expression and, 115–16
  secondary moral rules and, 102
  Paley, William and, 84
  public opinion and, 113–14
  rule-utilitarianism and, 103–8, 109, 126
Miller, Dale, 180
Miller, David, 107, 206
Montague, Philip, 180
Moore, George Edward, 128–9, 141, 147
  moral rules, 128
moral expression as legislation, 42, 112–18, 126,
  166, 192
morality as legislation, 24, 26, 46, 143, 151
  historical argument, review of, 151–5
  justifying the hybrid approach and, 20–2
  morality expressed as universal laws and,
    180
  necessary moral commitments of, 199–207
Morison, William Loutit, 100
motive-consequentialism, 187

Nowell-Smith, Patrick, 135

O'Flaherty, Michael, 83
orthodoxy, utilitarian, *see* utilitarianism,
  orthodoxy and

Paley, William, 8, 18, 22, 23, 26, 47, 81, 92, 94, 98,
  101, 153, 161, 190
  Austin, John and, 99–100
  consequentialism of, 84, 87, 99
  divorce laws, views on, 88
  God, role of, 84–7
  greatest good, promotion of, 89
  property, views on, 88
  religious toleration and establishment, views
    on, 90–2
  rule-based approach of, 83
  rules, principles for evaluating, 90
  self-defense, views on, 89
  suicide, views on, 90
Parfit, Derek, 159, 181, 197
  consequentialism, self-defeating, 19
  Kantian contractualism, 183–8
paternalism, 111, 112, 114
Pettit, Philip, 179, 212
political context, *see* context, political

Portmore, Douglas, 202
Proast, Jonas, 53–6
Pufendorf, Samuel von, 33, 48

Rawls, John, 5, 6, 20, 103, 136, 141, 150, 172, 176,
  178, 202–3, 205
religion, 74, 76, 161, 195, 213
  Austin, John and, 100
  benevolence and, 8
  Bentham, Jeremy and, 99
  divine legislation and, 8
  Hutcheson, Francis and, 67
  legislative perspective and, 29, 200
  Mill, John Stuart and, 116
  morality as legislation and, 25
  Paley, William and, 84, 90–2
  rule-utilitarianism and, 7
  sanctions, *see* sanctions, divine
  Sidgwick, Henry and, 118, 119
  toleration and, 34, 47, 53–6, 57, 62, 71, 152,
    205, 207
  utilitarianism and, 18, 26, 127
Rosen, Frederick, 24, 77
Ross, William David, 130, 133, 154, 201
rule-consequentialism, 8, 12, 17, 27, 28, 44, 46, 56,
  100, 124, 127, 137, 161, 163, 165, 169, 186, 192,
  193, 198
  Brandt, Richard and, 137
  Hooker, Brad and, 174–80, 203
  legislative forms of, 54
  Locke, John and, 34, 47–51, 54–6, 57
  Parfit, Derek and, 183–9
rule-utilitarianism, 5, 7, 8, 11, 17, 18, 24, 27, 83,
  124, 127–8, 137
  Brandt, Richard and, 137–8, 149–51
  consistency of, 6
  critics of, twentieth century, 138–43
  development of, early twentieth century,
    128–32
  development of, mid-twentieth century,
    132–8
  Hare, Richard Mervyn and, 144–7
  Harsanyi, John and, 148–9
  Mill, John Stuart and, 6, 103–9, 126
  religion and, 7, 74
  rules, exceptions to, 132–5

sanctions, 13, 64, 65, 93, 120, *see also* sanction-
  utilitarianism
  conscience and, 27, 106–8
  divine, 17, 18, 27, 45, 65, 67, 81, 85, 93, 95, 101
  legal, 93, 98, 102, 109, 114
  reputational, 27, 93, 97, 98, 102, 113–6, 153,
    213, 215
sanction-utilitarianism, 106–8